A TEXT BOOK OF

MICROPROCESSORS

FOR

Semester – III

Second Year Degree Course in
Computer Science and Engineering

As Per New Revised Syllabus of Shivaji University, Kolhapur
(Effective form 2014)

Dr. ST Patil
M. Tech. CSE PhD. Computer
Professor, Computer Engineering
Vishwakarma Institute of Technology (VIT),
PUNE – 411 037

MICROPROCESSORS (S.E. COMP. SCI. & ENGG. SEM. III - SU)   ISBN 978-93-5164-241-1
First Edition : September 2014
© : Author

The text of this publication, or any part thereof, should not be reproduced or transmitted in any form or stored in any computer storage system or device for distribution including photocopy, recording, taping or information retrieval system or reproduced on any disc, tape, perforated media or other information storage device etc., without the written permission of Authors with whom the rights are reserved. Breach of this condition is liable for legal action.

Every effort has been made to avoid errors or omissions in this publication. In spite of this, errors may have crept in. Any mistake, error or discrepancy so noted and shall be brought to our notice shall be taken care of in the next edition. It is notified that neither the publisher nor the authors or seller shall be responsible for any damage or loss of action to any one, of any kind, in any manner, therefrom.

Published By :
NIRALI PRAKASHAN
Abhyudaya Pragati, 1312, Shivaji Nagar,
Off J.M. Road, PUNE – 411005
Tel - (020) 25512336/37/39, Fax - (020) 25511379
Email : niralipune@pragationline.com

Printed at
Repro Knowledgecast Limited
India

DISTRIBUTION CENTRES
PUNE

Nirali Prakashan
119, Budhwar Peth, Jogeshwari Mandir Lane
Pune 411002, Maharashtra
Tel : (020) 2445 2044, 66022708, Fax : (020) 2445 1538
Email : bookorder@pragationline.com

Nirali Prakashan
S. No. 28/25, Dhyari,
Near Pari Company, Pune 411041
Tel : (022) 24690204 Fax : (020) 24690316
Email : dhyari@pragationline.com
bookorder@pragationline.com

MUMBAI
Nirali Prakashan
385, S.V.P. Road, Rasdhara Co-op. Hsg. Society Ltd.,
Girgaum, Mumbai 400004, Maharashtra
Tel : (022) 2385 6339 / 2386 9976, Fax : (022) 2386 9876
Email : niralimumbai@pragationline.com

DISTRIBUTION BRANCHES

NAGPUR
Pratibha Book Distributors
Above Maratha Mandir, Shop No. 3, First Floor,
Rani Jhanshi Square, Sitabuldi, Nagpur 440012,
Maharashtra, Tel : (0712) 254 7129

BENGALURU
Pragati Book House
House No. 1, Sanjeevappa Lane, Avenue Road Cross,
Opp. Rice Church, Bengaluru – 560002.
Tel : (080) 64513344, 64513355,
Mob : 9880582331, 9845021552
Email:bharatsavla@yahoo.com

JALGAON
Nirali Prakashan
34, V. V. Golani Market, Navi Peth, Jalgaon 425001,
Maharashtra, Tel : (0257) 222 0395
Mob : 94234 91860

KOLHAPUR
Nirali Prakashan
New Mahadvar Road,
Kedar Plaza, 1st Floor Opp. IDBI Bank
Kolhapur 416 012, Maharashtra. Mob : 9855046155

CHENNAI
Pragati Books
9/1, Montieth Road, Behind Taas Mahal, Egmore,
Chennai 600008 Tamil Nadu, Tel : (044) 6518 3535,
Mob : 94440 01782 / 98450 21552 / 98805 82331, Email : bharatsavla@yahoo.com

RETAIL OUTLETS
PUNE

Pragati Book Centre
157, Budhwar Peth, Opp. Ratan Talkies,
Pune 411002, Maharashtra
Tel : (020) 2445 8887 / 6602 2707, Fax : (020) 2445 8887

Pragati Book Centre
Amber Chamber, 28/A, Budhwar Peth,
Appa Balwant Chowk, Pune : 411002, Maharashtra,
Tel : (020) 20240335 / 66281669
Email : pbcpune@pragationline.com

Pragati Book Centre
676/B, Budhwar Peth, Opp. Jogeshwari Mandir,
Pune 411002, Maharashtra
Tel : (020) 6601 7784 / 6602 0855

PBC Book Sellers & Stationers
152, Budhwar Peth, Pune 411002, Maharashtra
Tel : (020) 2445 2254 / 6609 2463

MUMBAI
Pragati Book Corner
Indira Niwas, 111 - A, Bhavani Shankar Road, Dadar (W), Mumbai 400028, Maharashtra
Tel : (022) 2422 3526 / 6662 5254, Email : pbcmumbai@pragationline.com

PREFACE

It gives me immense pleasure to present this book on **'Microprocessors'** to the Students of Second Year of Degree in Computer Science and Engineering Course of Shivaji University, Kolhapur. It is strictly written as per New Revised Syllabus 2014.

The text includes information about basic concepts of 8085 Microprocessor. It Various building blocks of the 8085 Microprocessor Architecture are explained in detail. Programming treatment of various concepts are given wherever necessary. Number of solved programs and exercises are given to strengthens the concepts. The working of Microprocessor system is explained with extensive instructions and programming to get an insight into the subject.

My sincere hope is that the material presented in the book will be useful in understanding the subject as well as for attempting examination questions.

I take this opportunity to express my thanks to **Shri. Dineshbhai Furia** and **Shri. Jignesh Furia** and **Shri. M.P. Munde** for publishing this book in time.

I also take this opportunity to express my thank all the staff members of Nirali Prakashan namely Mrs. Ulka Chavan, Mrs. Shilpa Kale, Mrs. Pratibha Bele and Miss. Mandakini Jadhvar for their tremendous dedication and hard work in bringing out this book in an excellent form.

I also thankful to **Mr. Virdhaval Shinde**, Branch Manager, Kolhapur Offcie and **Mr. Ashok Nanaware**, Branch Manager, Sangli District for their valuable help and efforts for promotion of my book.

My special thanks to my family members, students and all those who directly or indirectly supported me in this project.

Any suggestions and feedback shall be appreciated and acknowledged.

September 2014   **Dr. ST PATIL**
Pune

SYLLABUS

Unit 1: Intel 8085 Architecture and Programming (6)

1.1 Architecture of 8085

1.2 Instruction set & Execution in 8085

1.3 Classification of Instructions

1.4 Instruction set of 8085

1.5 Sample Programs

1.6 Assembler

1.7 Assembly Language Programs

Unit 2: Microprocessor and Architecture (6)

2.1 The Microprocessor Based Personal Computer System.

2.2 Internal Microprocessor Architecture

2.3 Real Mode Memory Addressing

2.4 Introduction to Protected Mode memory Addressing

2.5 Memory Paging

Unit 3: Addressing Modes and Data Movement Instructions (6)

3.1 Data Addressing Modes

3.2 Program Memory Addressing Mode

3.3 Stack Memory Addressing Mode

3.4 MOV Revisited

3.5 PUSH/POP

3.6 Load Effective Address

3.7 String Data Transfer

3.8 Miscellaneous Data Transfer Instruction

3.9 Segment Override Prefix

3.10 Assembler Details

Unit 4: Arithmetic, Logic and Program Control Instructions (6)

    4.1 Addition, Subtraction and Comparison

    4.2 Multiplication and Division

    4.3 BCD and ASCII Arithmetic

    4.4 Basic Logic Instructions

    4.5 Shift and Rotate

    4.6 The Jump Group

    4.7 Controlling the Flow of program

    4.8 Machine control and Miscellaneous Instructions

Unit 5: Interrupts and The 80386 Microprocessor (6)

    5.1 Basic Interrupt Processing

    5.2 Hardware Interrupt

    5.3 The 80386 Microprocessor: The memory System

    5.4 Special 80386 Registers

    5.5 80386 Memory Management

    5.6 Virtual 8086 Mode

    5.7 The Memory Paging Mechanism

Unit 6: Pentium, Pentium Pro and Pentium 4 Microprocessor (4)

    6.1 The Pentium Microprocessor : The Memory System

    6.2 Special Pentium Registers

    6.3 Pentium Memory Management

    6.4 The Pentium Pro Microprocessor : Internal structure of the Pentium Pro

    6.5 The Pentium 4 : Memory Interface, Register Set, Hyper Threading Technology CPUID

CONTENTS

1. **Intel 8085 Architecture and Programming** — 1.1 – 1.26

2. **Microprocessor and Architecture** — 2.1 – 2.32

3. **Addressing Modes and Data Movement Instructions** — 3.1 – 3.38

4. **Arithmetic, Logic and Program Control Instructions** — 4.1 – 4.36

5. **Interrupts and The 80386 Microprocessor** — 5.1 – 5.28

6. **Pentium, Pentium Pro and Pentium 4 Microprocessor** — 6.1 – 6.28

Unit - I

INTEL 8085 ARCHITECTURE AND PROGRAMMING

1.1 INTRODUCTION

The Intel 8085 is an 8-bit microprocessor introduced by Intel in 1977. It was backward binary compatible with the more-famous Intel 8080 required less supporting hardware, thus allowing simpler and less expensive microcomputer systems to be built.

The "5" in the model number came from the fact that the 8085 requires only a +5-Volt (V) power supply by using depletion mode transistors, rather than requiring the +5 V, −5 V and +12 V supplies the 8080 needed. These processors were sometimes used in computers running the CP/M operating system.

The Intel 8085 required at least an external ROM and RAM and an 8 bit address latch (both latches combined in the Intel 8755 2K × 8 EPROM / 2 × 8 I/O, Intel 8155 256-byte RAM and 22 I/O and 14 bit programmable Timer/Counter) so cannot technically be called a microcontroller.

Both designs (8080/8085) were eclipsed for desktop computers by the compatible Zilog Z80, which took over most of the CP/M computer market as well as taking a share of the booming home computer market in the early-to-mid-1980s.

The 8085 had a long life as a controller. Once designed into such products as the DEC tape controller and the VT100 video terminal in the late 1970s, it served for new production throughout the life span of those products (generally longer than the product life of desktop computers).

Microprocessing unit is synonymous to central processing unit, CPU used in traditional computer. Microprocessor (MPU) acts as a device or a group of devices which do the following tasks.
- Communicate with peripherals devices
- Provide timing signal
- Direct data flow
- Perform computer tasks as specified by the instructions in memory

1.2 ARCHITECTURE OF 8085 MICROPROCESSOR

The 8085 microprocessor is an 8-bit general purpose microprocessor which is capable to address 64k of memory. This processor has forty pins, requires +5 V single power supply and a 3-MHz single-phase clock.

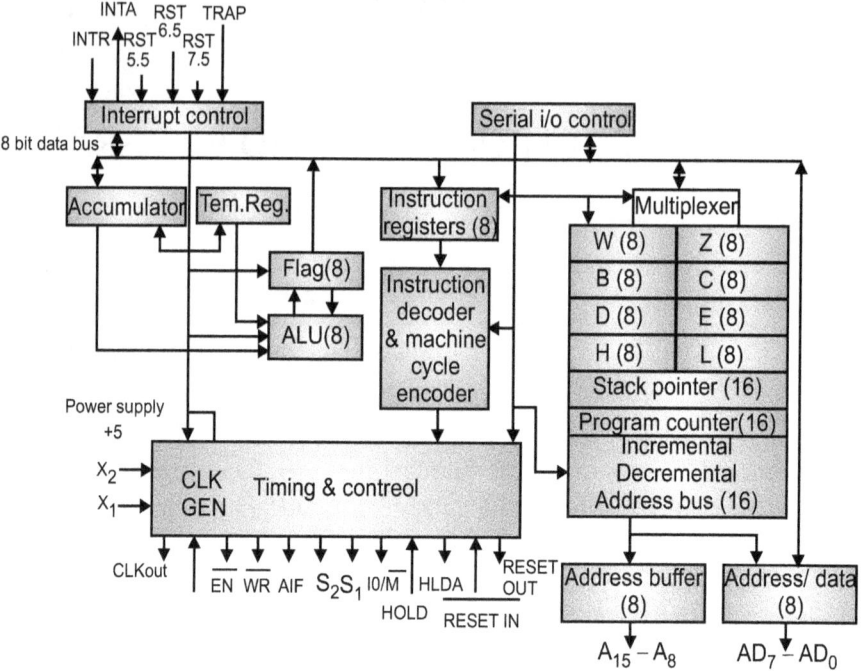

Fig. 1.1 : Architecture of 8085

1.2.1 ALU

The ALU perform the computing function of microprocessor. It includes the accumulator, temporary register, arithmetic & logic circuit & and five flags. Result is stored in accumulator & flags.

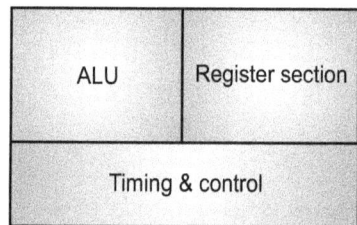

Fig. 1.2 : Arithmatic and logic unit

1.2.2 Accumulator

It is an 8-bit register that is part of ALU. This register is used to store 8-bit data & in performing arithmetic & logic operation. The result of operation is stored in accumulator.

1.2.3 Flags

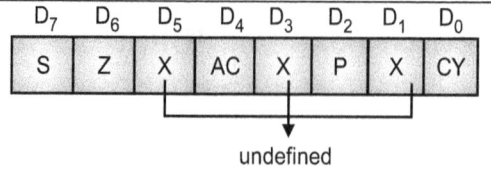

Fig. 1.3

The register are programmable. It can be used to store and transfer the data from the registers by using instruction. The ALU includes five flip-flops that are set & reset acc. to data condition in accumulator and other registers.

- **S (Sign) Flag** : After the execution of an arithmetic operation, if bit D_7 of the result is 1, the sign flag is set. It is used to signed number. In a given byte, if D_7 is 1 means negative number. If it is zero means it is a positive number.
- **Z (Zero) Flag** : The zero flag is set if ALU operation result is 0.
- **AC (Auxiliary Carry) Flag** : In arithmetic operation, when carry is generated by digit D3 and passed on to digit D_4, the AC flag is set. This flag is used only internally BCD operation.
- **P (Parity) Flag** : After arithmetic or logic operation, if result has even no. of 1s, the flag is set. If it has odd no. of 1s, flag is reset.
- **C (Carry) Flag** : If arithmetic operation result in a carry, the carry flag is set, otherwise it is reset.

1.2.4 Register Section

It is a basically storage device & transfer data from registers by using instruction.

- **Stack Pointer (SP)** : The stack pointer is also a 16-bit register which is used as a memory pointer. It points to a memory location in Read/Write memory known as stack. In between execution of program, some time data to be stored in stack. The beginning of the stack is defined by loading a 16-bit address in the stack pointer.
- **Program Counter (PC)** : This 16-bit register deals with fourth operation to sequence the execution of instruction. This register is also a memory pointer. Memory location have 16-bit address. It is used to store the execution address. The function of the program counter is to point to memory address from which next bytes is to be fetched.
- **Storage Registers** : These registers store 8-bit data during a program execution. These register are identified as B,C,D,E,H,L. They can be combined as register pair BC, DE and HL to perform some 16 bit operations.

1.2.5 Timing and Control Section

This unit is responsible to synchronize Microprocessor operation as per the clock pulse and to generate the control signals which are necessary for smooth communication between Microprocessor and peripherals devices. The RD bar and WR bar signal are syncronous pulses which indicates whether data is available on the data bus or not. The control unit is responsible to control the flow of data between microprocessor, memory and peripheral devices.

1.3 PIN DIAGRAM OF 8085 MICROPROCESSOR

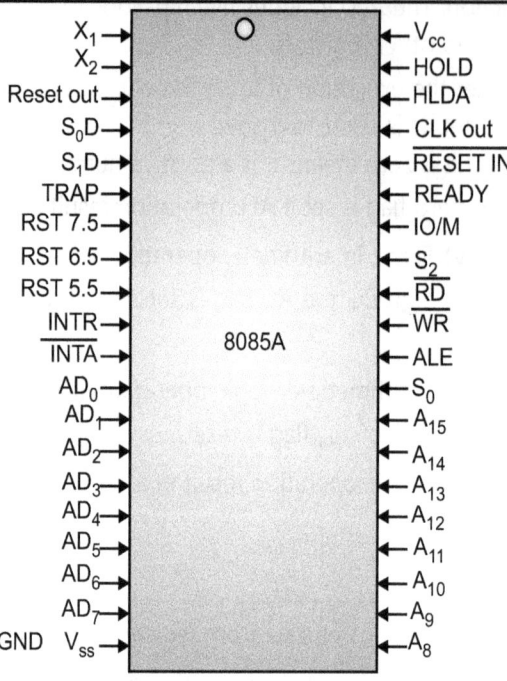

Fig. 1.4 : Pin diagram

All the signal can be classified into six groups

Table 1.1

S.N.	Group	Description
1	Address bus	• The 8085 microprocessor has 8 signal line, A_{15} - A_8 which are unidirectional & used as a high order address bus.
2	Data bus	• The signal line AD7 - AD0 are bidirectional for dual purpose. They are used as low order address bus as well as data bus.
3	Control signal and Status signal	Control Signal • **RD Bar** - It is a read control signal (active low). It is active then memory read the data. • **WR Bar** - It is write control signal (active low). It is active when written into selected memory. Status signal • **ALU (Address Latch Enable)** - When ALU is high. 8085 microprocessor is use address bus. When ALU is low. 8085 microprocessor is use data bus. • **IO/M Bar** - This is a status signal used to differentiate between i/o and memory operation. When it is high, it

		indicate an i/o operation and low, it indicate memory operation. • **S_1 and S_0** - These status signal, similar to i/o and memory bar, can identify various operation, but they are rarely used in small system.
4	**Power supply and frequency signal**	• **V_{cc}** - +5v power supply. • **V_{ss}** - ground reference. • **X, X** - A crystal is connected at these two pins. The frequency is internally divided by two operate system at 3-MHz, the crystal should have a frequency of 6-MHz. • **CLK Out** - This signal can be used as the system clock for other devices.
5	**Externally initiated signal**	• **INTR(i/p)** - Interrupt request. • **INTA Bar (o/p)** - It is used as acknowledge interrupt. • **TRAP(i/p)** - This is non maskable interrupt and has highest priority. • **HOLD(i/p)** - It is used to hold the executing program. • **HLDA(o/p)** - Hold acknowledge. • **READY(i/p)** - This signal is used to delay the microprocessor read or write cycle until a slow responding peripheral is ready to accept or send data. • **RESET IN Bar** - When the signal on this pin goes low, the program counter is set to zero, the bus are tri-stated, & MPU is reset. • **RESET OUT** - This signal indicate that MPU is being reset. The signal can be used to reset other devices. • **RST 7.5, RST 6.5, RST 5.5 (Request Interrupt)** - It is used to transfer the program control to specific memory location. They have higher priority than INTR interrupt.
6	**Serial I/O ports**	• The 8085 microprocessor has two signals to implement the serial transmission serial input data and serial output data.

1.4 INSTRUCTION FORMAT

Each instruction is represented by a sequence of bits within the computer. The instruction is divided into group of bits called field. The way of instruction is expressed is known as instruction format. It is usually represented in the form of rectangular box. The instruction format may be of the following types.

1.4.1 Variable Instruction Formats

These are the instruction formats in which the instruction length varies on the basis of opcode & address specifiers. For Example, VAX instructions vary between 1 and 53 bytes while X86 instruction vary between 1 and 17 bytes.

Format

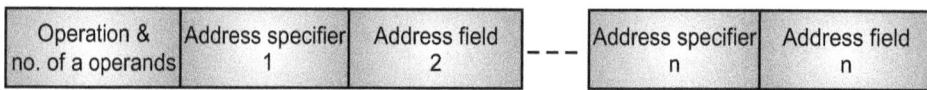

Fig. 1.5

Advantage
- These formats have good code density.

Disadvantage
- These instruction formats are very difficult to decode & pipeline.

1.4.2 Fixed Instruction Formats

In this type of instruction format, all instruction are same size. For Example, MIPS, Power PC, Alpha, ARM.

Format

| Operation | Address field 1 | Address field 2 | Address field 3 |

Fig. 1.6

Advantage
- They are easy to decode & pipeline.

Disadvantage
- They don't have as good code density.

1.4.3 Hybrid Instruction Formats

In this type of instruction formats, we have multiple format length specified by opcode. For example, IBM 360/70, MIPS 16, Thumb.

Format

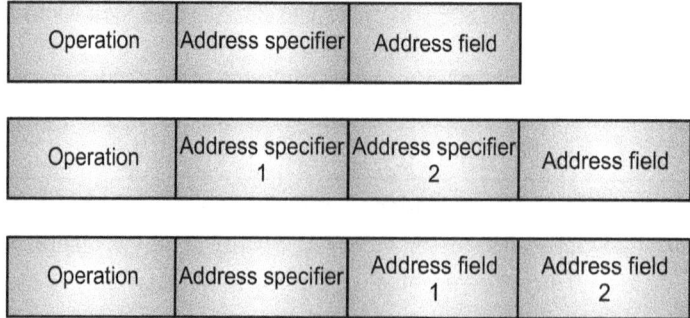

Fig. 1.7

Advantage
- These compromise between code density & instruction of these type are very easy to decode.

1.5 INSTRUCTION SET OF 8085

An Instruction is a command given to the computer to perform a specified operation on given data. The instruction set of a microprocessor is the collection of the instructions that the microprocessor is designed to execute. The instructions described here are of Intel 8085. These instructions are of Intel Corporation. They cannot be used by other microprocessor manufactures. The programmer can write a program in assembly language using these instructions. These instructions have been classified into the following groups:

1. Data Transfer Group
2. Arithmetic Group
3. Logical Group
4. Branch Control Group
5. I/O and Machine Control Group

1. Data Transfer Group

Instructions, which are used to transfer data from one register to another register, from memory to register or register to memory, come under this group. Examples are: MOV, MVI, LXI, LDA, STA etc. When an instruction of data transfer group is executed, data is transferred from the source to the destination without altering the contents of the source. For example, when MOV A, B is executed the content of the register B is copied into the register A, and the content of register B remains unaltered. Similarly, when LDA 2500 is executed the content of the memory location 2500 is loaded into the accumulator. But the content of the memory location 2500 remains unaltered.

Data Transfer Group Instructions

Instruction	Description	Operation
MOV r1, r2	(Move Data; Move the content of the one register to another)	[r1] <-- [r2]
MOV r, m	(Move the content of memory register).	r <-- [M]
MOV M, r	(Move the content of register to memory)	M <-- [r]
MVI r, data	(Move immediate data to register).	[r] <-- data
MVI M, data	(Move immediate data to memory)	M <-- data
LXI rp, data 16	(Load register pair immediate)	[rp] <-- data 16 bits, [rh] <-- 8 LSBs of data
LDA addr	(Load Accumulator direct)	[A] <-- [addr].

STA addr.	(Store accumulator direct)	[addr] <-- [A]
LHLD addr.	(Load H-L pair direct)	[L] <-- [addr], [H] <-- [addr+1]
SHLD addr.	(Store H-L pair direct)	[addr] <-- [L], [addr+1] <-- [H]
LDAX rp.	(LOAD accumulator indirect)	[A] <-- [[rp]]
STAX rp.	(Store accumulator indirect)	[[rp]] <-- [A]
XCHG	(Exchange the contents of H-L with D-E pair)	[H-L] <--> [D-E]

2. Arithmetic Group

The instructions of this group perform arithmetic operations such as addition, subtraction; increment or decrement of the content of a register or memory. Examples are: ADD, SUB, INR, DAD etc.

Arithmetic Group Instructions :

Instruction	Description	Operation
ADD r	(Add register to accumulator)	[A] <-- [A] + [r]
MOV r, m	(Move the content of memory register).	r <-- [M]
ADD M	(Add memory to accumulator)	[A] <-- [A] + [[H-L]]
ADC r	(Add register with carry to accumulator)	[A] <-- [A] + [r] + [CS]
ADC M	(Add memory with carry to accumulator)	[A] <-- [A] + [[H-L]] [CS]
ADI data	(Add immediate data to accumulator)	[A] <-- [A] + data
ACI data	(Add with carry immediate data to accumulator)	[A] <-- [A] + data + [CS]
DAD rp	(Add register paid to H-L pair)	[H-L] <-- [H-L] + [rp]
SUB r	(Subtract register from accumulator)	[A] <-- [A] – [r]
SUB M	(Subtract memory from accumulator)	[A] <-- [A] – [[H-L]]
SBB r	(Subtract register from accumulator with borrow)	[A] <-- [A] – [r] – [CS]
SBB M	(Subtract memory from accumulator with borrow)	[A] <-- [A] – [[H-L]] – [CS]
SUI data	(Subtract immediate data from accumulator)	[A] <-- [A] – data
SBI data	(Subtract immediate data from accumulator with borrow)	[A] <-- [A] – data – [CS]

INR r	(Increment register content)	[r] <-- [r] +1
INR M	(Increment memory content)	[[H-L]] <-- [[H-L]] + 1
DCR r	(Decrement register content)	[r] <-- [r] – 1
DCR M	(Decrement memory content)	[[H-L]] <-- [[H-L]] – 1
INX rp	(Increment register pair)	[rp] <-- [rp] – 1
DCX rp	(Decrement register pair)	[rp] <-- [rp] -1
DAA	(Decimal adjust accumulator)	-

The instruction DAA is used in the program after ADD, ADI, ACI, ADC, etc instructions. After the execution of ADD, ADC, etc instructions the result is in hexadecimal and it is placed in the accumulator. The DAA instruction operates on this result and gives the final result in the decimal system. It uses carry and auxiliary carry for decimal adjustment. 6 is added to 4 LSBs of the content of the accumulator if their value lies in between A and F or the AC flag is set to 1. Similarly, 6 is also added to 4 MSBs of the content of the accumulator if their value lies in between A and F or the CS flag is set to 1. All status flags are affected. When DAA is used data should be in decimal numbers.

3. Logical Group

The Instructions under this group perform logical operation such as AND, OR, compare, rotate etc. Examples are: ANA, XRA, ORA, CMP, and RAL etc.

Logical Group Instructions :

Instruction	Description	Operation
ANA r	(AND register with accumulator)	[A] <-- [A] ^ [r]
ANA M	(AND memory with accumulator)	[A] <-- [A] ^ [[H-L]]
ANI data	AND (immediate data with accumulator)	[A] <-- [A] ^ data
ORA r	(OR register with accumulator)	[A] <-- [A] v [r]
ORA M	(OR memory with accumulator)	[A] <-- [A] v [[H-L]]
ORI data	OR immediate data with accumulator	() [A] <-- [A] v data
XRA r	(EXCLUSIVE – OR register with accumulator)	[A] <-- [A] v [r]
XRA M	(EXCLUSIVE-OR memory with accumulator)	[A] <-- [A] v [[H-L]]
XRI data	(EXCLUSIVE-OR immediate data with accumulator)	[A] <-- [A]
CMA	(Complement the accumulator)	[A] <-- [A]
CMC	(Complement the carry status)	[CS] <-- [CS]
STC	(Set carry status)	[CS] <-- 1

CMP r	(Compare register with accumulator)	[A] – [r]
CMP M	(Compare memory with accumulator)	[A] – [[H-L]]
CPI data	(Compare immediate data with accumulator)	[A] – data

The 2nd byte of the instruction is data, and it is subtracted from the content of the accumulator. The status flags are set according to the result of subtraction. But the result is discarded. The content of the accumulator remains unchanged.

- RLC (Rotate accumulator left) [An+1] <-- [An], [A0] <-- [A7],[CS] <-- [A7].

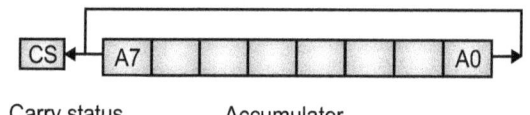

Carry status   Accumulator

Fig. 1.8

The content of the accumulator is rotated left by one bit. The seventh bit of the accumulator is moved to carry bit as well as to the zero bit of the accumulator. Only CS flag is affected.

- RRC. (Rotate accumulator right) [A7] <-- [A0], [CS] <-- [A0], [An] <-- [An+1].

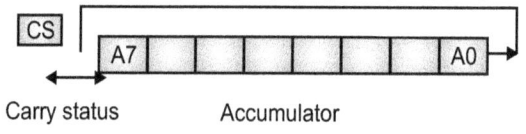

Carry status   Accumulator

Fig. 1.9

The content of the accumulator is rotated right by one bit. The zero bit of the accumulator is moved to the seventh bit as well as to carry bit. Only CS flag is affected.

- RAL. (Rotate accumulator left through carry) [An+1] <-- [An], [CS] <-- [A7], [A0] <-- [CS].
- RAR. (Rotate accumulator right through carry) [An] <-- [An+1], [CS] <-- [A0], [A7] <-- [CS]

4. Branch Control Group

This group includes the instructions for conditional and unconditional jump, subroutine call and return, and restart. Examples are: JMP, JC, JZ, CALL, CZ, RST etc.

Branch Group Instructions

- JMP addr (label). (Unconditional jump: jump to the instruction specified by the address). [PC] <-- Label.
- Conditional Jump addr (label): After the execution of the conditional jump instruction the program jumps to the instruction specified by the address (label) if the specified condition is fulfilled. The program proceeds further in the normal sequence if the specified condition is not fulfilled. If the condition is true and program jumps to the

specified label, the execution of a conditional jump takes 3 machine cycles: 10 states. If condition is not true, only 2 machine cycles; 7 states are required for the execution of the instruction.

Instruction	Description
JZ addr (label).	(Jump if the result is zero)
JNZ addr (label).	(Jump if the result is not zero)
JC addr (label).	(Jump if there is a carry)
JNC addr (label).	(Jump if there is no carry)
JP addr (label).	(Jump if the result is plus)
JM addr (label).	(Jump if the result is minus)
JPE addr (label).	(Jump if even parity)
JPO addr (label).	(Jump if odd parity)

- CALL addr (label) (Unconditional CALL: call the subroutine identified by the operand) CALL instruction is used to call a subroutine. Before the control is transferred to the subroutine, the address of the next instruction of the main program is saved in the stack. The content of the stack pointer is decremented by two to indicate the new stack top. Then the program jumps to subroutine starting at address specified by the label.
- RET (Return from subroutine)
- RST n (Restart) Restart is a one-word CALL instruction. The content of the program counter is saved in the stack. The program jumps to the instruction starting at restart location.

5. **I/O and Machine Control Group**

   This group includes the instructions for input/output ports, stack and machine control. Examples are: IN, OUT, PUSH, POP, and HLT etc.

Stack, I/O and Machine Control Group Instructions :

Instruction	Description	Operation
IN port-address.	(Input to accumulator from I/O port)	[A] <-- [Port]
OUT port-address.	(Output from accumulator to I/O port)	[Port] <-- [A]
PUSH rp.	(Push the content of register pair to stack)	
PUSH PSW.	(PUSH Processor Status Word)	
POP rp.		
POP PSW.	(Pop Processor Status Word)	
HLT (Halt).		

XTHL.	(Exchange stack-top with H-L)	
SPHL.	(Move the contents of H-L pair to stack pointer)	
EI.	(Enable Interrupts)	
DI.	(DISABLE♂ Interrupts)	
SIM.	(Set Interrupt Masks)	
RIM.	(Read Interrupt Masks)	
NOP.	(No Operation)	

1.6 ASSEMBLY LANGUAGE PROGRAMS

Program 1.1: Assembly Language program to Store the data byte 32H into memory location 4000H.

```
MVI A, 32H    : Store 32H in the accumulator
STA 4000H     : Copy accumulator contents at address 4000H
HLT           : Terminate program execution
```

Program 1.2: Assembly Language Program to add two 8-bit numbers.

```
MVI A, 24H    // load Reg A=ACC with 24H
MVI B , 56H   // load Reg B with 56H
ADD B         // ACC= ACC+B
OUT 01H       // Display ACC contents on port 01H
HALT          // End the program
```
Result: 7A (All are in Hex)

Program 1.3: Assembly Language Program to Multiply two 16-bit numbers

```
LDA 2000   // Load multiplicant to accumulator
MOV B A,   // Move mul i li t p cant from A( ) acc to B register
LDA 2001   // Load multiplier to accumulator
MOV C A,   // Move multiplier multiplier from A to C
MVI A,00   // Load immediate value 00 to a
L: ADD B   // Add B( p) multiplier) with A
DCR C      // Decrement C, it act as a counter
JNZ L      // Jump to L if C reaches 0
STA 2010   // Store result in to memory
HLT        // End
```

Program 1.4: Assembly Language Program to Exchange the contents of memory locations 2000H and 4000H

LDA 2000H	: Get the contents of memory location 2000H into accumulator
MOV B, A	: Save the contents into B register
LDA 4000H	: Get the contents of memory location 4000H intoaccumulator
STA 2000H	: Store the contents of accumulator at address 2000H
MOV A, B	: Get the saved contents back into A register
STA 4000H	: Store the contents of accumulator at address 4000H

Program 1.5: Subtract the contents of memory location 4001H from the memory location 2000H and place the result in memory location 4002H.

First number = (4000H) = 51H
Second number = (4001H) = 19H
Result = 51H - 19H = 38H

LXI H, 4000H	: HL points 4000H
MOV A, M	: Get first operand
INX H	: HL points 4001H
SUB M	: Subtract second operand
INX H	: HL points 4002H
MOV M, A	: Store result at 4002H.
HLT	: Terminate program execution

Program 1.6: Add two 16-bit numbers

(4000H) = 15H
(4001H) = 1CH
(4002H) = B7H
(4003H) = 5AH
Result = 1C15 + 5AB7H = 76CCH
(4004H) = CCH
(4005H) = 76H

LHLD 4000H	: Get first I6-bit number in HL
XCHG	: Save first I6-bit number in DE
LHLD 4002H	: Get second I6-bit number in HL
MOV A, E	: Get lower byte of the first number
ADD L	: Add lower byte of the second number
MOV L, A	: Store result in L register
MOV A, D	: Get higher byte of the first number

ADC H	: Add higher byte of the second number with CARRY
MOV H, A	: Store result in H register
SHLD 4004H	: Store 16-bit result in memory locations 4004H and 4005H.
HLT	: Terminate program execution

Program 1.7: Add the contents of memory locations 40001H and 4001H and place the result in the memory locations 4002H and 4003H.

(4000H) = 7FH
(4001H) = 89H
Result = 7FH + 89H = 108H
(4002H) = 08H
(4003H) = 01H

LXI H, 4000H	: HL Points 4000H
MOV A, M	: Get first operand
INX H	: HL Points 4001H
ADD M	: Add second operand
INX H	: HL Points 4002H
MOV M, A	: Store the lower byte of result at 4002H
MVI A, 00	: Initialize higher byte result with 00H ADC A : Add carry in the high byte result
INX H	: HL Points 4003H
MOV M, A	: Store the higher byte of result at 4003H
HLT	: Terminate program execution

Program 1.8: Subtract the 16-bit number in memory locations 4002H and 4003H from the 16-bit number in memory locations 4000H and 4001H. The most significant eight bits of the two numbers are in memory locations 4001H and 4003H. Store the result in memory locations 4004H and 4005H with the most significant byte in memory location 4005H.

(4000H) = 19H
(4001H) = 6AH
(4004H) = 15H (4003H) = 5CH
Result = 6A19H - 5C15H = 0E04H, (4004H) = 04H, (4005H) = 0EH

LHLD 4000H	: Get first 16-bit number in HL
XCHG	: Save first 16-bit number in DE
LHLD 4002H	: Get second 16-bit number in HL
MOV A, E	: Get lower byte of the first number
SUB L	: Subtract lower byte of the second number

MOV L, A	: Store the result in L register
MOV A, D	: Get higher byte of the first number
SBB H	: Subtract higher byte of second number with borrow
MOV H, A	: Store 16-bit result in memory locations 4004H and 4005H.
SHLD 4004H	: Store 16-bit result in memory locations 4004H and 4005H.
HLT	: Terminate program execution

Program 1.9: Find the 1's complement of the number stored at memory location 4400H and store the complemented number at memory location 4300H.

(4400H) = 55H // Any number, Result = (4300H) = AAH

LDA 4400B	: Get the number
CMA	: Complement number
STA 4300H	: Store the result
HLT	: Terminate program execution

Program 1.10: Find the 2's complement of the number stored at memory location 4200H and store the complemented number at memory location 4300H.

(4200H) = 55H, Result = (4300H) = AAH + 1 = ABH

LDA 4200H	: Get the number
CMA	: Complement the number
ADI, 01 H	: Add one in the number
STA 4300H	: Store the result
HLT	: Terminate program execution

Program 1.11: Calculate the sum of series of numbers. The length of the series is in memory location 4200H and the series begins from memory location 4201H. Consider the sum to be 8 bit number. So, ignore carries. Store the sum at memory location 4300H. and Consider the sum to be 16 bit number. Store the sum at memory locations 4300H and 4301H

4200H = 04H
4201H = 10H
4202H = 45H
4203H = 33H
4204H = 22H

Result = 10 + 41 + 30 + 12 = H, 4300H = H

Source program:

LDA 4200H	
MOV C, A	: Initialize counter
SUB A	: sum = 0

LXI H, 4201H	: Initialize pointer
BACK	: ADD M : SUM = SUM + data
INX H	: increment pointer
DCR C	: Decrement counter
JNZ BACK	: if counter 0 repeat
STA 4300H	: Store sum
HLT	: Terminate program execution

Program 1.12: Multiply two 8-bit numbers stored in memory locations 2200H and 2201H by repetitive addition and store the result in memory locations 2300H and 2301H.

(2200H) = 03H
(2201H) = B2H
Result = B2H + B2H + B2H = 216H, (2300H) = 16H, (2301H) = 02H

LDA 2200H	
MOV E, A	
MVI D, 00	: Get the first number in DE register pair
LDA 2201H	
MOV C, A	: Initialize counter
LXI H, 0000 H	: Result = 0
BACK: DAD D	: Result = result + first number
DCR C	: Decrement count
JNZ BACK	: If count 0 repeat
SHLD 2300H	: Store result
HLT	: Terminate program execution

Program 1.13: Divide 16 bit number stored in memory locations 2200H and 2201H by the 8 bit number stored at memory location 2202H. Store the quotient in memory locations 2300H and 2301H and remainder in memory locations 2302H and 2303H.

(2200H) = 60H
(2201H) = A0H
(2202H) = 12H
Result = A060H/12H = 8E8H Quotient and 10H remainder
(2300H) = E8H
(2301H) = 08H
(2302H= 10H
(2303H) 00H

Source program

```
LHLD 2200H      : Get the dividend
LDA 2202H       : Get the divisor
MOV C, A
LXI D, 0000H    : Quotient = 0
BACK: MOV A, L
SUB C           : Subtract divisor
MOV L, A        : Save partial result
JNC SKIP        : if CY 1 jump
DCR H           : Subtract borrow of previous subtraction
SKIP: INX D     : Increment quotient
MOV A, H
CPI, 00         : Check if dividend < divisor
JNZ BACK        : if no repeat
MOV A, L
CMP C
JNC BACK
SHLD 2302H      : Store the remainder
XCHG
SHLD 2300H      : Store the quotient
HLT             : Terminate program execution
```

Program 1.14: Find the number of negative elements (most significant bit 1) in a block of data. The length of the block is in memory location 2200H and the block itself begins in memory location 2201H. Store the number of negative elements in memory location 2300H

(2200H) = 04H (2201H) = 56H
(2202H) = A9H
(2203H) = 73H
(2204H) = 82H

Result = 02 since 2202H and 2204H contain numbers with a MSB of 1.

Source program

```
LDA 2200H
MOV C, A        : Initialize count
MVI B, 00       : Negative number = 0
LXI H, 2201H    : Initialize pointer
```

```
BACK: MOV A, M    : Get the number
ANI 80H           : Check for MSB
JZ SKIP           : If MSB = 1
INR B             : Increment negative number count
SKIP: INX H       : Increment pointer
DCR C             : Decrement count
JNZ BACK          : If count 0 repeat
MOV A, B
STA 2300H         : Store the result
HLT               : Terminate program execution
```

Program 1.15: Find the largest number in a block of data. The length of the block is in memory location 2200H and the block itself starts from memory location 2201H. Store the maximum number in memory location 2300H. Assume that the numbers in the block are all 8 bit unsigned binary numbers.

(2200H) = 04
(2201H) = 34H
(2202H) = A9H
(2203H) = 78H
(2204H) = 56H
Result = (2202H) = A9H

Source program

```
LDA 2200H
MOV C, A          : Initialize counter
XRA A             : Maximum = Minimum possible value = 0
LXI H, 2201H      : Initialize pointer
BACK: CMP M       : Is number> maximum
JNC SKIP          : Yes, replace maximum MOV A, M
SKIP: INX H
DCR C
JNZ BACK
STA 2300H         : Store maximum number
HLT               : Terminate program execution
```

Program 1.16: Write a program to count number of 1's in the contents of D register and store the count in the B register.

Source program:

```
MVI B, 00H
MVI C, 08H
MOV A, D
BACK: RAR
JNC SKIP
INR B
SKIP: DCR C
JNZ BACK
HLT
```

Program 1.17: Write a program to sort given 10 numbers from memory location 2200H in the ascending order.

MVI B, 09	: Initialize counter
START	: LXI H, 2200H: Initialize memory pointer
MVI C, 09H	: Initialize counter 2
BACK: MOV A, M	: Get the number
INX H	: Increment memory pointer
CMP M	: Compare number with next number
JC SKIP	: If less, don't interchange
JZ SKIP	: If equal, don't interchange
MOV D, M	
MOV M, A	
DCX H	
MOV M, D	
INX H	: Interchange two numbers
SKIP:DCR C	: Decrement counter 2
JNZ BACK	: If not zero, repeat
DCR B	: Decrement counter 1
JNZ START	
HLT	: Terminate program execution

Program 1.18: Calculate the sum of series of even numbers from the list of numbers. The length of the list is in memory location 2200H and the series itself begins from memory location 2201H. Assume the sum to be 8 bit number so you can ignore carries and store the sum at memory location

Sample problem:

2200H= 4H
2201H= 20H
2202H= 15H
2203H= 13H
2204H= 22H
Result 2210H= 20 + 22 = 42H
= 42H

Source program:

LDA 2200H	
MOV C, A	: Initialize counter
MVI B, 00H	: sum = 0
LXI H, 2201H	: Initialize pointer
BACK: MOV A, M	: Get the number
ANI 01H	: Mask Bit 1 to Bit 7
JNZ SKIP	: Don't add if number is ODD
MOV A, B	: Get the sum
ADD M	: SUM = SUM + data
MOV B, A	: Store result in B register
SKIP: INX H	: increment pointer
DCR C	: Decrement counter
JNZ BACK	: if counter 0 repeat
STA 2210H	: store sum
HLT	: Terminate program execution

Program 1.19: Find the square of the given numbers from memory location 6100H and store the result from memory location 7000H

LXI H, 6200H	: Initialize lookup table pointer
LXI D, 6100H	: Initialize source memory pointer
LXI B, 7000H	: Initialize destination memory pointer
BACK: LDAX D	: Get the number
MOV L, A	: A point to the square
MOV A, M	: Get the square
STAX B	: Store the result at destination memory location
INX D	: Increment source memory pointer

INX B	: Increment destination memory pointer
MOV A, C	
CPI 05H	: Check for last number
JNZ BACK	: If not repeat
HLT	: Terminate program execution

Program 1.20: Divide the 16-bit unsigned number in memory locations 2200H and 2201H (most significant bits in 2201H) by the B-bit unsigned number in memory location 2300H store the quotient in memory location 2400H and remainder in 2401H

Assumption: The most significant bits of both the divisor and dividend are zero.

MVI E, 00	: Quotient = 0
LHLD 2200H	: Get dividend
LDA 2300	: Get divisor
MOV B, A	: Store divisor
MVI C, 08	: Count = 8
NEXT: DAD H	: Dividend = Dividend x 2
MOV A, E	
RLC	
MOV E, A	: Quotient = Quotient x 2MOV A, H
SUB B	: Is most significant byte of Dividend > divisor
JC SKIP	: No, go to Next step
MOV H, A	: Yes, subtract divisor
INR E	: and Quotient = Quotient + 1
SKIP:DCR C	: Count = Count - 1
JNZ NEXT	: Is count =0 repeat
MOV A, E	
STA 2401H	: Store Quotient
Mov A, H	
STA 2410H	: Store remainder
HLT	: End of program

Program 1.21: Transfer ten bytes of data from one memory to another memory block. Source memory block starts from memory location 2200H where as destination memory block starts from memory location 2300H

```
LXI H, 4150       : Initialize memory pointer
MVI B, 08         : count for 8-bit
MVI A, 54
LOOP              : RRC
JC LOOP1
MVI M, 00         : store zero it no carry
JMP COMMON
LOOP2: MVI M, 01: store one if there is a carry
COMMON: INX H
DCR B             : check for carry
JNZ LOOP
HLT               : Terminate the program
```

1.7 ASSEMBLER

Assembler is system software which is used to convert an assembly language program to its equivalent object code. The input to the assembler is a source code written in assembly language (using mnemonics) and the output is the object code. The design of an assembler depends upon the machine architecture as the language used is mnemonic language.

Basic Assembler Functions:

The basic assembler functions are:
- Translating mnemonic language code to its equivalent object code.
- Assigning machine addresses to symbolic labels.

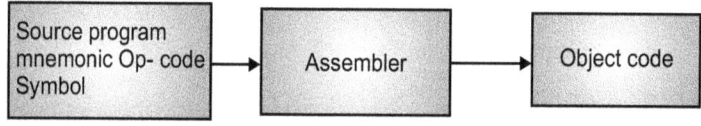

Fig. 1.10

The design of assembler can be to perform the following:
- Scanning (tokenizing)
- Parsing (validating the instructions)
- Creating the symbol table
- Resolving the forward references
- Converting into the machine language

The design of assembler in other words:
- Convert mnemonic operation codes to their machine language equivalents
- Convert symbolic operands to their equivalent machine addresses

- Decide the proper instruction format Convert the data constants to internal machine representations
- Write the object program and the assembly listing

So for the design of the assembler we need to concentrate on the machine architecture of the SIC/XE machine. We need to identify the algorithms and the various data structures to be used.

According to the above required steps for assembling the assembler also has to handle assembler directives, these do not generate the object code but directs the assembler to perform certain operation. These directives are:

START: Specify name & starting address.

END: End of the program, specify the first execution instruction.

BYTE, WORD, RESB, RESW

End of record: a null char(00)

End of file: a zero length record

The assembler design can be done in two ways:
- Single pass assembler
- Multi-pass assembler

Single-Pass Assembler :

In this case the whole process of scanning, parsing, and object code conversion is done in single pass. The only problem with this method is resolving forward reference. This is shown with an example below:

10	1000	FIRST	STL	RET	ADR	141033
--						
--						
95	1033	RETADR		RESW		1

In the above example in line number 10 the instruction STL will store the linkage register with the contents of RETADR. But during the processing of this instruction the value of this symbol is not known as it is defined at the line number 95. Since I single-pass assembler the scanning, parsing and object code conversion happens simultaneously. The instruction is fetched; it is scanned for tokens, parsed for syntax and semantic validity. If it valid then it has to be converted to its equivalent object code. For this the object code is generated for the opcode STL and the value for the symbol RETADR need to be added, which is not available.

Due to this reason usually the design is done in two passes. So a multi-pass assembler resolves the forward references and then converts into the object code. Hence the process of the multi-pass assembler can be as follows:

Pass-1
- Assign addresses to all the statements
- Save the addresses assigned to all labels to be used in Pass-2

- Perform some processing of assembler directives such as RESW, RESB to find the length of data areas for assigning the address values.
- Defines the symbols in the symbol table(generate the symbol table)

Pass-2
- Assemble the instructions (translating operation codes and looking up addresses).
- Generate data values defined by BYTE, WORD etc.
- Perform the processing of the assembler directives not done during pass-1.
- Write the object program and assembler listing.

Assembler Design :

The most important things which need to be concentrated is the generation of Symbol table and resolving forward references.

Symbol Table :
- This is created during pass - 1
- All the labels of the instructions are symbols
- Table has entry for symbol name, address value.

Forward Reference :

Symbols that are defined in the later part of the program are called forward referencing.
- There will not be any address value for such symbols in the symbol table in pass - 1.

Example Program :

The example program considered here has a main module, two subroutines Purpose of example program
- Reads records from input device (code F1)
- Copies them to output device (code 05)
- At the end of the file, writes EOF on the output device, then RSUB to the OS

Data transfer (RD, WD)
- A buffer is used to store record
- Buffering is necessary for different I/O rates
- The end of each record is marked with a null character $(00)_{16}$
- The end of the file is indicated by a zero-length record

Subroutines (JSUB, RSUB)
- RDREC, WRREC
- Save link register first before nested jump

1.7.1 Simple SIC Assembler

The program below is shown with the object code generated. The column named LOC gives the machine addresses of each part of the assembled program (assuming the program is

starting at location 1000). The translation of the source program to the object program requires us to accomplish the following functions:
- Convert the mnemonic operation codes to their machine language equivalent. Convert symbolic operands to their equivalent machine addresses.
- Build the machine instructions in the proper format.
- Convert the data constants specified in the source program into their internal machine representations in the proper format.
- Write the object program and assembly listing.

All these steps except the second can be performed by sequential processing of the source program, one line at a time. Consider the instruction

```
10 1000   LDA    ALPHA00 -----
```

This instruction contains the forward reference, i.e. the symbol ALPHA is used is not yet defined. If the program is processed (scanning and parsing and object code conversion) is done line-by-line, we will be unable to resolve the address of this symbol. Due to this problem most of the assemblers are designed to process the program in two passes.

In addition to the translation to object program, the assembler has to take care of handling assembler directive. These directives do not have object conversion but gives direction to the assembler to perform some function. Program of directives are the statements like BYTE and WORD, which directs the assembler to reserve memory locations without generating data values. The other directives are START which indicates the beginning of the program and END indicating the end of the program.

The assembled program will be loaded into memory for execution. The simple object program contains three types of records: Header record, Text record and end record. The header record contains the starting address and length. Text record contains the translated instructions and data of the program, together with an indication of the addresses where these are to be loaded.

The end record marks the end of the object program and specifies the address where the execution is to begin.

The assembler can be designed either as a single pass assembler or as a two pass assembler. The general description of both passes is as given below:

Pass 1 (Define Symbols)
- Assign addresses to all statements in the program
- Save the addresses assigned to all labels for use in Pass 2
- Perform assembler directives, including those for address assignment, such as BYTE
- and RESW

Pass 2 (Assemble Instructions and Generate Object Program)
- Assemble instructions (generate opcode and look up addresses)
- Generate data values defined by BYTE, WORD

- Perform processing of assembler directives not done during Pass 1
- Write the object program and the assembly listing.

QUESTIONS

1. Draw and explain architecture of 8085 microprocessor.
2. What are the different types of registers used in 8085 microprocessor.
3. Explain different types of flags used in 8085 microprocessor.
4. What are the different types of instructions used in 8085 microprocessor.
4. Explain the function of following instructions

   | STA addr | LDAX rp | SBB M | DAA | ANA M |
   | CMP r | RRC | JC | CALL | PUSH |

6. Explain the addressing modes in 8085 microprocessor.
7. What is assembler? Why it Is required?
8. Write an assembly language program to add / substact / multiply / division / block transfer / finding largest number etc.

✠ ✠ ✠

Unit - II

MICROPROCESSOR AND ARCHITECTURE

2.1 INTRODUCTION

A microprocessor is one of the most exciting technological innovations in electronics since the appearance of the transistor in 1948. This wonder device has not only set in the process of revolutionizing the field of digital electronics, but it is also getting entry into almost every sphere of human life. Applications of microprocessors range from the very sophisticated process controllers and supervisory control equipment to simple game machines and even toys.

It is, therefore, imperative for every engineer, specially electronics engineer, to know about microprocessors. Every designer of electronic products needs to learn how to use microprocessors. Even if he has no immediate plans to use a microprocessor, he should have knowledge of the subject so that he can intelligently plan his future projects and can make sound engineering judgments when the time comes.

The subject of microprocessors is overviewed here with the objective that a beginner gets to know what a microprocessor is, what it can do, how it fits in a system and gets an overall idea of the various components of such a system. Once he has understood signam of each component and its place in the system, he can go deeper into the working details and design of individual components without difficulty.

To an engineer who is familiar with mainframe and mini computers, a microcomputer is simply a less powerful mini computer. Microcomputers have smaller instruction sets and are slower than mini computers, but then they are far less expensive and smaller too. To an engineer with a hardware background and no computer experience, a microcomputer will look like a sequential state machine that can functionally replace thousands of random logic chips, but occupies a much lesser space, costs much lesser and the number of device interconnections being fewer in it, is much more reliable.

A microcomputer is primarily suited, because of its very low cost and very small size, to dedicated applications. On the same grounds, the mainframe computer is as a rule suitable as a general purpose computer. Mini computer finds applications in both areas.

2.2 MICROPROCESSOR BASED PERSONAL COMPUTER SYSTEM

2.2.1 Microprocessor-Based Computer System

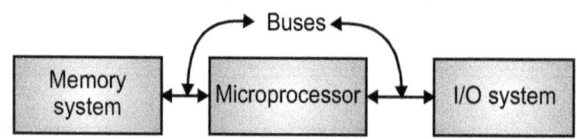

Fig. 2.1 : The block diagram of a microprocessor-based computer system

Dynamic RAM (DRAM)	8085, 8086, 8088	Mouse
Static RAM (SRAM)	80186, 801486	Keyboard
Cache	Pentium, Pentium II	Printer
Read-only (ROM)	Pentium III, Pentium 4	Hard disk drive
Flash memory EEPROM	Core2duo, dual core	Monitor
SDRAM	I-3, I-5.	Scanner

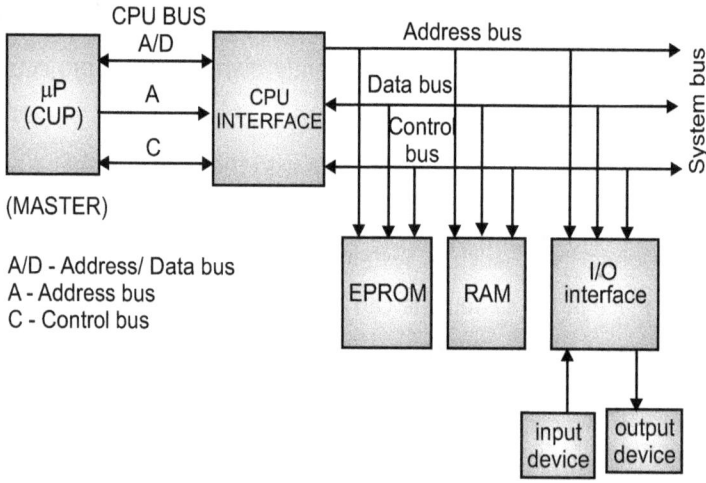

A/D - Address/ Data bus
A - Address bus
C - Control bus

Fig. 2.2 : Microprocessor based system (organization of microcomputer)

There are many different kinds of microprocessors and microprocessor based systems, most microprocessors are designed following the same architecture. The most popular computer architecture used nowadays is von Neumann architecture. More complex systems uses Harvard architecture (to be explained in the later lecture). von Neumann architecture divides the computer system into five parts: computation unit, control unit, memory, input, and output. Most today's systems put computation unit and control unit together and call it CPU, and put input and output together and call it I/O component.

It consists of 4 main parts

1. **Central Processing Unit (CPU)**

   CPU has two main components Arithmetic and logic unit (ALU) Responsible for computation only,‹ Control unit Responsible for sending and gathering information from memory and I/O Responsible for coordinating the sequence and timing of the activities on the whole system.„ CPU also has several storage places called registers.

   CPU is the "brain" of the microcomputer. It provides the decision making ability for the computer. CPU has two parts, the arithmetic and logic unit (ALU), and control unit. ALU is responsible for arithmetic and logic operations. Control unit is responsible for coordinating the data flow and to control the sequence and timing of circuit operations in the system. Registers are a very small but fast accessing storage space that hold very essential information for program execution and decision making. In program execution, the CPU reads and executes the programs instructions one by one from the main memory. The execution of instructions may involve the arithmetic/logic operations and/or transfer data between CPU and main memory (or I/O ports).

2. **Memory**

Primary (or main) memory
- Volatile memory: RAM - random access memory
- Non-volatile memory: ROM - read only memory EPROM, EEPROM, FLASH

„ Secondary memory

Hard disks, CD, floppy disks, tape

Memory is responsible for storing programs and the data that are needed by the program. To make the concept clear, we divide the computer memory to main memory (or primary memory) and secondary memory. The main memory is the memory that the CPU can access directly. Examples of main memory include RAM, ROM, etc.. The secondary memory cannot be addressed directly (cannot access specified memory location) by the CPU. Examples of secondary include floppy disk, hard disk, CD, etc.. The information in the secondary memory must be copied to the main memory so that CPU can access it. Secondary memory is much cheaper than primary memory. There are two types of primary memories: volatile and nonvolatile. Volatile memory is the type of memory that will lose data when the power supply to the memory is gone. Random access memory (RAM) is one type of volatile memory.

Nonvolatile memory keeps the data in the memory even it is not powered up. Nonvolatile memory includes read only memory (ROM), one time programmable memory (OTP), erasable programmable memory (EPROM), electrically erasable programmable read only memory (EEPROM), and flash memory. ROM can only be programmed by the chip manufacturer. OTP can be programmed only once by the user. EPROM can be programmed and reprogrammed by the user. The erasing process usually takes 10 to 30 minutes. EEPROM and flash memory can be programmed and erased electrically. The memory erasing and reprogramming process for EEPROM and flash memory is fast (takes a few minutes). EEPROM can be programmed and erased byte by byte. Flash memory can only be erased block (many bytes) by block.

(i) Memory Management

microprocessor, memory management becomes extremely important. Memory management is required due to the following two reasons.

1. Limitation of Physical Memory

A microprocessor has limited number of address lines. Hence the physical memory addressability is limited. Increasing the number of address lines is not attractive as it makes the architecture and design complex without significant gain. Packaging becomes difficult and expensive. Memory Management Unit (MMU) solves this problem by translating the virtual memory address into the physical memory address. Virtual memory can be many times larger than the physical memory. Only the programs currently required are brought from the secondary storage such as a hard disk to, the physical memory (RAM) for execution.

2. Need for Protection

In a multi-user operating system, there is a possibility that a user program can corrupt the operating system area or the area of some other user unless a protection mechanism is built. Hence each user should be protected from other users and the operating system should be protected from other user (task). The user (task) should be allowed to have a controlled access to the operating system resources. Hence various privilege levels are defined. For example, in a situation having 4 privilege levels, 0 is the highest privilege and 3 has the lowest privilege as shown in the fig. The fig. shows a typical Unix operating system layout.

It has to be noted that the user is at the lowest privilege level, i.e., privilege level 3 and the operating system Kernel is at the highest privilege level, i.e., privilege level 0.

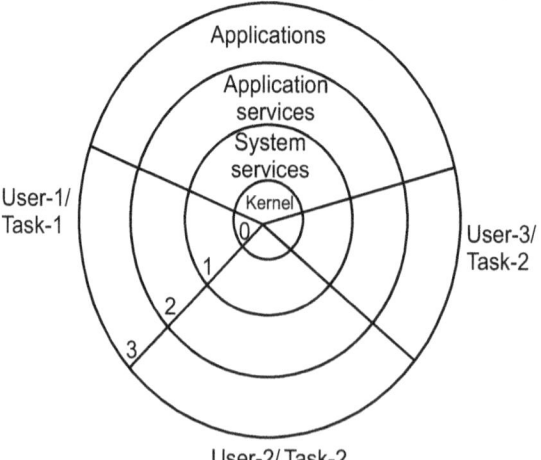

Fig. 2.3 : Protection mechanism and privilege levels

Kernel, System services and Application services constitute the operating system. The user or task sits at the lowest privilege level and can not access the resource available at higher privilege levels directly. Similarly, Task-1, Task-2 and Task-3 occupy different memory blocks and they are protected from each other. A microprocessor such as 8086 does not provide this kind of protection. The Memory Management Unit (MMU) of advanced microprocessors such as 80286 incorporates this kind of protection for a multi-user operating system.

(ii) Role of Memory Management Unit (MMU):

The virtual address space of a microprocessor may be many times larger than the actual physical address space. This is desirable as a microprocessor is supposed to store large programs and data which can not be accommodated in the physical memory space. Usually programs and data are stored in a secondary storage such as a hard disk. The hard disk is in the virtual or logical address space but not in the physical address space. Faster memory such as RAM is used as the physical memory (Primary Storage).

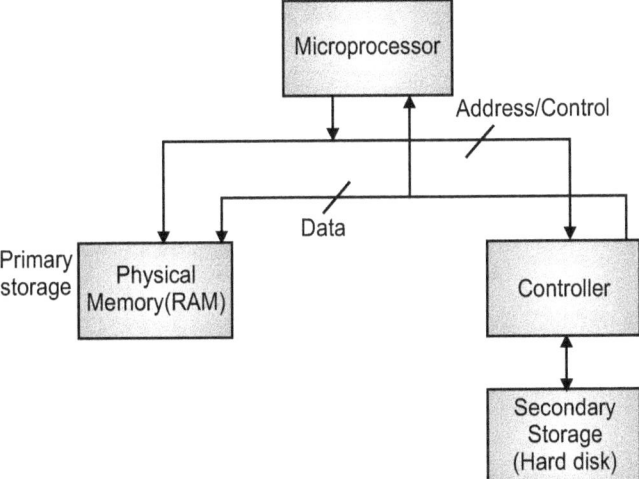

Fig. 2.4 : Microprocessor interfacing with primary storage and secondary storage

When a microprocessor is to execute a program, it checks whether the program is available in the physical memory (RAM). If the program is not available in the physical memory, it is brought from the secondary memory to the physical memory for execution. If available space is inadequate in the physical memory, some less important or unused program can be swapped back to the secondary memory to create space.

(iii) Memory Management Unit (MMU)

Memory Management Unit within a microprocessor converts the virtual memory address into a physical memory address. Virtual memory address is sometimes referred as logical memory address.

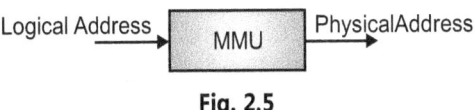

Fig. 2.5

MMU can convert logical address into physical address in two ways.

1. Segment Oriented Approach :

In this case, the logical memory space consists of memory segments of variable length. Each segment contains some data/ program as is described by a "descriptor". The segment "descriptor" contains the base address of the segment, segment size and other attributes. The descriptors of all segments are stored in a "descriptor table" located in the physical memory.

The logical address of a memory location contains two parts, viz, segment selector and offset. The segment selector points to the segment "descriptor" in the descriptor table. From the "descriptor", the base address of the segment is obtained. The offset part of the logical address is added to the segment base to generate physical address of the memory.

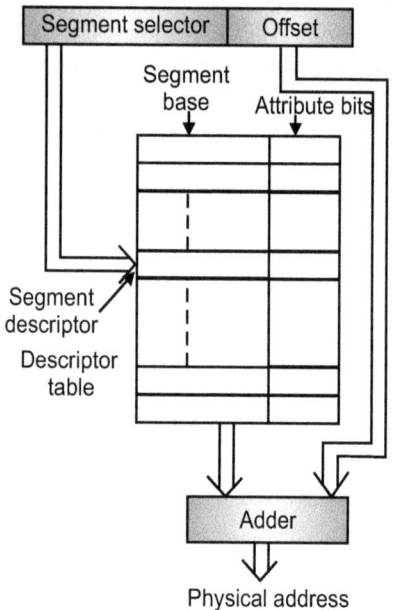

Fig. 2.6

2. **Page Oriented Approach**

In page oriented approach, the logical address space is divided into pages of fixed length. A page has 4 Kbytes. Since the MMU deals with smaller chunk of memory (4 Kbytes), it is easier and faster to swap back and forth between the secondary storage and the physical memory.

3. **Input / Output**

Input ports:‹ Mouse, Keyboard, switches, sensors

„ Output ports:‹ Monitor,‹ Printer,

„ Bi-directional ports:‹ Modem,‹ Disk,‹ Networks

I/O is responsible for interfacing between CPU and operators (or external devices). I/O includes any device that converts binary data in the computer into another form of data that are used by human beings. Examples of I/O devices include monitors, keyboards, printers, modems, mice, hard disks, floppy disks, etc.. Each computer system may have many I/O ports. Each input port has a unique address and each output port has a unique address. Some microprocessors assign the memory and I/O with separate address space (e.g., Intel x86 processors). In this case, one may use memory address X and also I/O address X the same time. Some microprocessors make the memory and I/O use the same address space (e.g., Motorola 68HC12). In this case, if memory uses address X, I/O cannot use address X.

4. Buses

Components need to be connected, Wires connecting the components are called buses,,, There are three types buses:‹ Address bus,‹ Data bus,‹ Control Bus

We have mentioned that a microcomputer includes three fundamental components, Central Processing Unit (CPU), Main Memory (MM), and Input/output (I/O). These three components are connected by a set of parallel electric conductors (wires), called buses. A bus is a set of parallel connections between components. There are three types of buses in a microcomputer: address bus, data bus and

(i) Control Bus:

- "CPU needs to indicate not only the address of interested information, but also what to be done for that information, e.g., ‹ to read from or write to a memory address, ‹ to read from or write to an I/O port, ‹ etc.

- "Control bus is a set of wires to carry the command from CPU to memory or I/O and to receive response or request information from memory or I/O" The number of wires on control bus depends on the complexity of the system.

- Control bus carries the control signals between CPU and memory/IO. There are many control signals for computer operations. Some control signals are related and must be considered in parallel. Some control signals are independent and unrelated to other control signals. Not all the control signals need to be utilized. Therefore, the width of the control bus depend not only on the CPU but also on the complexity of the application system. That is the reason that we usually do not mention the width of the control bus.

- The address bus is used mainly by the microprocessors to indicate which particular address in the main memory or I/O need to be accessed. The data bus is used for retrieving information from main memory or I/O to the microprocessor, or store the information from the microprocessor to memory or I/O. The control bus is responsible for transmitting task commands (e.g., read, write, etc.) to the memory and I/O and receiving corresponding responses from memory and I/O components.

(ii) Address Bus

- The information for computation is stored in memory,,, Some information for computation are obtained from input ports,,, The size of memory and I/O are usually defined in the unit of BYTEs.

- A CPU needs to access thousands or millions of memory and I/O addresses. A CPU should indicate which particular memory or I/O address need to be accessed. Address bus carries the signal that indicates the address of the interested information. The signals on the address bus always go from CPU to memory or I/O.

- We have learned that CPU is responsible for executing the program and memory is responsible for storing program and data. It is obvious that the desired program and data need to be moved from memory to CPU for execution. Since CPU controls the activities of the whole system, CPU should indicate which address of the memory or I/O is interested. The address is carried by the address bus. The address information always goes from CPU to memory and I/O. All memory and I/O components that are connected to the address bus should monitor the information on the address bus all the time. Each memory and I/O has a unique set of addresses. Only one of the memory or I/O component can respond to the CPU's request at each time.

Address

In a binary digital circuit, each wire can indicate one of two states at any time instance,,, The two states are 1 (High) and 0 (Low),,, Therefore, at any time instance.‹ One wire can indicate two different addresses,‹ Two wires can indicate 2^2 different states (00, 01, 10, 11).‹ Three wires can indicate 2^3 different states (000, 001, 010, 011, 100, 101, 110, 111).‹ N wires can indicate 2^N different states .,, If a system has M memory addresses, its address bus should have at least log2M (or bits)

In the digital computer system, the information are transmitted based on the two voltage levels (high and low). Therefore, all the information are represented by binary numbers. A memory or I/O address is represented by a binary number too. There are two ways to transmit information: sequential and parallel. In sequential transmit ion, one wire can be used to send 1 bit information at one time and another bit information at another time. In parallel transmission, many wires are used in parallel to transmit many bits at the same time. Address bus uses parallel transmission.

If a CPU supports more memory addresses, it should have wider address bus. In the other words, based on the number of bits of an address bus, we can calculate the addressable space of a microprocessor. As computers ranging from simple to complex, the number of wires on the address buses for different system ranges from 12 bits to 32 bits. 8085 uses 16 bit address, 8086 uses 20 bit address and 68HC12 microprocessor used in this course has 16 bit address bus.

(iii) Data bus

CPU needs to store or retrieve information in memory or I/O.,, These information are represented in electric voltage and carried by a set of wires called data bus.,, The number of wires on the data bus is the number of bits to be transmitted in parallel between memory and CPU at each time.,, Wider data bus can reduce the number of data transfer ,, The data bus for 8085 is 8 bit, 8086 has 16 bit and 68HC12 can be either 8 bits or 16 bits. Besides providing address information to Memory and I/O through address bus, CPU also need a way to move the content of memory addresses to and from memory and I/O. Data can be moved one bit at a time or hundreds bits at a time. The width of the data bus determines how many bits are moved at each time. The common width of the data bus ranges from 8 bit to 32 bit. Some advanced microprocessors have 64 or even 128 bit wide data bus. The data bus for 68HC12 can be either 8 bit or 16 bits. If the data bus of a CPU is at most 8 bit wide, the CPU is an 8-bit CPU. If the data bus of a CPU is at most 32 bit wide, the CPU is a 32-bit CPU. 68HC12 is a 16-bit CPU.

Data

From CPU point of view, any information needed from memory and I/O is called data. Data can be the information needed by a program (as we commonly think what data is). Data can also be program instructions.

Since CPU just does calculation, from CPU point of view, any information needed from the memory and I/O are considered as data and obtained through data bus. Some data are the program instructions and some data are the information needed to execute the program instructions. From programmer's point of view, data is only the information needed by the program. Therefore, it is important to clarify what do we mean when talking about data.

2.2.2 CPU and its Supporting Circuits

Power and ground, Reset, Clock, Signal de-multiplexing, Signal buffering (bus driver) are CPU supporting circuits.

In the rest of this chapter, we will describe the CPU and its connection to buses. In order to make a CPU work, several supporting circuits are needed. Although the actual implementation of these circuits in a particular system may be different, the concept used in these circuits are the same for all different kind of microprocessors. We will try to show these concepts on different microprocessors.

Power and Ground

CPUs usually have multiple power and ground connections. The purpose of multiple power and ground connections is to avoid interference between various CPU internal circuits for computation, control and drivers.

All microprocessors need power supply and ground. A microprocessor may use either 3 volt power or 5 volt power. If re-programmable memory (EEPROM, flash memory) is included in the microprocessor, 11 to 12 volt power supply may be needed. A microprocessor may use multiple power lines and multiple ground pins. The purpose of using separate power and ground pins is to reduce electrical interference between different circuits that are responsible for computation, control, analog to digital conversion, and port drivers.

Clock Circuit

All CPU circuits work according to a fast and accurate clock.„ The ideal clock signal is actually a square wave with fixed duty cycles.

Fig. 2.7

The clock signal usually is originated from a crystal. The maximum and minimum frequency of the clock is specified by the CPU. Each CPU has a suggested circuits for crystal connection.

All CPU circuitry operates according to the system clock. Some CPU circuits work according to the rising edge of the clock and some on the falling edge of the clock. The ideal clock is a square wave with specified duty cycle. The required duty cycles (100% * time of high in a period/ period) for the clock input differ from different microprocessors. Each CPU specifies a maximum clock speed and minimum clock speed. The source of clock can be from a quartz crystal, or an RC circuits, or an external circuit. Most CPUs are driven by quartz crystal. Each CPU has its own suggested ways to connect a clock source to it. The frequency of the crystal should be chosen as an integer multiple of the desired system clock frequency (depends on the given CPU).

2.3 INTERNAL MICROPROCESSOR ARCHITECTURE

The processor, also called the **Central Processing Unit (CPU)**, interprets and carries out the basic instructions that operate a computer. The processor significantly impacts overall computing power and manages most of a computer's operations. On the larger computers, such as mainframes and supercomputers, the various functions performed by the processor extend over many separate chips and often multiple circuit boards. On a personal computers, such as mainframes and supercomputers, the various functions performed by the processor extend over many separate chips and often multiple circuit boards. On a personal computer, all functions of the processor usually are on a single chip. Some computer and chip manufacturers use the term microprocessor to refer to a personal computer processor chip.

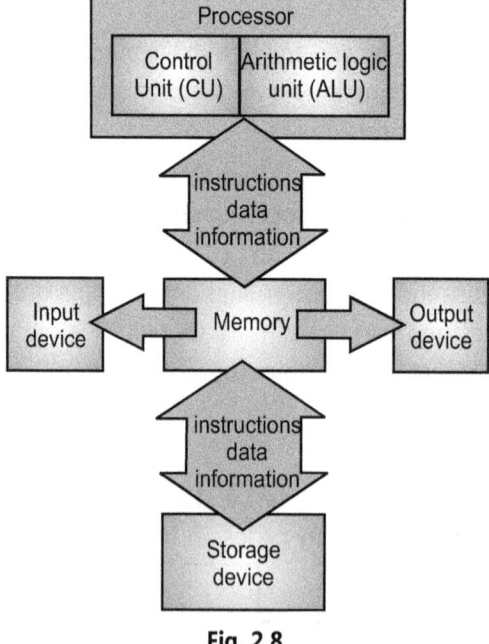

Fig. 2.8

The underlying principles of all computer processors are the same. It does not matter of the brand, age, software or broadband set-up. Fundamentally, they all take signals in the form of binary (0s and 1s), manipulate them according to a set of instructions, and produce output in the form of binary. The voltage on the line at the time and signal is sent determines whether the signal is a 0 or 1. On a 3.3-volt system, an application of 3.3-volts means that it's 1, while an application of 0 volts means it's a 0.

Processors work by reacting to an input of 0s and 1s in specific ways and then returning an output based on the decision. The decision itself happens in a circuit called a logic gate, each of which requires at least one transistor, with the inputs and outputs arranged differently by different operations. The fact that today's processors contain millions of transistors offer a clue as to how complex the logic system is. The processor's logic gates work together to make decisions using Boolean Logic, which is based on the algebraic system establish by mathematician George Boole. For more information regarding Boolean logic.

A processor contains small, high-speed storage locations, called registers, that temporarily hold data and instructions. Registers are part of the processor, not part of memory or a permanent storage device. Processors have many different types of registers, each with a specific storage function. Register functions include storing the location from where an instruction was fetched, storing and instruction while the control unit decodes it, storing the data while the ALU computes it, and storing the results of a calculation.

To summarise registers are locations where data or control information is temporarily stored. It's like a drawer in which you keep your files and papers. The CPU is made up for two main parts; Arithmetic Logic Unit and Control Unit.

The control unit is the component of the processor that directs and coordinates most of the processor that directs and coordinates most of the operations in the computer. The control unit has a role much like a traffic light: it interprets each instruction issued by a program and then initiates the appropriate action to carry out the instruction. Types of internal components that the control unit directs include the arithmetic/logic unit, registers, and buses.

The functions performed by the control unit vary greatly by the internal architecture of the CPU, since the control unit really implements this architecture of the CPU, since the control unit implements this architecture. On a regular processor that executes x86 instructions natively the control unit performs the tasks of fetching, decoding, managing execution and then storing results.

The Arithmetric Logic Unit (ALU), another component of the processor, performs arithmetic, comparison, and other operations.

Arithmetic operations include basic calculations such as addition, subtraction, multiplication, and division. Comparison operations involve comparing one data item with another to determine whether the first item is greater than, equal to, or less than the other item is greater than, equal to, or less than the other item. Depending on the results of the comparison, different actions may occur.

For every instruction, a processor repeats a set of four basic operations, which comprise a machine cycle.

- **Step 1: Fetching** : Fetching is the process of obtaining a program instruction or data item from memory.
- **Step 2: Decoding** : The term decoding refers to the process of translating the instruction into signals the computer can execute.
- **Step 3: Executing** : Executing is the process of carrying out the commands.
- **Step 4: Storing (if necessary)** : Storing, in this context, means writing the result to memory (not to a storage medium).

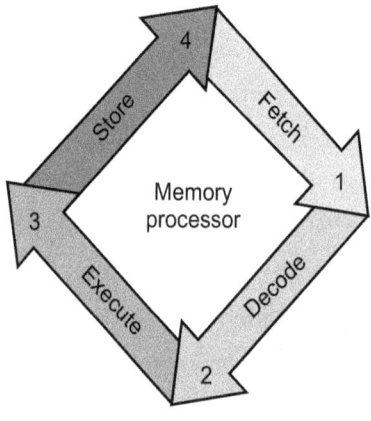

Fig. 2.9

In some computers, the processor fetches, decodes, executes, and stores only one instruction at a time. In these computers, the processor waits until an instruction completes all four stages of the machine cycle (fetch, decode, execute, and store) before beginning work on the next instruction.

Most of today's personal computers support a concept called pipelining. With pipelining, the processor begins fetching a second instruction before it completes the machine cycle for the first instruction. Processors that use pipelining are faster because they do not have to wait for one instruction to complete the machine cycle before fetching the next. Think of a pipeline as an assembly line. By the time the first instruction is in the last stage of the machine cycle, three other instructions could have been fetched and started through the machine cycle.

Machine cycle (without pipeline):

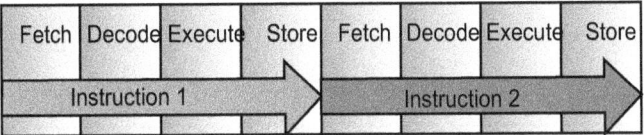

Machine cycle (with pipeline):

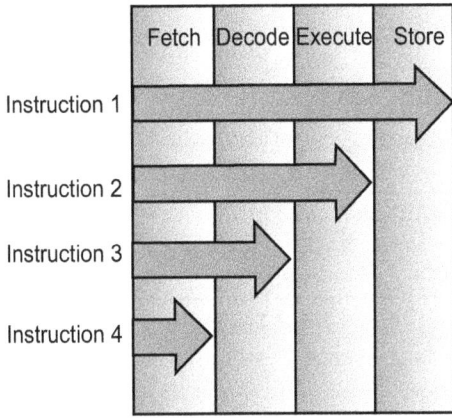

Fig. 2.10

Most modern computers support pipelining. With pipelining, the processor fetches a second instruction before the first instruction.

2.3.1 System Clock

The processor relies on a small quartz crystal circuit called the system clock to control the timing of all computer operations. Just as your heart beats at a regular rate to keep your body functioning, the system clock generates regular electronic pulses, or ticks, that set the operating pace of components of the system unit.

Each tick equates to a clock cycle. In the past, processors used on or more clock cycles to execute each instruction. Processors today often are superscalar, which means they can execute more than one instruction per clock cycle.

The pace of the system clock, called the clock speed, is measured by the number of ticks per second. Current personal computer processors have clock speeds in the gigahertz range. Giga is a prefix that stands for billion, and a hertz is one cycle per second. Thus, one gigahertz (GHz) equals one billion ticks of the system clock per second. A computer that operates at 3 Ghz has 3 billion (giga) clock cycles in one second (hertz).

The faster the clock speed, the more instructions the processor can execute per second. The speed of the system clock has no effect on devices such as a printer or disk drive. The speed of the system clock is just one factor that influences a computer's performance. Other factors, such as the type of processor chip, amount of cache, memory access time, bus width, and bus clock speed.

2.3.2 Cache

Most of today's computers improve processing times with **cache** (pronounced cash). Two types of cache are memory cache and disk cache.

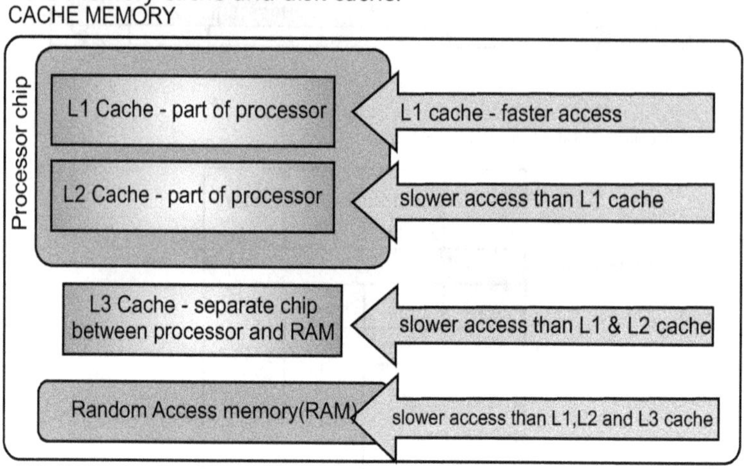

```
                    CACHE MEMORY

Processor chip
    ┌─ L1 Cache - part of processor ─┐  ← L1 cache - faster access
    │                                │
    └─ L2 Cache - part of processor ─┘  ← slower access than L1 cache

       L3 Cache - separate chip
       between processor and RAM       ← slower access than L1 & L2 cache

       Random Access memory(RAM)       ← slower access than L1, L2 and L3 cache
```

Fig. 2.11

Memory Cache helps speed the processes of the computer because it stores frequently used instructions and data. Most personal computers today have two types of memory cache: L1 cache and L2 cache. Some also have L3 Cache.

- **L1 Cache :** L1 Cache is built directly in the processor chip. L1 cache usually has a very small capacity, ranging from 8Kb to 128Kb. The more common sizes for personal computers are 32Kb or 64Kb.
- **L2 Cache :** L2 Cache is slightly slower than L1 cache but has a much larger capacity, ranging from 64 Kb to 16 Mb. When discussing cache, most users are referring to L2 cache. Current processor include advanced transfer cache (ATC), a type of L2 cache built directly on the processor chip. Processors that use ATC perform at much faster rates than those that do not use it.
- **L3 Cache :** L3 Cache is a cache on the motherboard that is separate from the processor chip. L3 cache exists only on computers that use L2 advanced transfer cache (ATC). Personal computers often have up to 8 Mb of L3 cache; servers and workstations have from 8 Mb to 24 Mb of L3 cache.

  Cache speeds up processing time because it stores frequently used instructions and data. When the processor needs an instruction or data, it searches memory in this order: L1 cache, then L2 cache, then L3 cache (if it exists), then RAM with a greater delay in processing for each level of memory it must search.

  If the instruction or data is not found in memory, then it must search a slower speed storage medium such as a hard disk, CD, or DVD. Windows Vista users can increase the size of cache through Windows Ready Boost, which can allocate up to 4 GB of removable flash memory devices as additional cache. Examples of removable flash memory include USB flash drives, Compact Flash cards, and SD (Secure Digital) cards.

2.4 ARCHITECTURE OF 8086

Unlike microcontrollers, microprocessors do not have inbuilt memory. Mostly Princeton architecture is used for microprocessors where data and program memory are combined in a single memory interface. Since a microprocessor does not have any inbuilt peripheral, the circuit is purely digital and the clock speed can be anywhere from a few MHZ to a few hundred MHZ or even GHZ. This increased clock speed facilitates intensive computation that a microprocessor is supposed to do.

We will discuss the basic architecture of Intel 8086 before discussing more advanced microprocessor architectures.

Intel 8086 is a 16 bit integer processor. It has 16-bit data bus and 20-bit address bus. The lower 16-bit address lines and 16-bit data lines are multiplexed (AD0-AD15). Since 20-bit address lines are available, 8086 can access up to 1 Giga byte of physical memory.

The basic architecture of 8086 is shown below.

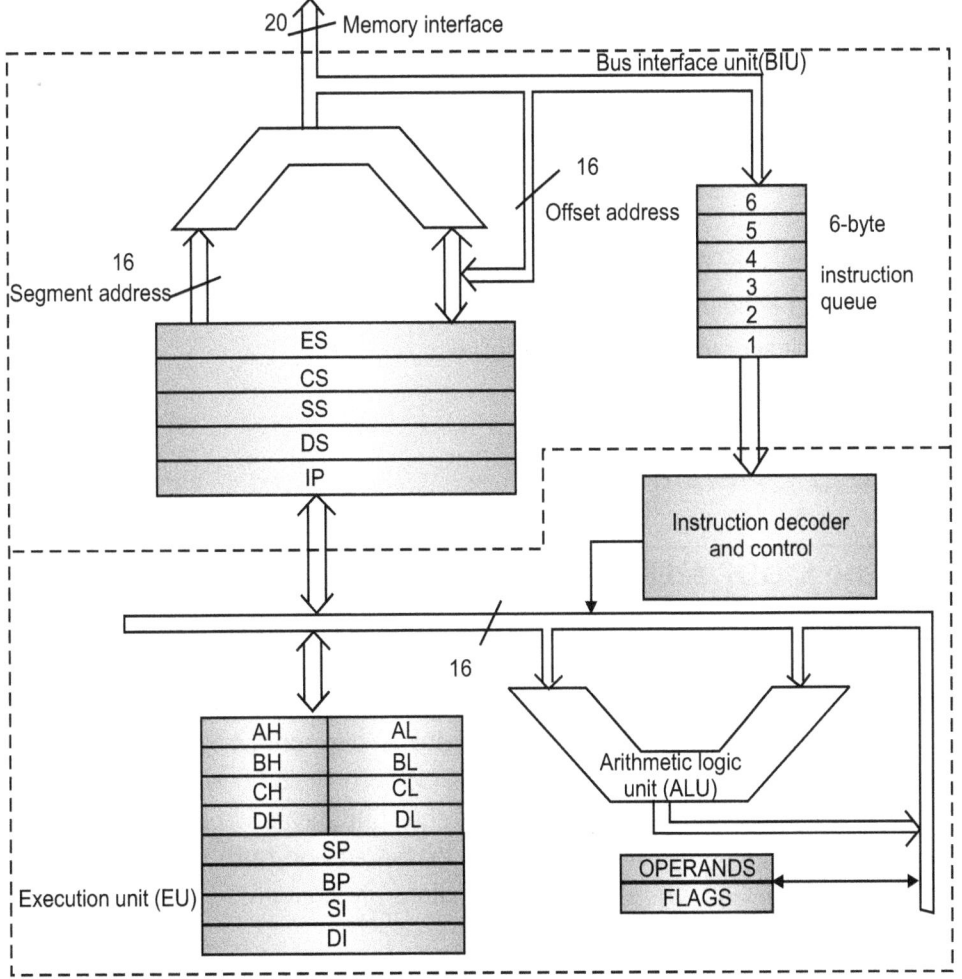

Fig. 2.12 : Basic architecture of 8086 microprocessor

The internal architecture of Intel 8086 is divided into two units, viz., Bus Interface Unit (BIU) and Execution Unit (EU).

Bus Interface Unit (BIU)

The Bus Interface Unit (BIU) generates the 20-bit physical memory address and provides the interface with external memory (ROM/RAM). As mentioned earlier, 8086 has a single memory interface. To speed up the execution, 6-bytes of instruction are fetched in advance and kept in a 6-byte Instruction Queue while other instructions are being executed in the Execution Unit (EU). Hence after the execution of an instruction, the next instruction is directly fetched from the instruction queue without having to wait for the external memory to send the instruction. This is called pipe-lining and is helpful for speeding up the overall execution process.

8086's BIU produces the 20-bit physical memory address by combining a 16-bit segment address with a 16-bit offset address. There are four 16-bit segment registers, viz., the code segment (CS), the stack segment (SS), the extra segment (ES), and the data segment (DS). These segment registers hold the corresponding 16-bit segment addresses. A segment address is the upper 16-bits of the starting address of that segment. The lower 4-bits of the starting address of a segment is always zero. The offset address is held by another 16-bit register. The physical 20-bit address is calculated by shifting the segment address 4-bit left and then adding that to the offset address.

For Example:

Code segment Register CS holds the segment address which is 4569 H

Instruction pointer IP holds the offset address which is 10A0 H

The physical 20-bit address is calculated as follows.

Segment address :   45690 H
Offset address   : + 10A0 H
Physical address :   46730 H

2.5 REAL MODE MEMORY ADDRESSING

Intel processors start executing code in the real-mode operating environment. Since real-mode is fully compatible with the 8086 architecture, it enables execution of MS-DOS applications on newer processors such as the Pentium and Pentium Pro. Unfortunately, along with the numerous benefits of real-mode, there is also one major drawback to this mechanism. That is, a processor running in real-mode can exploit only the lowest 20 bits of its address bus and is therefore limited to the meagre 1MB memory space of the 8086. IBM's decision to reserve the upper 384KB of the PC for ISA add-on cards (and the BIOS), made things even worst since it left real-mode applications (including MS-DOS itself) with barely 640 KB of RAM to work with.

As you already know, a processor requires a minimum of 20 address lines to have the ability to access 1MB of memory. When Intel engineers designed the 8086, it was impracticle to implement a 20 bit address register to hold the generated addresses. So instead, Intel decided to divide address space into 64 KB segments and coordinate memory access through the use of two 16 bit values - a **Segment** and an **Offset**.

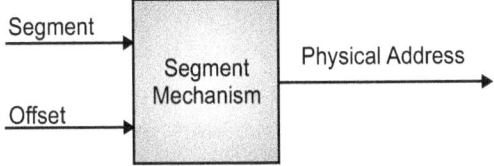

Fig. 2.13

Four dedicated Segment Registers were created in order to hold the segment portion of the processor generated addresses. Each of these registers was designated to serve as a base pointer to a unique segment in the processor physical address space.

Segment Register	Designated Role
CS	**Code Segment Register** This register points to the currently active code segment. Used in conjunction with the IP register to point to the next instruction to be fetched and executed by the processor.
DS	**Data Segment Register** This register usually points to the default data segment which contains the global and static variables of the active application.
ES	**Extra Segment Register** General purpose segment register used mostly for data transfers between different segments.
SS	**Stack Segment Register** This register points to the segment containing the active stack. The top of stack is located at address SS:SP.
FS GS	**General Purpose Segment Registers** First introduced on the 80386, these segment registers can be used for any purpose in your application code.

The value set into a segment register identifies a specific 64 KB region of memory, where as the offset part points to an exact location within that region. To calculate a physical address, the processor shifts the content of the segment register four bits to the left (thus multiplying its value by 16) and adds the offset.

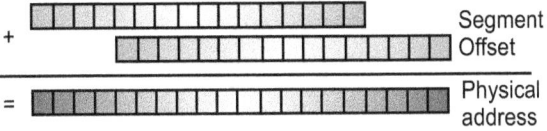

Fig. 2.14 : Physical memory calculation in real-mode

The notation adopted by Intel for address representation in real-mode is segment offset. For an example consider address A359:B3FD which is located at segment A359h and has an offset which equals B3FDh. This notation was chosen since it serves the need to pinpoint an exact location within the physical address space of the processor while allowing the programmer to examine the internal composition of the address value.

Interesting to note is the fact that although segments are 64 KB in size, they are spaced 16 bytes apart in memory. This should make perfect sense to you if you understand the procedure taken by the processor when it calculates physical addresses in real-mode. Since the content of a segment register forms the 16 high-order bits of a physical address, it is always divisible by 16 and has its lowest four bits set to zero.

This concept is clearly depicted in the following Fig. 2.15.

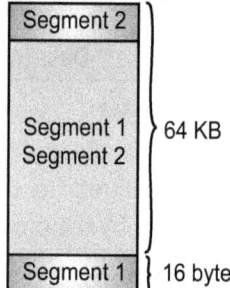

Fig. 2.15 : Consecutive segments

Note that there is an area of overlap between segments in real-mode, so each physical address is accessible using many different combinations of segment and offset values. For instance, if we load one of the segment registers with 1234H and use an offset which equals 5 H, we can read the content of physical address 12345H.

    Mov BX, 1234H

    Mov ES, BX

    Mov BX, 5H

    Mov AL, [ES:BX]

In this case, the processor will shift 1234H four bits to the left (12340H) and add the offset 5H. Alternatively, we could load ES with 1233H and use an offset which equals 15H to get a pointer which corresponds to the same physical memory location.

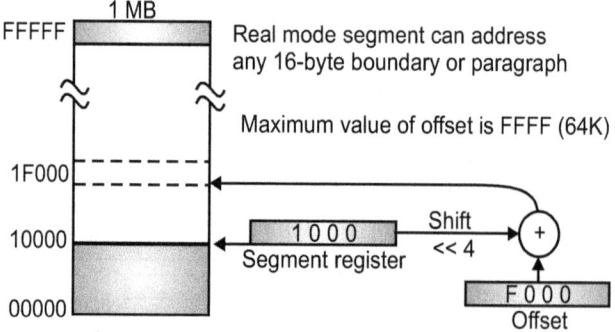

Fig. 2.16

In real mode, the effective memory address is the same as the linear, or physical, memory address. The segment register operates by specifying the base of a 64 kb region of memory, each region overlapping the other by 16 bytes.

In protected mode, the effective address is translated by the page table which provides a larger region size and more memory addressability. The segment register, a/k/a selector, selects the particular page table to use.

In the 8086-type processors, memory is organized into bytes (8 bits=1 byte). When dealing with quantities larger than eight bits, the 8086 stores the least significant byte in the lowest address. While that sounds logical, it's confusing when you're reading listings or memory dumps because the numbers seem backwards. For instance, the computer stores the word B800H as two bytes: 00H followed by B8H.

The Intel family of processors use a memory-addressing technique known as segmentation. A segment is a region of memory. The computer can handle multiple segments. In real mode (the one in which DOS normally runs), each segment is 64 K long and there are 65536 possible segments. But these segments overlap so that each starts 16 bytes after the one before it. This is why DOS cannot address more than 1MB directly (65536 * 16 = 1048576 = 1MB). The 8086 and 8088 can only address 1MB anyway. The 286, 386+ can accommodate much more memory, but DOS cannot access it directly.

Segments are numbered from 0000H to FFFFH. Since each segment is 64KB long, we use a value called an offset, to specify the byte we want to address. A complete 8086 address always contains a segment and an offset.

2.6 PROTECTED MODE MEMORY ADDRESSING

When the processor is running in protected-mode, two mechanisms are involved in the memory translation process: Segmentation and Paging. Although working in tandem, these two mechanisms are completely independent of each other. In fact, the paging unit can be disabled by clearing a single bit in an internal processor register. In this case, the linear addresses which are generated by the segmentation unit pass transparently through the paging unit and straight to the processor address bus.

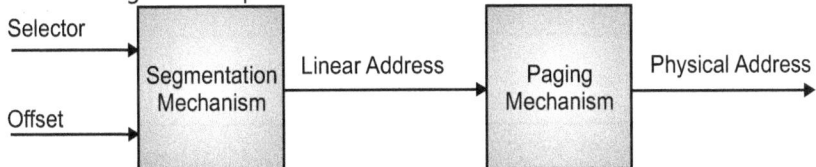

Fig. 2.17 : Protected-mode address translation process

2.6.1 Segmentation

The role of the segmentation unit is the same as on the 8086 processor. It allows the operating system to divide programs into logical blocks and place each block in a different memory region. This makes it possible to regulate access to critical sections of the application and help identify bugs during the development process. The implementation of the segmentation unit on the 80386 (and above) is simply an extension of the old 8086 unit.

It includes several new features such as the ability to define the exact location and size of each segment in memory and set a specific privilege level to a segment which protects its content from unauthorized access.

Not only real-mode applications use segment registers for accessing memory. The same process takes place under protected-mode. However, there are several differences which should be considered. First, there is a slight change in terminology. Under protected-mode, segment registers receive the name Selectors which reflects their new role in the memory translation process. Although still 16-bit in size, their interpretation by the processor is inherently different. Fig. 2.18 presents the structure of a selector along with the various bit-fields which comprise it.

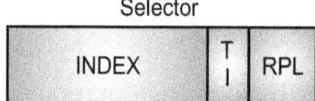

RPL - Requestor privilege level
TI - Table indicator
INDEX - Index into descriptor table

Fig. 2.18 : Internal composition of a selector

Instead of shifting segment registers (selectors) four bits to the left and adding an offset (like in real-mode), the processor treats each selector as an index to a Descriptor Table.

2.6.2 Descriptor Tables

Descriptor tables reside in system memory and are used by the processor to perform address translation. Each entry in a descriptor table is 8 bytes long and represents a single segment in memory. A descriptor entry contains both a pointer to the first byte in the associated segment and a 20-bit value which represents the size of the segment in memory. Several other fields contain special attributes such as a privilege level and the segment's type. Fig. 2.19 presents the exact structure of a descriptor entry along with a description of each of its internal fields.

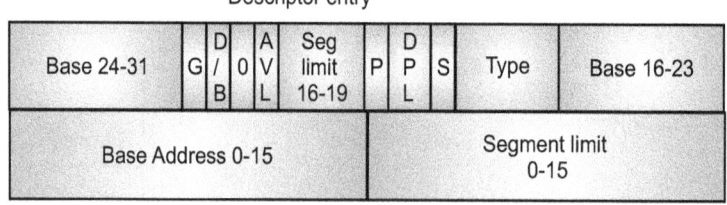

AVL - Available for use by the operating system
BASE - Segment base address
D/B - Default segment size(16/32 bits)
DPL - Descriptor privilege level
G - Granularity
LIMIT - Segment limit
P - Present bit
S - Descriptor type (System/Application)
Type-Segment Type

Fig. 2.19 : Structure of a descriptor entry

Table 2.1 contains a complete list of all descriptor fields and their functionality.

Field	Designated Role
BASE	Segment Base Address (32-bits) This field points to the segment's starting location in the 4 GB linear address space.
D/B	Segment Size Bit When the descriptor entry describes a code segment, this bit is used to specify the default length of operands and addresses. When the bit is set, the processor assumes a 32-bit segment. When the bit is clear, a 16-bit segment is assumed. When the descriptor entry describes a data segment, this bit is used to control the operation of the stack. When this bit is set, stack operations use the ESP register. When this bit is clear, stack operations use the SP register.
DPL	Descriptor Privilege Level (2-bits) This field defines the segment privilege level. It is used by the protection mechanism built into the processor to restrict access to the segment.
G	Granularity Bit This bit controls the resolution of the segment limit field. When this bit is clear, the resolution is set to one byte. When this bit is set, the resolution is set to 4 KB.
LIMIT	Segment Limit (20-bits) This field determines the size of the segment in units of one byte (When the granularity bit is clear) or in units of 4KB (When the granularity bit is set).
P	Segment Present Bit This bit specifies whether the segment is present in memory. When this bit is clear, a segment-not-present exception is generated whenever a selector for the descriptor is loaded into one of the segment registers. This is used to notify the operating system of any attempt to access a segment which has been swapped to disk (virtual memory support) or which was not previously allocated (a protection violation).
S	Descriptor Type Bit This bit determines whether this is a normal segment or a system segment. When this bit is set, this is either a code or a data segment. When this bit is clear, this is a system segment.

...Cont.

Type	**Segment Type (4-bits)** When the descriptor entry describes a code segment, this field determines the type of the segment: execute-only or execute-read, conforming or non-conforming. When the descriptor entry describes a data segment, this field determines the type of the segment: read-only or read-write, expand-down or expand-up. Accessesing an expand-up segment with an offset which exceeds the segment limit value, causes an exception. The limit field in expand-down data segments is treated differently by the processor. Offsets which cause an exception to occur in expand-up segments are valid in expand-down segments. An access into an expand-down segment must be done with an offset larger than the segment limit or else an exception is generated. Decreasing the segment limit value in an expand-down segment causes memory to be allocated at the bottom of the segment. This is very useful for stacks since they tend to grow toward lower memory addresses.

Since each selector points to a specific descriptor entry, there is a one to one relationship between selectors and segments in memory. This concept is demonstrated in the following Fig. 2.20.

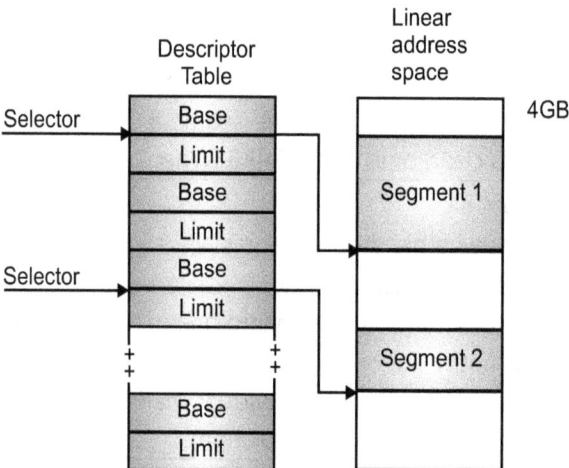

Fig. 2.20 : Relationship between selectors and segments

As Fig. 2.21 shows, linear address calculation (which can be the physical address if paging is disabled) is done by using the selector as an index to the descriptor table, getting the base address of the segment, and adding the offset.

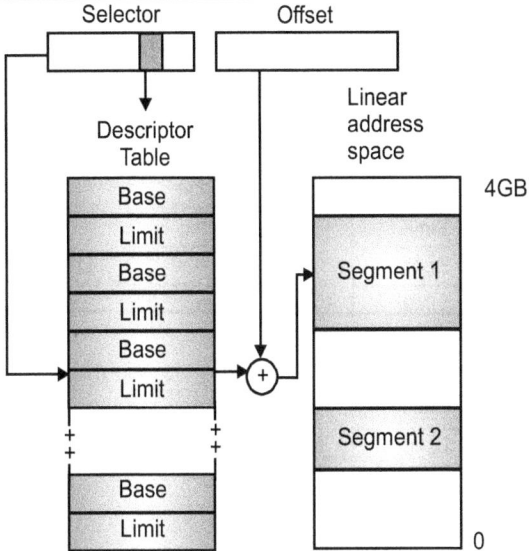

Fig. 2.21 : Virtual to linear address translation

Two types of descriptor tables are used by the processor when working in protected-mode. The first is known as the GDT (Global Descriptor Table) and is used mainly for holding descriptor entries of operating system segments. The second type is known as the LDT (Local Descriptor Table) and contains entries of normal application segments (although not necessarily). During initialization, the kernel creates a single GDT which is kept in memory until either the operating system terminates or until the processor is switched back to real-mode.

Whenever the user starts an application, the operating system creates a new LDT to hold the descriptor entries which represent the segments used by the new task. This makes it possible for the operating system to isolate each task's address space by enabling a different LDT whenever a task switch occurs. Bugs and other errors in the application cannot affect other running processes and are limited in scope to the currently mapped memory segments.

Note that not all operating systems behave exactly as described above (for instance, all Windows applications share a single LDT). However, this is the recommended programming practice as offered by Intel.

When looking for a specific descriptor entry, the addressing unit in the processor uses the TI bit (which is part of the selector) to decide which descriptor table should be used (the GDT or the currently active LDT). Fig. 2.22 shows this process in clarity.

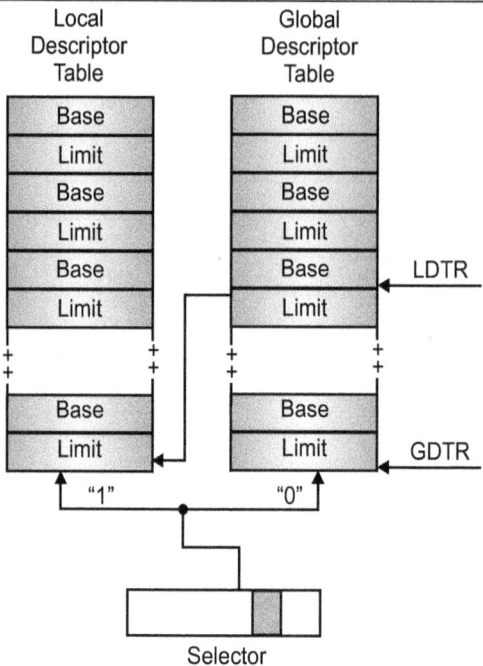

Fig. 2.22 : The table indicator bit

The linear address and size of the GDT itself are stored in a special processor register called GDTR. During bootstrap, the operating system initializes this register to point to the newly created GDT and does not modify its value during the entire session. In much the same manner, the LDTR register contains the size and position of the currently active LDT in memory (In fact, it serves as a selector to the GDT, pointing to a descriptor entry which contains all the relevant information). The fact that the LDTR register serves as a selector to the GDT rather than contain specific values, makes it possible for the operating system to switch easily between different LDTs and prevent inter-task memory corruptions.

In order to clarify the operation of the segmentation mechanism in protected-mode, I'll use a small C code snippet:

```
char far   *pChar;
pChar      = GlobalAlloc(GMEM_FIXED, 100);
pChar[50] = 'A';
```

This piece of code asks Windows to allocate a 100 bytes buffer and store its address in a far pointer called pChar. If you examine the code inside GlobalAlloc, you will see that Windows allocates a selector in its LDT whenever you call this function in your application. So pChar actually contains both a selector and an offset. To modify the allocated buffer, the processor uses the LDTR register to index its GDT and find the currently active LDT descriptor. Then, it accesses the LDT by using the selector part of pChar as an index to retrieve the segment base address. The offset (50) is added to the retrieved segment base address and the letter 'A' is written to the calculated memory location.

Note that the information presented above applies only to the 16-bit implementation of Windows. The behavior of GlobalAlloc on the Win32 platforms is inherently different.

2.7 ADVANTAGES OF PROTECTED MODE MEMORY ADDRESSING

All the 386's special features become available in the processor's protected mode. Some of the extra powers of this mode are mentioned here...

1. **Access to 4 Gigabytes of Memory** - This is the most obvious difference between protected mode and real mode. Protected mode programs can use up to 4 GB of memory for data, code and stack space. Using some undocumented features of the 8086 processors, it is possible for real-mode programs to access memory above the 1MB limit for data storage. However, using these techniques for code and stack space is generally impractical. Of course, you probably won't have 4GB of memory installed on your system. That brings us to the next feature.

2. **Virtual Memory** - The Memory Management Unit (MMU) on the 386 allows virtual memory to be implemented, which makes a program think that it has 4GB of memory when it has less (actually much less). The 386 and special operating system software simulate the extra memory using a mass storage (like a hard disk drive). Of course, you need about 4GB of free disk storage space, but that's another problem.

3. **Address Translation** - The MMU also allows addresses to be translated, or mapped, before use. For example, you might want to translate all references to a 4KB block at a segment B800H (the CGA text buffer) to a data buffer in your program. Later, your program could copy the buffer to the screen. This is useful when redirecting the output of a program that directly writes to the screen. Translation can also simulate expanded memory without an expanded memory board. But there are also certain functions in the later versions of EMS which can't be emulated by the MMU. But you will hardly require those functions even if your program is advanced.

   Programs work with logical addresses. The 386 converts these logical addresses into 32-bit linear (non-segmented addresses). The MMU then converts linear addresses to physical addresses. If the MMU isn't active, linear and physical addresses are equivalent. Applying this terminology to real mode, the address B800:0010 is a logical address. Its equivalent linear address is B8010H. Since real mode doesn't use the MMU, the physical address is the same as the linear address.

4. **Improved Segmentation** - In real mode, all segments are 64KB long and are in fixed locations. In protected mode, segments can be as short as one byte or as long as 4GB. The function **_djgpp_nearptr_enable()** uses this feature. Attempting to access memory past the end of a segment will cause an error. If the segment is 4GB long, then the addresses get wrapped if a program tries to access beyond the 4GB limit. Segments may start off at any location. In addition, the programmer determines each segment's intended use, which the 386 enforces. That is, if the program attempts to write data into a segment meant for code, the 386 will force an error. You also can define a segment that covers the entire address range of 4GB and effectively dispense with segments

altogether. All memory references are then via 32-bit non-segmented pointers. These flat pointers correspond directly to linear addresses.

5. **Memory Protection** - The 386 allows memory to be protected. For example, a user's program may not be able to overwrite operating system data. This, combined with the checks on segments, protects programs against bugs that would crash the computer.
6. **Process Protection** - In a similar fashion to memory protection, different programs (or parts of a program) can be protected from each other. One program might not have access to another program's data, while the operating system might have access to everyone's data. Conversely, user programs may have only limited access to the operating system's data. This is actually implemented using the page protection mechanism provided by the MMU.
7. **32-Bit Registers** - All general-purpose registers on the 386 are 32-bits wide. Except for the E prefix (ex: EAX instead of AX), these registers have the same names as in the 8086. Two new segment registers (FS and GS) are also available; they are accessible from all modes but are most useful in protected mode programs. Real-mode programs can also access these 32-bit registeres, but they won't use them for indexing purposes. And using 32-bit registers in protected mode (32-bit protected mode) will cut down the size of the code generally.
8. **Improved Addressing Modes** - In real mode, programs can only form addresses with constant values, the BX or BP register, and the SI or DI register. In protected mode programs, any register can form addresses. An index can include a scale factor of two, four or eight. This allows you to write instructions like MOV EBX, [EDI][EAX*8]+2.
9. **Multitasking Support** - The 386 has special provisions to save the current processor state and switch to a new task (known as context switch). A single instruction can switch contexts rapidly. This has important ramifications for operating systems and real-time processing. The 386 also supports nested tasks. A task can return to its original task using a back-link.
10. **Hardware Debugging** - The 386 has special hardware for implementing single-step code and data breakpoints. This hardware is available in real mode with some special techniques.

2.8 ENTERING PROTECTED MODE

The lowest 5 bits of the control register CR0 contain 5 flags that determine how the system is going to function. This status register has 1 flag that we are particularly interested in: the "Protected Mode Enable" flag (PE). Here are the general steps to entering protected mode:
- Create a Valid GDT (Global Descriptor Table)
- Create a 6 byte pseudo-descriptor to point to the GDT
    - If paging is going to be used, load CR3 with a valid page table, PDBR, or PML4.
    - If PAE (Physical Address Extension) is going to be used, set CR4.PAE = 1.
    - If switching to long mode, set IA32_EFER.LME = 1.

- Disable Interrupts (CLI).
- Load an IDT pseudo-descriptor that has a null limit (this prevents the real mode IDT from being used in protected mode)
- Set the PE bit (and the PG bit if paging is going to be enabled) of the MSW or CR0 register
- Execute a far jump (in case of switching to long mode, even if the destination code segment is a 64-bit code segment, the offset must not exceed 32-bit since the far jump instruction is executed in compatibility mode)
- Load data segment registers with valid selector(s) to prevent GP exceptions when interrupts happen
- Load SS:(E)SP with a valid stack
- Load an IDT pseudo-descriptor that points to the IDT
- Enable Interrupts.

2.9 REAL MODE VS PROTECTED MODE

Superficially protected mode and real mode don't seem to be very different. Both use memeory segmentation, interrupts and device drivers to handle the hardware. But there are differences which justify the existence of two separate modes. In real mode, we can view memory as 64k segments atleast 16bytes apart. Segmentation is handled through the use of an internal mechanism in conjunction with segment registers. The contents of these segment registers (CS,DS,SS...) form part of the physical address that the CPU places on the addresss bus. The physical address is generated by multiplying the segment register by 16 and then adding a 16 bit offset. It is this 16 bit offset that limits us to 64k segments.

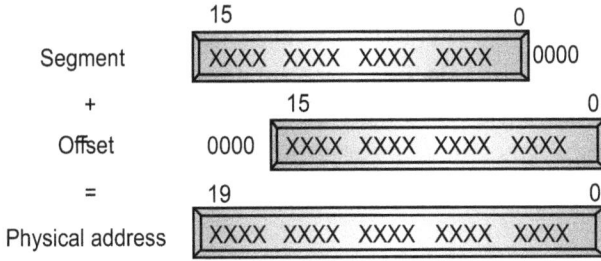

Fig. 2.23 : Real mode addressing

In protected mode, segmentation is defined via a set of tables called descriptor tables. The segment registers contain pointers into these tables. There are two types of tables used to define memory segmentation : The Global Descriptor Table and The Local Descriptor Table. The GDT contains the basic descriptors that all applications can access. In real mode one segment is 64k big followed by the next in a 16 byte distance. In protected mode we can have a segment as big as 4Gb and we can put it wherever we want. The LDT contains segmentation information specific to a task or program. An OS for instance could set up a GDT with its system descriptors and for each task an LDT with appropriate descriptors. Each descriptor is 8 bytes long. The format is given below (fig 3). Each time a segment register is loaded, the base address is fetched from the appropriate table entry. The contents of the descriptor is stored in a programmer invisible register called shadow registers so that future references to the same segment can use this information instead of referencing the table each time. The physical address is formed by adding the 16 or 32 bit offset to the base address in the shadow register. These differences are made clear in fig. 1 and 2.

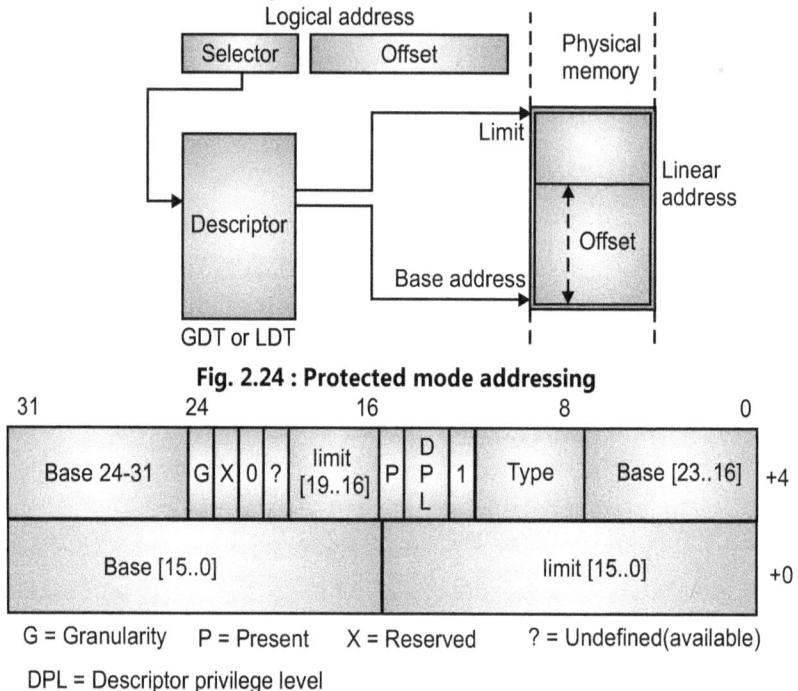

Fig. 2.24 : Protected mode addressing

Fig. 2.25 : Segment descriptor format

G = Granularity   P = Present   X = Reserved   ? = Undefined(available)
DPL = Descriptor privilege level

We have yet another table called the interrupt descriptor table or the IDT. The IDT contains the interrupt descriptors. These are used to tell the processor where to find the interrupt handlers. It contains one entry per interrupt, just like in Real Mode, but the format of these entries is totally different.

2.10 MEMORY PAGING

Paging is a method of writing data to, and reading it from, secondary storage for use in primary storage, also known as main memory. Paging plays a role in memory management for a computer's OS (operating system).

In computer operating systems, paging is one of the memory-management schemes by which a computer can store and retrieve data from secondary storage for use in main memory. In the paging memory-management scheme, the operating system retrieves data from secondary storage in same-size blocks called pages. The main advantage of paging over memory segmentation is that it allows the physical address space of a process to be noncontiguous. Before paging came into use, systems had to fit whole programs into storage contiguously, which caused various storage and fragmentation problems.

Paging is an important part of virtual memory implementation in most contemporary general-purpose operating systems, allowing them to use secondary storage for data that do not fit into physical random-access memory (RAM).

In a memory management system that takes advantage of paging, the OS reads data from secondary storage in blocks called pages, all of which have identical size.

The physical region of memory containing a single page is called a frame. When paging is used, a frame does not have to comprise a single physically contiguous region in secondary storage. This approach offers an advantage over earlier memory management methods, because it facilitates more efficient and faster use of storage.

Paging is a mechanism which helps the operating system to create unique virtual address spaces while it also has a major role in memory simulation using disk space - A process commonly known as Virtual Memory support.

The 32-bit linear address generated by the segmentation unit can be optionally fed into the paging unit to undergo a second address manipulation process. There is no mathematical correlation between a linear address and its associated physical counterpart but instead, special tables in memory known as the Page Tables assist the paging unit in transforming the input linear address into a physical address which is sent to the processor bus.

Applications live inside a 4GB linear address space and have no indication of how physical memory is organized. This has numerous benefits since no application can see or modify other applications data structures - One of the features required by most multitasking operating systems.

The paging unit treats the linear and physical address spaces as a collection of consecutive 4KB pages (The Pentium and Pentium Pro can also handle 4MB pages). A linear page can be mapped to any of the physical pages or it can be marked as non-present to make it sensitive to memory accesses. Trying to read or modify a non-present page causes the processor to generate a Page Fault Exception(exception 0xEh) which is usually handled by the operating system internal code.

This is exacly the essence of virtual memory. When programs consume all available memory, the operating system attempts to free memory by swapping least recently used (LRU) pages of memory to disk. The swapped pages are marked as non-present so when they are later accessed by their owning application, they would be automatically reloaded from disk by the operating system (The code handling the page exception is responsible for loading these pages and mapping them back to physical memory). You can think of this process as if the operating system "steals" memory from background tasks in order to give it to the currently active application.

The real impressive characteristic of the virtual memory mechanism is that it is completely transparent to application code. After loading a page from disk and remapping it to physical memory, the operating system reexecutes the instruction which caused the page fault exception to occur, so the running application is not even aware of the fact that part of its memory was stored temporarily on disk.

Before enabling the paging unit, the operating system must construct a table in memory known as the page directory table. The 1024 DWORD entries of the page directory table hold physical addresses of another set of paging tables called page tables. Page tables participate in the last stage of the address translation process since they actually contain the physical addresses of the 4KB chunks of memory.

A close examination of the paging process reveals that the processor breaks the linear address into three components before turning it into a physical one. The top 10 bits of the linear address are used by the processor to index the page directory table. The processor retrieves the entry from the table and uses it to find the physical address of a page table. The next 10 bits of the linear address serve as an index into the corresponding page table. By adding the page table entry value (which represents the physical address of a physical page in memory) and the 12 lower bits of the linear address (the offset into the page), the processor can locate the requested physical address and send it to its address bus. Fig. 7 shows the internal structure of a linear address and its interpretation by the processor.

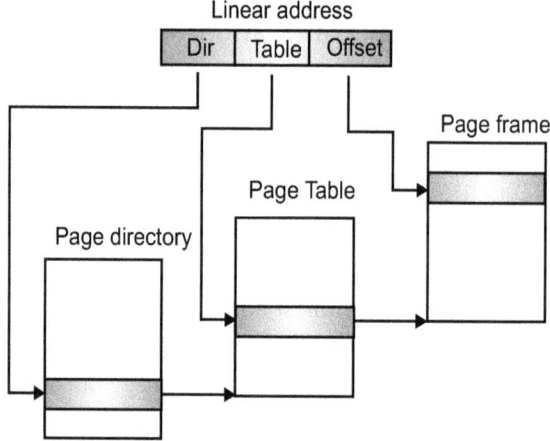

Fig. 2.26 : Components of a linear address

The two-level address indirection mechanism (page directory and page table) was chosen to solve the problem related to the memory occupied by the page tables themselves. Since each page table (including the page directory table) occupies 4KB of physical memory (1024 entries * 4 bytes each), 1024 page tables (one page table for each entry in the page directory) would require 4MB of memory - An awful waste of valuable memory bytes. The use of the page directory table solves this problem since each entry (which represents a 4KB page table) can be marked as non-present. Non-present page tables eliminate the need to allocate a chunk of 4KB physical memory to hold their content.

Under Windows 95, each running 32-bit process is mapped to the 4MB-2GB range of linear address space. Although 32-bit applications share the same linear address space, Windows loads each application to a different physical memory location (if enough memory is available). Whenever a task switch occurs, Windows modifies its page tables to reflect the new linear to physical mapping scheme and swaps least recently used pages of memory to disk.

Paging is memory management technique which widely uses virtual memory concept. When paging is used, the processor divides the linear address space into fixed-size pages (of 4KBytes, 2 MBytes, or 4 MBytes in length) that can be mapped into physical memory and/or disk storage. When a program (or task) references a logical address in memory, the processor translates the address into a linear address and then uses its paging mechanism to translate the linear address into a corresponding physical address.

2.10.1 Linear Page Translation during Paging

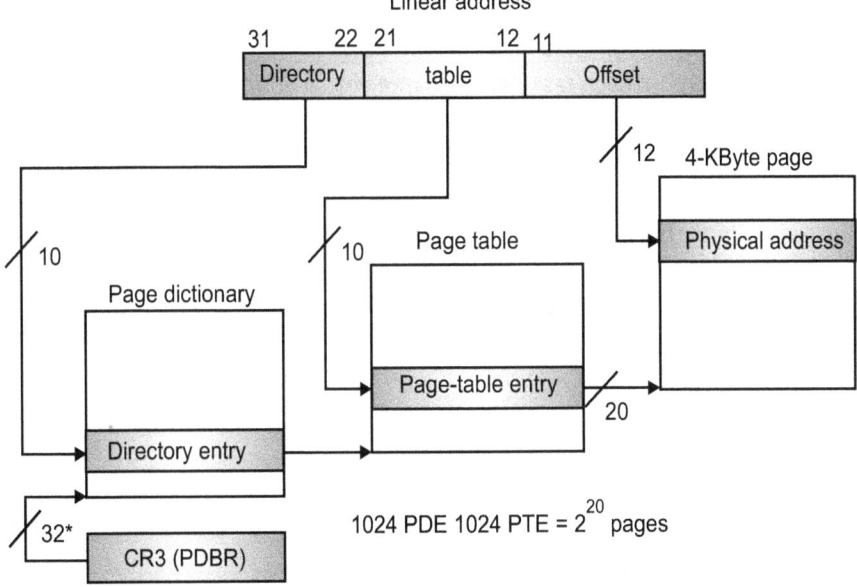

Fig. 2.27

If the page containing the linear address is not currently in physical memory, the processor generates a page-fault exception (#14). The exception handler for the page-fault exception typically directs the operating system to load the page from disk storage into physical memory. When the page has been loaded in physical memory, a return from the exception handler causes the instruction that generated the exception to be restarted. The information that the processor uses to map linear addresses into the physical address space and to generate page-fault exceptions (when necessary) is contained in page directories and page tables stored in memory.

2.10.2 Page-Directory and Page-Table Entries

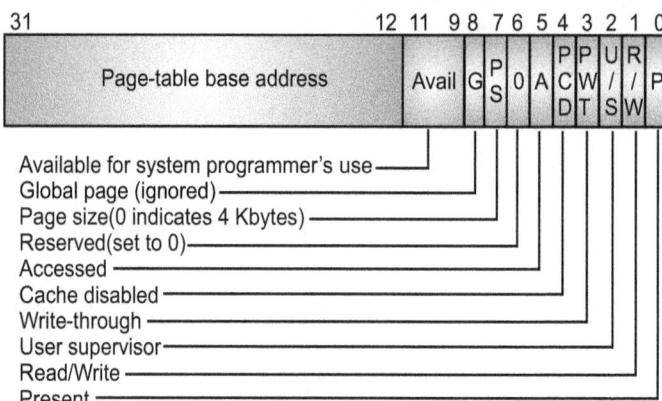

Fig. 2.28

2.10.3 Advantages of Paging

- Address translation: each task has the same virtual address
- Address translation: turns fragmented physical addresses into contiguous virtual addresses
- Memory protection (buggy or malicious tasks can't harm each other or the kernel)
- Shared memory between tasks (a fast type of IPC, also conserves memory when used for DLLs)
- Demand loading (prevents big load on CPU when a task first starts running, conserves memory)
- Memory mapped files
- Virtual memory swapping (lets system degrade gracefully when memory required exceeds RAM size)

QUESTIONS

1. Explain microprocessor based personal computer.
2. What is the function of CPU?
3. Explain memory organization?
4. What are the different types of buses? Explain with neat diagram.
5. Compare real mode and protected mode memory addressing.
6. Describe real mode memory management.
7. Describe protected mode memory management.
8. Explain memory paging in details.
9. What is the function of cache.
10. Describe switching of protected mode.

✠ ✠ ✠

Unit - III

ADDRESSING MODES AND DATA MOVEMENT INSTRUCTIONS

3.1 INTRODUCTION

Like the 8085 processors described in the previous chapter, the 8085 / 8086 processors let you access memory in many different ways. The 8085 / 8086 memory addressing modes provide flexible access to memory, allowing you to easily access variables, arrays, records, pointers, and other complex data types. Mastery of the 8085 / 8086 addressing modes is the first step towards mastering 8085 / 8086 assembly language.

When Intel designed the original 8086 processor, they provided it with a flexible, though limited, set of memory addressing modes. Intel added several new addressing modes when it introduced the 80386 microprocessor. Note that the 80386 retained all the modes of the previous processors; the new modes are just an added bonus. If you need to write code that works on 80286 and earlier processors, you will not be able to take advantage of these new modes. However, if you intend to run your code on 80386 sx or higher processors, you can use these new modes. Since many programmers still need to write programs that run on 80286 and earlier machines, it's important to separate the discussion of these two sets of addressing modes to avoid confusing them.

When 8086 executes an instruction, it performs the specified function on data. These data are called its operands and may be part of the instruction, reside in one of the internal registers of the microprocessor, stored at an address in memory or held at an I/O port, to aces these different types of operands, the 8086 is provided with various addressing modes (Data Addressing Modes).

3.2 DATA ADDRESSING MODES OF 8086

The 8086 has 12 addressing modes. The various 8086 addressing modes can be classified into five groups.

- Addressing modes for accessing immediate and register data (register and immediate modes).
- Addressing modes for accessing data in memory (memory modes)
- Addressing modes for accessing I/O ports (I/O modes)
- Relative addressing mode
- Implied addressing mode

3.2.1 Register Addressing Modes

Most 8086 instructions can operate on the 8086's general purpose register set. By specifying the name of the register as an operand to the instruction, you may access the contents of that register. Consider the 8086 mov (move) instruction:

>   mov   destination, source

This instruction copies the data from the source operand to the destination operand. The eight and 16 bit registers are certainly valid operands for this instruction. The only restriction is that both operands must be the same size. Now let's look at some actual 8086 mov instructions:

>   mov   ax, bx   ;Copies the value from BX into AX
>   mov   dl, al   ;Copies the value from AL into DL
>   mov   si, dx   ;Copies the value from DX into SI
>   mov   sp, bp   ;Copies the value from BP into SP
>   mov   dh, cl   ;Copies the value from CL into DH
>   mov   ax, ax   ;Yes, this is legal!

Remember, the registers are the best place to keep often used variables. As you'll see a little later, instructions using the registers are shorter and faster than those that access memory. Throughout this chapter you'll see the abbreviated operands reg and r/m (register/memory) used wherever you may use one of the 8086's general purpose registers.

In addition to the general purpose registers, many 8086 instructions (including the mov instruction) allow you to specify one of the segment registers as an operand. There are two restrictions on the use of the segment registers with the mov instruction. First of all, you may not specify cs as the destination operand, second, only one of the operands can be a segment register. You cannot move data from one segment register to another with a single mov instruction. To copy the value of cs to ds, you'd have to use some sequence like:

>   mov   ax, cs
>   mov   ds, ax

You should never use the segment registers as data registers to hold arbitrary values. They should only contain segment addresses. But more on that, later. Throughout this text you'll see the abbreviated operand sreg used wherever segment register operands are allowed (or required).

Example 3.1 :
> MOV DX (Destination Register) , CX (Source Register)
> Which moves 16 bit content of CS into DX.

Example 3.2 :
> MOV CL, DL
> Moves 8 bit contents of DL into CL

3.2.2 Memory Addressing Modes

The 8086 provides 17 different ways to access memory. This may seem like quite a bit at first, but fortunately most of the address modes are simple variants of one another so they're very easy to learn. And learn them you should! The key to good assembly language programming is the proper use of memory addressing modes.

The addressing modes provided by the 8086 family include displacement-only, base, displacement plus base, base plus indexed, and displacement plus base plus indexed. Variations on these five forms provide the 17 different addressing modes on the 8086. See, from 17 down to five. It's not so bad after all !

3.2.3 The Displacement Only Addressing Mode

The most common addressing mode, and the one that's easiest to understand, is the displacement-only (or direct) addressing mode. The displacement-only addressing mode consists of a 16 bit constant that specifies the address of the target location. The instruction mov al,ds:[8088h] loads the al register with a copy of the byte at memory location 8088h. Likewise, the instruction mov ds:[1234h],dl stores the value in the dl register to memory location 1234h:

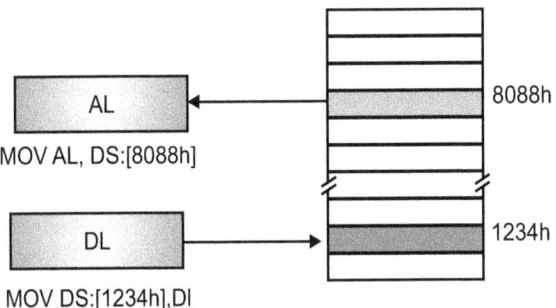

Fig. 3.1

The displacement-only addressing mode is perfect for accessing simple variables. Of course, you'd probably prefer using names like "I" or "J" rather than "DS:[1234h]" or "DS:[8088h]". Well, fear not, you'll soon see it's possible to do just that.

Intel named this the displacement-only addressing mode because a 16 bit constant (displacement) follows the mov opcode in memory. In that respect it is quite similar to the direct addressing mode on the x86 processors. There are some minor differences, however. First of all, a displacement is exactly that- some distance from some other point. On the x86, a direct address can be thought of as a displacement from address zero. On the 80x86 processors, this displacement is an offset from the beginning of a segment. Don't worry if this doesn't make a lot of sense right now. You'll get an opportunity to study segments to your heart's content a little later in this chapter. For now, you can think of the displacement-only addressing mode as a direct addressing mode. The examples in this chapter will typically access bytes in memory. Don't forget, however, that you can also access words on the 8086 processors :

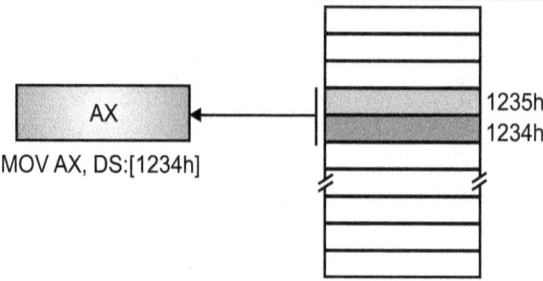

Fig. 3.2

By default, all displacement-only values provide offsets into the data segment. If you want to provide an offset into a different segment, you must use a segment override prefix before your address. For example, to access location 1234h in the extra segment you would use an instruction of the form mov ax,es:[1234h]. Likewise, to access this location in the code segment you would use the instruction mov ax, cs:[1234h]. The ds: prefix in the previous examples is not a segment override. The CPU uses the data segment register by default. These specific examples require ds: because of MASM's syntactical limitations.

3.2.4 The Register Indirect Addressing Modes

The 8086 CPUs let you access memory indirectly through a register using the register indirect addressing modes. There are four forms of this addressing mode on the 8086, best demonstrated by the following instructions:

    mov   al, [bx]
    mov   al, [bp]
    mov   al, [si]
    mov   al, [di]

As with the x86 [bx] addressing mode, these four addressing modes reference the byte at the offset found in the bx, bp, si, or di register, respectively. The [bx], [si], and [di] modes use the ds segment by default. The [bp] addressing mode uses the stack segment (ss) by default.

You can use the segment override prefix symbols if you wish to access data in different segments. The following instructions demonstrate the use of these overrides:

    mov   al, cs:[bx]
    mov   al, ds:[bp]
    mov   al, ss:[si]
    mov   al, es:[di]

Intel refers to [bx] and [bp] as base addressing modes and bx and bp as base registers (in fact, bp stands for base pointer). Intel refers to the [si] and [di] addressing modes as indexed addressing modes (si stands for source index, di stands for destination index). However, these addressing modes are functionally equivalent. This text will call these forms register indirect modes to be consistent.

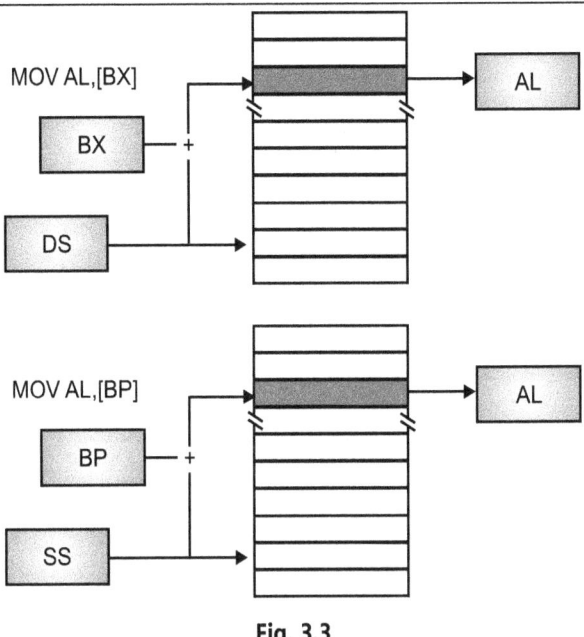

Fig. 3.3

Note: the [si] and [di] addressing modes work exactly the same way, just substitute si and di for bx above.

3.2.5 Indexed Addressing Modes

The indexed addressing modes use the following syntax:

    mov   al, disp[bx]
    mov   al, disp[bp]
    mov   al, disp[si]
    mov   al, disp[di]

If bx contains 1000h, then the instruction mov cl,20h[bx] will load cl from memory location ds:1020h. Likewise, if bp contains 2020h, mov dh,1000h[bp] will load dh from location ss:3020.

The offsets generated by these addressing modes are the sum of the constant and the specified register. The addressing modes involving bx, si, and di all use the data segment, the disp[bp] addressing mode uses the stack segment by default. As with the register indirect addressing modes, you can use the segment override prefixes to specify a different segment:

    mov   al, ss:disp[bx]
    mov   al, es:disp[bp]
    mov   al, cs:disp[si]
    mov   al, ss:disp[di]

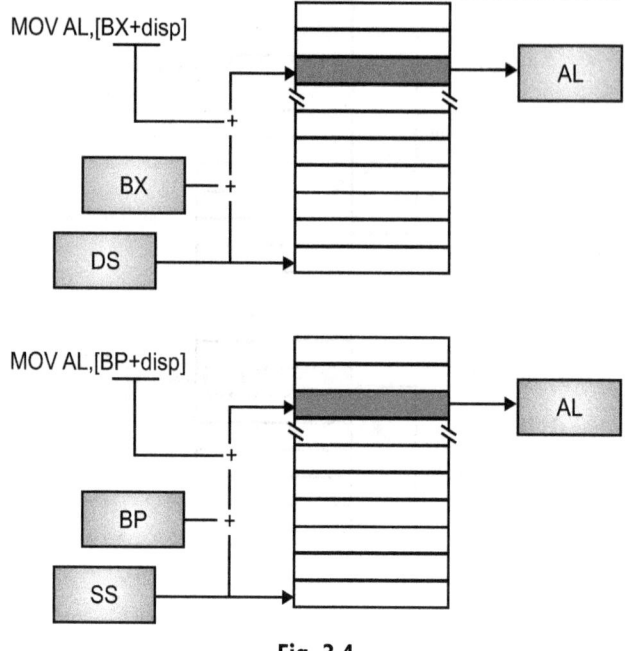

Fig. 3.4

You may substitute si or di in the figure above to obtain the [si+disp] and [di+disp] addressing modes.

Note that Intel still refers to these addressing modes as based addressing and indexed addressing. Intel's literature does not differentiate between these modes with or without the constant. If you look at how the hardware works, this is a reasonable definition. From the programmer's point of view, however, these addressing modes are useful for entirely different things. Which is why this text uses different terms to describe them. Unfortunately, there is very little consensus on the use of these terms in the 80x86 world.

3.2.6 Based Indexed Addressing Modes

The based indexed addressing modes are simply combinations of the register indirect addressing modes. These addressing modes form the offset by adding together a base register (bx or bp) and an index register (si or di). The allowable forms for these addressing modes are

```
mov    al, [bx][si]
mov    al, [bx][di]
mov    al, [bp][si]
mov    al, [bp][di]
```

Suppose that bx contains 1000h and si contains 880h. Then the instruction

```
mov    al,[bx][si]
```

would load al from location DS:1880h. Likewise, if bp contains 1598h and di contains 1004, mov ax,[bp+di] will load the 16 bits in ax from locations SS:259C and SS:259D.

The addressing modes that do not involve bp use the data segment by default. Those that have bp as an operand use the stack segment by default.

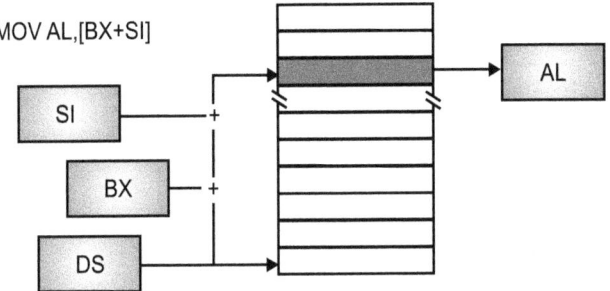

Fig. 3.5

You substitute di in the figure above to obtain the [bx+di] addressing mode.

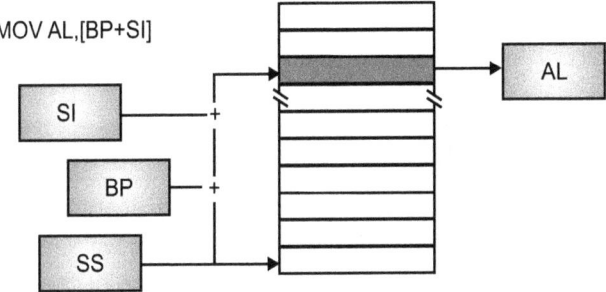

Fig. 3.6

You substitute di in the figure above for the [bp+di] addressing mode.

3.2.7 Based Indexed Plus Displacement Addressing Mode

These addressing modes are a slight modification of the base/indexed addressing modes with the addition of an eight bit or sixteen bit constant. The following are some examples of these addressing modes:

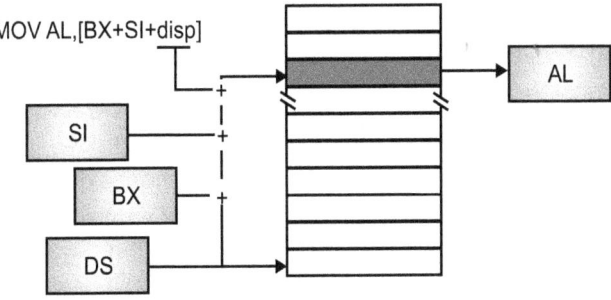

Fig. 3.7

```
mov    al, disp[bx][si]
mov    al, disp[bx+di]
mov    al, [bp+si+disp]
mov    al, [bp][di][disp]
```

You may substitute di in the figure above to produce the [bx+di+disp] addressing mode.

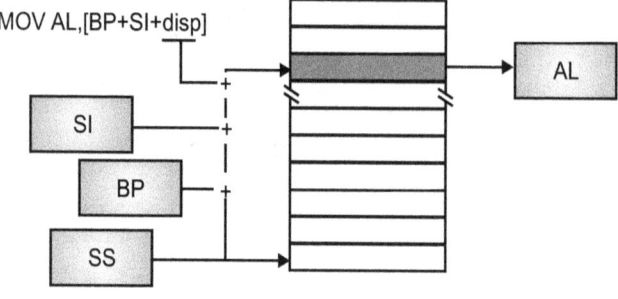

Fig. 3.8

You may substitute di in the figure above to produce the [bp+di+disp] addressing mode.

Suppose bp contains 1000h, bx contains 2000h, si contains 120h, and di contains 5. Then mov al,10h[bx+si] loads al from address DS:2130; mov ch,125h[bp+di] loads ch from location SS:112A; and mov bx,cs:2[bx][di] loads bx from location CS:2007.

3.3 MASM SYNTAX FOR 8086 MEMORY ADDRESSING MODES

Microsoft's assembler uses several different variations to denote indexed, based/indexed, and displacement plus based/indexed addressing modes. You will see all of these forms used interchangeably throughout this text. The following list some of the possible combinations that are legal for the various 80x86 addressing modes:

disp[bx], [bx][disp], [bx+disp], [disp][bx], and [disp+bx]

[bx][si], [bx+si], [si][bx], and [si+bx]

disp[bx][si], disp[bx+si], [disp+bx+si], [disp+bx][si], disp[si][bx], [disp+si][bx], [disp+si+bx], [si+disp+bx], [bx+disp+si], etc.

MASM treats the "[ ]" symbols just like the "+" operator. This operator is commutative, just like the "+" operator. Of course, this discussion applies to all the 8086 addressing modes, not just those involving BX and SI. You may substitute any legal registers in the addressing modes above.

An Easy Way to Remember the 8086 Memory Addressing Modes

There are a total of 17 different legal memory addressing modes on the 8086: disp, [bx], [bp], [si], [di], disp[bx], disp[bp], disp[si], disp[di], [bx][si], [bx][di], [bp][si], [bp][di], disp[bx][si], disp[bx][di], disp[bp][si], and disp[bp][di]. You could memorize all these forms so that you know which are valid (and, by omission, which forms are invalid). However, there is an easier way besides memorizing these 17 forms. Consider the chart:

DISP	[BX]	[SI]
	[BP]	[DI]

If you choose zero or one items from each of the columns and wind up with at least one item, you've got a valid 8086 memory addressing mode. Some examples:

- Choose disp from column one, nothing from column two, [di] from column 3, you get disp[di].
- Choose disp, [bx], and [di]. You get disp[bx][di].
- Skip column one & two, choose [si]. You get [si]
- Skip column one, choose [bx], then choose [di]. You get [bx][di]

Likewise, if you have an addressing mode that you cannot construct from this table, then it is not legal. For example, disp[dx][si] is illegal because you cannot obtain [dx] from any of the columns above.

The effective address is the final offset produced by an addressing mode computation. For example, if bx contains 10h, the effective address for 10h[bx] is 20h. You will see the term effective address in almost any discussion of the 8086's addressing mode. There is even a special instruction load effective address that computes effective addresses.

Not all addressing modes are created equal! Different addressing modes may take differing amounts of time to compute the effective address. The exact difference varies from processor to processor. Generally, though, the more complex an addressing mode is, the longer it takes to compute the effective address. Complexity of an addressing mode is directly related to the number of terms in the addressing mode. For example, disp[bx][si] is more complex than [bx]. See the instruction set reference in the appendices for information regarding the cycle times of various addressing modes on the different 80x86 processors.

The displacement field in all addressing modes except displacement-only can be a signed eight bit constant or a signed 16 bit constant. If your offset is in the range -128...+127 the instruction will be shorter than an instruction with a displacement outside that range. The size of the value in the register does not affect the execution time or size. So if you can arrange to put a large number in the register(s) and use a small displacement, that is preferable over a large constant and small values in the register(s).

If the effective address calculation produces a value greater than 0FFFFh, the CPU ignores the overflow and the result wraps around back to zero. For example, if bx contains 10h, then the instruction mov al,0FFFFh[bx] will load the al register from location ds:0Fh, not from location ds:1000Fh.

3.4 STACK ADDRESSING MODES

The stack is used to hold temporary variables and stores return addresses for procedures.
    push and pop instructions are used to manipulate it.
    call and ret also refer to the stack implicitly.
Two registers maintain the stack, esp and ss .
    A LIFO (Last-in, First-out) policy is used.
    The stack grows toward lower address.
    Data may be pushed from any of the registers or segment registers.

Data may be popped into any register except cs.

popfd	;Pop doubleword for stack to EFLAG
pushfd	;Pushes EFLAG register.
push 1234 H	;Pushes 1234H
push dword [ebx]	;Pushes double word in data esg.
pushad	;eax,ecx,edx,ebx,esp,ebp,esi,edi
pop eax	;Pops 4 bytes.

3.5 STACK OPERATIONS, INPUT/OUTPUT AND MACHINE CONTROL GROUP

Before going to study 'the instruction from this group it is necessary understand- what is a stack ? The stack is a part of Read/Write memory that is used for temporary storage of binary information during the execution of a program. The binary information is basically the intermediate results and the return address in case of subroutine programs.

- For the applicationthe, internal memory of the microprocessor (registers) is not programs sufficient to store the intermediate results. These intermediate results can be stored temporarily on the stack and can be referred back when required.

- A subroutine is a group of instructions, performs particular subtask which is executed number of times. It is written separately. The microprocessor executes this subroutine by transferring program control to the subroutine program. After completion of subroutine program execution, the program control is returned back to the main program. The use of subroutines is a very important technique in designing software for microprocessor systems because it eliminates more efficiently. For implementation of subroutine technique, it is necessary to define stack. In the. stack, -the address of instruction in the main program which follows the subroutine call is stored.

- The stack is a portion of Read/Write memory set aside by'the user for the purpose of storing information temporarily. When the information is written on the stack, the operation is called PUSH. When the information read -from stack, the operation is called a POP.

- The microprocessor stores the information, much like stacking plates. Using this analogy of stacking plates it is easy to illustrate the stack operation.

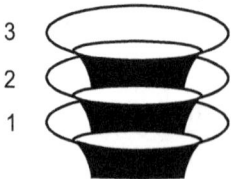

Fig. 3.9 : Stacked plates

Fig. 3.9 shows the stacked plates. Here, we realize that if it is desired to take out the first stacked plate we will have to remove all plates above the first plate in thee-reverse order. This means that to remove first plate we will have to remove the third plate, then the second plate :and finally the first plate. This means that, the first information pushed on the stack is the last information poped from the stack. This type of operation is known as a first in, last out (FILO). This stack is implemented with the help of special memory pointer register. The special pointer register is called the stack pointer. During PUSH and POP operation stack pointer register gives the address of memory where the information is to be stored or to be read. The stack pointer's contents are automatically manipulated to point to stack. The memory location currently pointed by stack pointer is called as top of stack.

The stack pointer SP, 'is a 16-bit register in the 8085A which is manipulated by the microprocessor's control section, during stack related instructions.

Stack Operations : This group consists of the following set of instructions
- LXI SP, data and SPHL
- PUSH and POP instructions
- CALL and RETURN instructions
- RESTART instructions
- XTHL
- SPHL

LXI SP, Data and SPHL : Initializes Stack Pointer.

Before execution of any stack related instruction, stack pointer must be initialized with the a valid memory address. The stack pointer can be initialized by two way.
- **Direct way ; LXI SP, data (16)**   ; Loads 16-bit data into SP
- **Indirect way ; C LXI H. data (16)** ; Load the bit data into HL
    SPHL   ; Loads the contents of HL into SP

Normally, the stack pointer is -initialized by the direct way. When a programmer wishes to set the stack pointer to a value that has been computed by the program, indirect way is used. The computed value is placed in H and L and the contents of HL register pair then moved into the stack pointer.,

SPHL	: Move data from HL to stack pointer.
Peration	: SP E ← HL
Description	: This-instruction copies the contents of HL register pair into the stack pointer. The contents of H register are copied to higher order byte of stack pointer and contents of L register are copied to the lower byte of stack pointer.
No. of bytes	: 1 byte. Opcode of SPHL.
Addressing Mode	: Register addressing.

Flags : Flags are not affected.
Example

: SP   2700H
: HL   2500H

SPHL ; This instruction will copy 2500H into stack pointer. So after ; execution of instruction stack pointer contents will be 2500H.

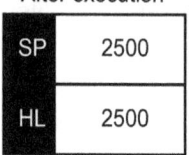

Fig. 3.10

Note :
1. The stack pointer can be initialized anywhere in the Read/Write memory map.. -However, as'a general practice, the stack pointer is initialized at the highest Read/Write memory location so that it will be less likely to interfere with a program.
2. Since the 8085A's stack pointer is decremented before data. is written to the stack, the stack pointer con actually be initialized to a value one higher than the highest Read/Write memory location available.

3.5.1 PUSH and POP Instructions

Temporary Stores the Contents of Register Pair and Program Internal Status Word

When programmer realizes the shortage of, the registers he, stores the present contents of the registers in the stack with the help of PUSH instruction and then uses the registers for other function. After completion of other function programmer loads the previous contents of the register from the stack with the help of POP instruction.

PUSH Operation

In PUSH operation, 16-bit data is stored in the. stack. This 16-bit data is stored in two operations. In the first then stack-pointer is decremented by one and byte of the 16-bit data is stored at the memory location pointed by stack pointer. In the second operation, stack pointer is again decremented by one, and then the lower byte of the 16-bit data is stored at the memory location pointed by stack pointer.

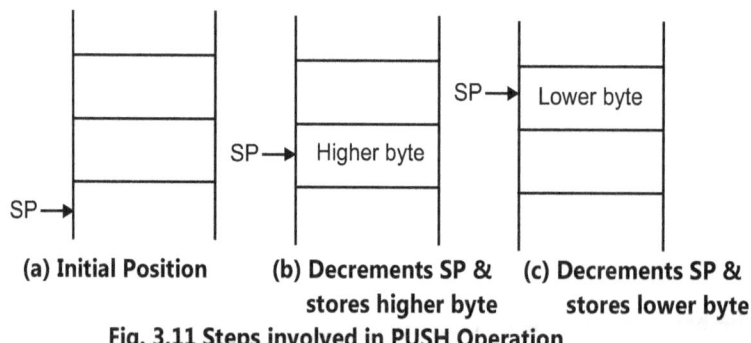

Fig. 3.11 Steps involved in PUSH Operation

PUSH Instructions

1. PUSH rp : Push specified register pair on the stack.

Operation : SP ← SP – 1, (SP) ← rpH, SP ← SP – 1, (SP) <– rpL. Description

This instruction decrements stack pointer by one and copies the higher byte of the register pair into the memory location pointed by stack pointer. It then decrements the stack pointer again by one and copies the lower byte of the register pair into the memory location pointer by stack pointer. The rp is 16-bit register pair such as BC, DE, HL, Only higher order register is to be specified within the instruction.

No. of Bytes : 1 byte.
Opcode of PUSH rp.

Addressing Mode : Register indirect addressing.

Flags : Flags are not affected.

Example : SP = 2000H, DE 1050H.

PUSH D : This instruction will decrement the stack pointer (2000H) by one (SP = IFFFH) and copies the contents of D register (10H) into the memory location 1FFFH. It then decrements the stack pointer again by one (SP = 1FFEH) and copies the contents of E register (50H) into the memory location 1FFEH.

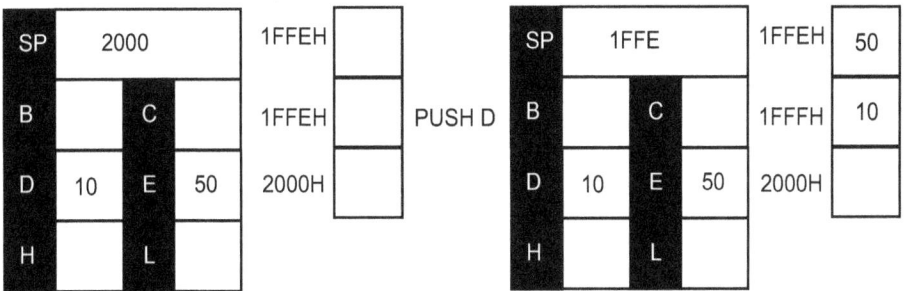

Fig. 3.12

2. PUSH PSW : Push program status word on the stack.

Operation : SP ← SP – 1
(SP) ← A
SP ← SP =,1
(SP) ← Flag register

Description : This instruction decrements stack pointer .byone and copies the accumulator contents into- the memory location pointed by stack pointer. It then decrements the stack pointer again by one and copies the flag register into the memory location pointed by the stack pointer.

No. of Bytes : I byte.
Opcode of PUSH PSW.
Addressing Mode : Register indirect addressing.
Flag : Flags are not affected„
Example : SP = 2000H, A = 20H, Flag register 80H
PUSH PSW : This instruction decrements the stack pointer (SP 2000H) by one (SP = IFFFH) and copies the contents of the accumulator (20H)into the memory location 1FFFH. Jt then decrements the stack pointer again by one (SP = 'IFFEH) and copies the contents of the flag register (80H) into the memory location I FFEH.

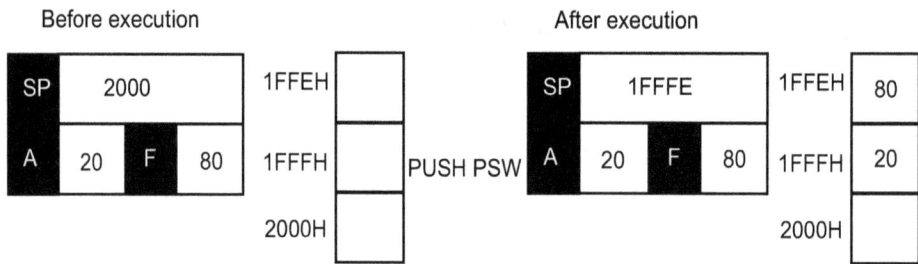

Fig. 3.13

POP Operation :

In POP operation, 16-bit data is read from the stack. This 16-bit data is read in two operations. In the first operation, the contents from the memory location pointed by stack pointer are loaded into lower byte of register pair and then the stack pointer is incremented by one. In the second operation, the contents from the memory location pointed by stack pointer are loaded into, higher byte of register pair and then the stack pointer is incremented by one.

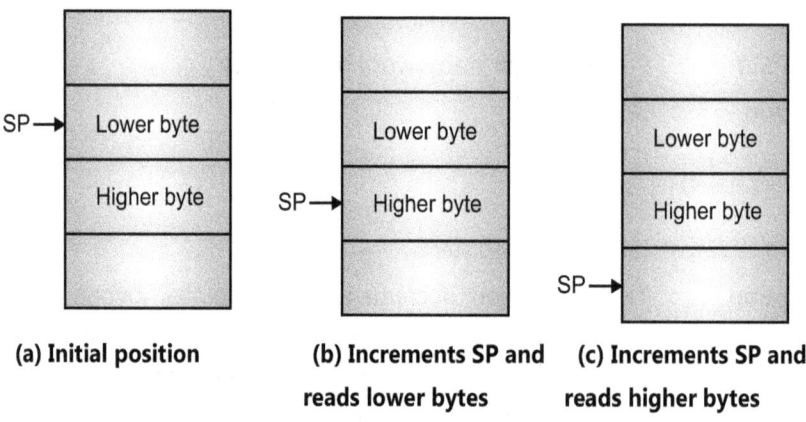

(a) Initial position (b) Increments SP and reads lower bytes (c) Increments SP and reads higher bytes

Fig. 3.14 : Stop Involved in POP Operation

POP Instructions :

1. POP rp : POP specified register pair of the stack.

Operation : rpL ← (SP)

SP ← SP + I

rpH ← (SP), SP ← SP + 1

Description : This instruction copies the contents of memory location pointed by the stack pointer into the lower byte of the specified register pair and increments the stack pointer by one. It then copies the contents of memory location pointed by stack pointer into the higher byte of the specified register pair and increments the stack pointer again by one. The rp is 16-bit register pair such-as BC, DE, HL. Only higher order register is to be specified within the instruction.

No. of Bytes : I byte.

Opcode of POP rp.

Addressing Mode : Register indirect Addressing.

Flags : Flags are not affected.

Example : SP 2000H, (2000H) = 30H, (2001H) 50H

POP B : This instruction will copy the contents of memory location pointed by stack pointer, 2000H (i.e. data 30H) into the C register. It will then increment the stack pointer by one, 2001H and will copy the contents of memory location pointed by stack pointer, 2001H (i.e. data 50H) into B register, and increment the stack pointer again by one.

Before execution

SP	2000
B	C

2000H	30
2001H	50
2002H	

POP B

After execution

SP	2002
B	50	C	30

2000H	30
2001H	50
2002H	

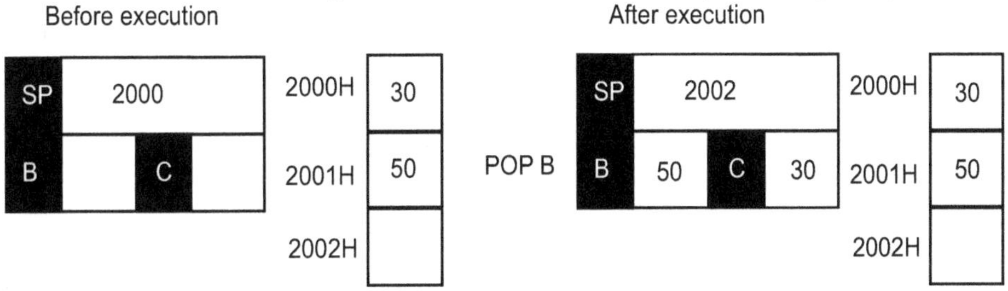

Fig. 3.15

2. POP PSW : POP program status word of the stack.

Operation : Flag register ← (SP)

SP ← SP + 1

A ← (SP)

SP ← SP + 1

Description : This instruction copies the contents of memory location pointed by the stack pointer into the flag register and increments the stack pointer by one. It then copies the contents- of memory location

		pointed by stack pointer into the accumulator and increments the stack pointer again by one.
No. of Bytes	:	I byte. Opcode of PORPSW.
Addressing Mode	:	Register indirect addressing.
Flags	:	Flags are not affected.
Example	:	SP = 2000H, (2000H) = 30H, (2001H) 50H
POP PSW	:	This instruction will copy the contents of memory location pointed by the stack pointer, 2000H (i.e. data 30H).into the flag register. It will then increment the stack pointer by one, 2001H and will copy the contents of memory location pointed by stack pointer into the accumulator and increment the stack pointer again by one.

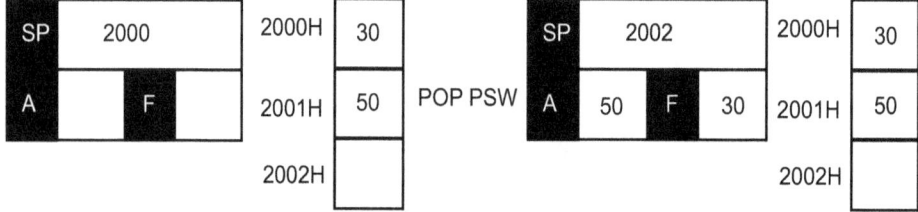

Fig. 3.16

3.5.2 CALL Address and RET : Implements Subroutines

Whenever we need to use a group of instructions several times throughout a program there are two ways to avoid rewriting of the group of instructions. One way is to write the group of instructions as a separate subroutine. We can then just CALL the subroutine whenever we need to execute that group of instructions. For calling the subroutine we have to store the return address onto the stack.

Subroutines

From the previous discussions, we know that the subroutine is a -group of instructions ructions stored as a separate program in the memory and it is called from the main program whenever required.

The 8085A microprocessor has two instructions to implement subroutines: CALL and RET. CALL instruction is used to call a subroutine in the main program and RET instruction is the last instruction in the subroutine to return it back to the main program. The CALL instruction saves the address of the instruction following it and then transfers the program control to the first instruction in the subroutine. When subroutine execution is completed the RET instruction reads s the return address from the stack and transfers control back to the instruction following the CALL.

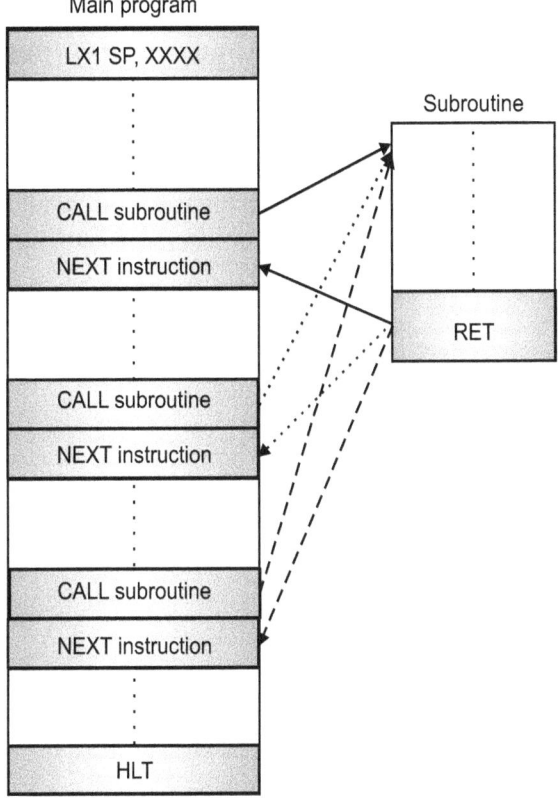

Fig. 3.17 : Program Flow

Main Program

6000H	LXI SP, 3000H
6003H	-
	-
	-
6010H	CALL DELAY (6500H)
6013H	

DELAY Subroutine

6500H DELAY	: MVI C, FFH
6502 BACK	: DCR C
6503 H	JNZ BACK
6503 H	RET

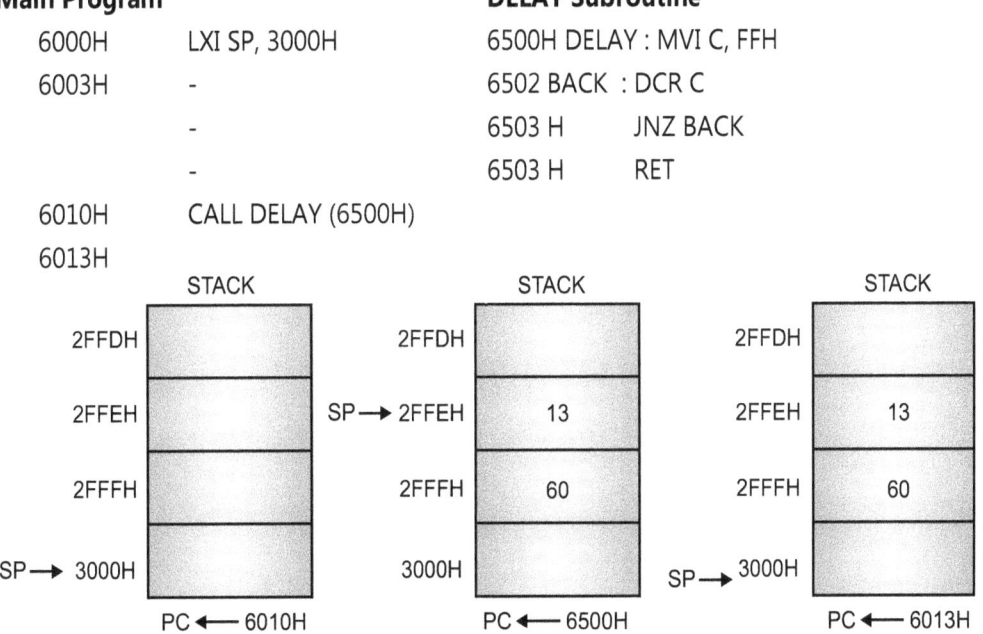

Fig. 3.18 : Details in the Execution of CALL and RETURN Instructions

Here, the main program initializes, stack pointer at 3000H memory location and executes instructions in sequence till the execution of CALL instruction. After execution of CALL instruction program control is transferred to the delay subroutine stored at memory address 6500H. Before transfer of control to the subroutine program, the address of the ,instruction (6013H) which is after the CALL instruction, is stored in the stack. At the end of delay subroutine RET instruction is executed, ted, which reads the return address (6013H) from-the stack and transfers the program control to the instruction which is after CALL instruction.

CALL

This is group consists of the following set of instructions.
1. CALL addr
2. C condition addr

1. CALL addr : Call unconditionally a subroutine whose starting address is given within the instruction.

Operation : $(SP - 1) \leftarrow PC_H$
$(SP - 1) \leftarrow PC_L$
$(SP \leftarrow SP - 2$
$PC \leftarrow addr$

Description : The CAC instruction is used to transfer program control to a subprogram or subroutine. This instruction pushes the current PC contents onto the stack and loads the given address into the PC. Thus the program control is transferred to the address given in the instruction. Stack pointer is decremented by two.

When the subroutine is called, the program control is transferred from calling program to the. subroutine. After execution of subroutine it is necessary to transfer program control back to the calling program. To do this processor must remember- the address of the instruction next to the CALL instruction. Processor saves this address on the stack when the CALL instruction is executed.

Note : The stack is a part of read/write memory set aside for storing intermediate results and addresses.

No. of Bytes : 3 bytes.
First byte : Opcode of CALL.
Second byte : Low order, byte of the address.
Third byte High order byte of the address.

Addressing Mode : Immediate register indirect addressing.

Flags : TVIags are not affected.

Example : Stack pointer = 3000H.

6000H CALL 2000H : This instruction will store the address of instruction next to

6003H : CALL (i.e. 6003H) onto stack and load PC with 2000H.

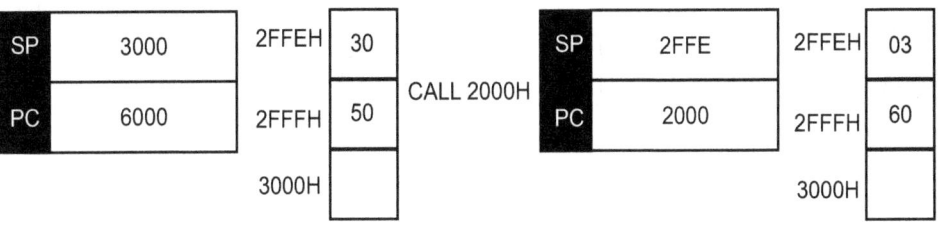

Fig. 3.19

RET	:	Return from the subroutine unconditionally.
Operation	:	PCL ← (SP)
		PC$_H$ ← (SP + 1)
		SP ← SP + 2
Description	:	This instruction pops the return addr (address of the instruction next to CALL in the main program) from the stack and loads program counter with this return address. Thus transfers program control to - the instruction next to CALL in the main program.

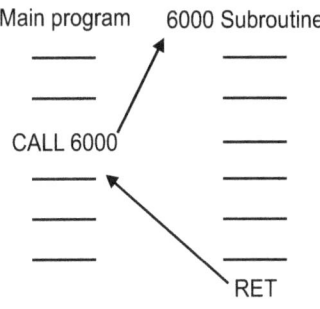

Fig. 3.20

No. of Bytes	:	1 byte.
		Opcode of RET.
Addressing Mode	:	Register indirect addressing.
Flags	:	Flag's are not affected.
Example	:	If SP = 27FDH and contents on the stack are as shown then

SP →	27FD	00
	27 FE	62
	27 FF	

RET : This instruction will load PC with 6200H and it will transfer program control to the address 6200H. It will also increment the stack pointer by two.

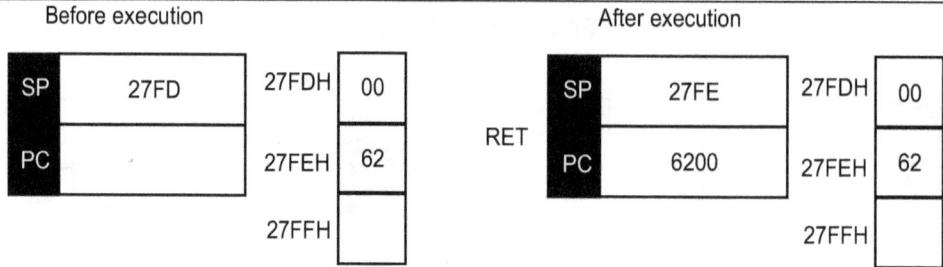

Fig. 3.21

3.5.3 Conditional Call and Return Instructions

In addition to the unconditional CALL and RET instructions, the 8085A instruction set includes eight conditional CALL instructions and eight conditional RET instructions. These conditions are checked by the reading the status of respective flags. If the condition associated with the conditional CALL is not' met, the instruction following the CALL is executed. If the condition ,is met, the program counter contents are saved on the stack, and the address contained in the CALL instruction is loaded into program counter. The number of machine cycles and T-states required by a conditional CALL depends on whether or not the condition is satisfied. When the condition is not. satisfied, two machine cycles with a total of nine T-state are required to fetch, decode -and execute the instruction. When the condition is satisfied, five machine T-states are required.

C condition addr : Call the subroutine conditionally at given addr.

Operation : If condition true $(SP - 1) \leftarrow PCH$
$(SP - 2) \leftarrow PC_L$
$SP \leftarrow SP - 2$
$PC \leftarrow addr$ else $PC \leftarrow PC + 3$

Description : This instruction calls the subroutine at the given address if a specified condition is satisfied. Before call it stores the address of instruction next to the call on the stack and decrements stack pointer by two. The table 3.1 shows the possible conditions for calls.

Table 3.1 : Conditional calls

Instruction code	Description	Condition for CALL
CC	Call on carry	CY = 1
CNC	Call on not carry	CY = 0
CP	Call on positive	S = 0
CM	Call on minus	S = 1
CPE	Call on parity even	P = 1
CPO	Call on parity odd	P = 0
CZ	Call on zero	Z = 1
CNZ	-Call on not zero	Z = A

No. of Bytes	: 3 bytes.
	First byte : Opcode of C condition.
	Second byte : Low. order byte of the, address.
	Third byte High order bytes of the address.
Addressing Mode	: Immediate register indirect addressing.
Flags	: Flags are not affected. Flags are checked.
Example	: Carry flag = 1, stack pointer = 4000H.
2000H CC 3000H	: This instruction will store the address of the next instruction i.e. 2003H on the stack and load the program
	; i.e. counter with 3000H.

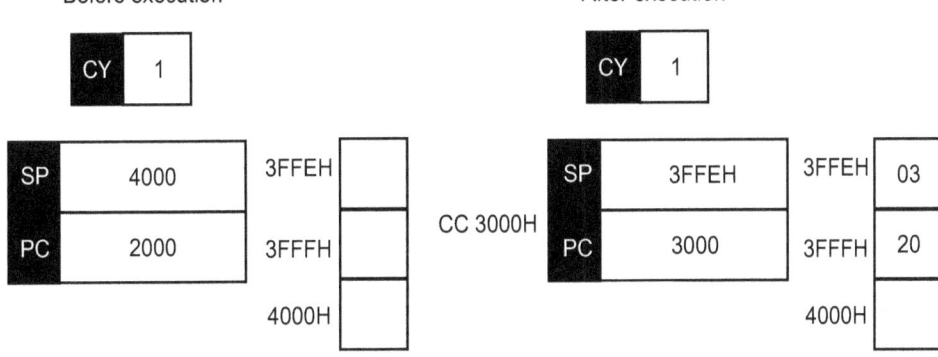

Fig. 3.22

R condition	: Return from the subroutine conditionally.
Operation	: If condition is true
	$PC_L \leftarrow (SP)$
	$PC_H \leftarrow (SP + 1)$
	$SP \leftarrow SP + 2$
	else
	$PC \leftarrow PC + 1$
Description	: This instruction returns the control to the main program if the specified condition is satisfied Table 3.2 shows the possible conditions for return.

Table 3.2 Conditions for return

Instruction code	Description	Condition for REF
RC	Return on carry	CY = 1
RNC	Return on not carry	CY = 0
RP	Return on positive	S = 0
RM	Return on minus	S = 1
RPE	Return on parity even	P = 1
RPO	Return on parity odd	P = 0
RZ	Return on zero	Z = 1
RNZ	Return on not zero	Z = 0

No. of Bytes : 1 byte.

Opcode of R condition

Addressing Mode : Register indirect addressing:

Flags : Flags are not affected.

RESTART

This oup consists of restart instructions.

1. RSTT n : Restart n (0 to 7)

Operation : (SP – 1) ← PCH

(SP – 2) ← PCL

SP ← SP – 2, PC ← (n × 8) in hex

Description : This instruction transfers the program control to the. specific memory address as shown in Table 3.3. This instruction is like a fixed address CALL instruction. These fixed addresses are also referred to as vector addresses. The processor multiplies the RST number by 8 to calculate these vector addresses. Before transferring the program control to the instruction following the vector address RST instruction saves the current program counter contents on the stack like CALL instruction.

Table 3.3 Vector addresses for return instructions

Instruction code	Vector Address
RST 0	0 × 8 = 0000H
RST 1	1 × 8 = 0008H
RST 2	2 × 8 = 0010ft
RST 3	3 × 8 = 0018H
RST 4	4 × 8 = 0020H
RST 5	5 × 8 = 0028H
RST 6	6 × 8 = 0030H
RST 7	7 × 8 = 0038H

No. of Bytes : I byte.

Opcode of RST n.

Addressing Mode : Register indirect addressing.

Flags : Flags are not, affected.

Example :

2000H RST 6   ; This instruction will save the current contents of the program
                     ; counter (i.e. address of next instruction 200111) on the stack and
                     ; it will load the program counter with vector address
                     ; $(6 \times 8 = 48_{10} = 30H)$ 0030H.

Before execution   After execution

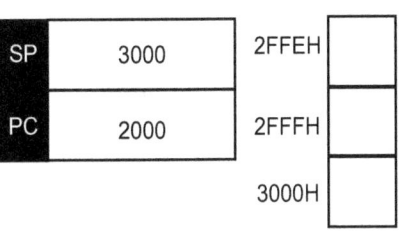 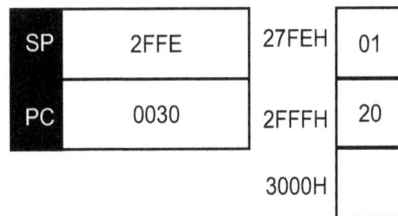

Fig. 3.23

Input/Output : This group consists of following set of instructions.

                       IN addr
                       OUT addr

1. IN addr (8-bit) : Copy data from input port into Accumulator.

Operation   : $A \leftarrow (addr)$

Description   : This instruction copies the data at the port whose address is specified in the instruction into the accumulator.

No. of Bytes.   : 2 bytes.
                       First byte Opcode of IN.
                       Second byte : 8-bit address.

Addressing Mode : Direct addressing.

Flags   : Flags are not affected.

Example   : Port address = 80H data stored at port address 80H, (80H) 10H

IN 80H   ; This instruction will copy the data stored at address 80H, i.e. data 1011 in the accumulator.

Before execution   After execution

   IN 80H   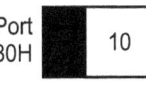

Fig. 3.24

2. OUT addr (8-bit) : Send data to the output port.

Operation   : $(addr) \leftarrow A$

Description   : This instruction sends the contents of accumulator to the output port whose address dress is specified within the instruction.

No. of Bytes   : 2 bytes.

First byte : Opcode of OUT.
Second byte : 8-bit address.
Addressing Mode : Direct addressing.
Flags : Flags are not affected.
Example : A = 40H
OUT 50H ; This instruction will send the contents of accumulator (4011) to the output port whose address is 50H.

Before execution   After execution

 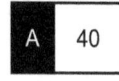 OUT 50H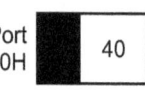

Fig. 3.25

3. **XTHL** : Exchange top of stack with H and L.
   Operation : L ↔ (SP)
   H ↔ (SP + 1)
   Description : This instruction' exchanges the contents of memory location pointed by the stack pointer with the contents of L register and the contents of. the next memory location with the contents of H register. This instruction does not modify stack pointer contents.
   No. of Bytes : I byte.
   Opcode of XTHL.
   Addressing Mode : Register indirect addressing.
   Flags : Flags are not affected.
   Example : HL = 3040H and SP = 2700H, (2700H) 50H, (2701H) = 60H
   XTHL : This instruction will exchange the contents of L register (40H) with the contents of memory location 2700H (i.e. 50H) and the contents of H register (30H) with the contents of memory location 2701H (i.e. 60H).

Before execution   After execution

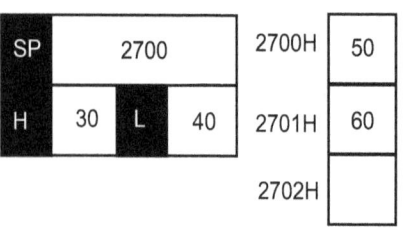   XTHL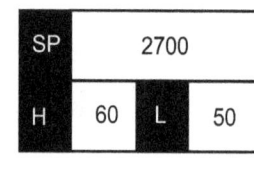

Fig. 3.26

4. **SPHL** : Move data from HL to stack pointer.
   Operation : SP ← HL

Description	:	This instruction -copies the contents of HL register pair into the stack pointer. The contents of H register are copied to higher order byte of stack pointer and contents of L register are copied to the lower byte of stack pointer.
No. of Bytes	:	1 byte., Opcode of SPHL.
Addressing Mode	:	Register addressing.
Flags	:	Flags are not affected.
Example	:	HL = 2500H
SPHL	:	This instruction will copy 2500H into stack pointer. So after execution of instruction stack pointer contents will be 2500H.

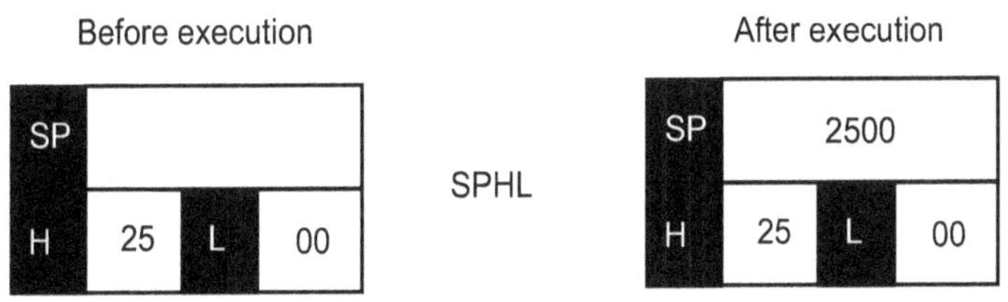

Before execution

After execution

SP

SP 2500

SPHL

H 25 L 00

H 25 L 00

Fig. 3.27

Machine Control : This group consists of following set of instructions.

(1) EI
(2) DI
(3) NOP
(4) HLT
(5) SIM
(6) RIM

1. EI	:	Enable Interrupt
Operation	:	IE (F/F) ← 1
Description	:	This instruction sets the interrupt enable flip flop to enable interrupts. When the microprocessor is reset or after interrupt acknowledge, the interrupt. enable flip-flop is reset. This instruction is used to reenable the interrupts.
No. of Bytes	:	1 byte. Opcode of EI.
Addressing Mode	:	None.
Flags	:	Flags are not affected.

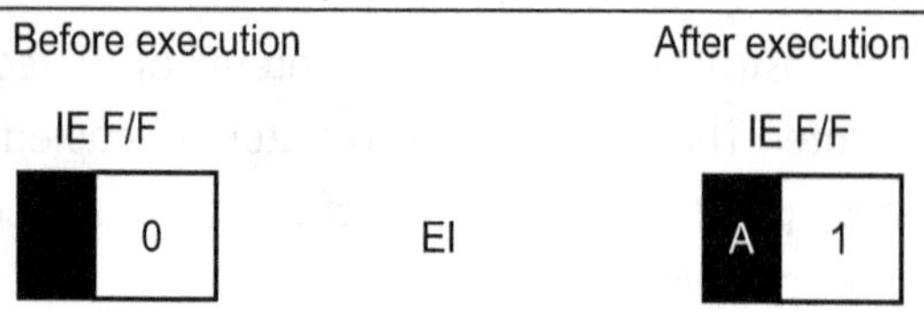

	Before execution		After execution
	IE F/F		IE F/F
	■ 0	EI	A 1

Fig. 3.28

2. DI : Disable Interrupts

Operation : IE (F/F) ← 0

Description : This instruction resets the interrupt enable flip flop to disable interrupts. This instruction disables all interrupts except TRAP since TRAP is non-maskable interrupt (cannot be disabled.. It is always enabled).

No. of Bytes : 1 byte.

Opcode of DI.

Addressing Mode : None,

Flags : Flags are . not affected.

3. NOP : No operation.

Description : No operation is performed.

No. of Bytes : 1 byte.

Opcode of NOP.

Addressing Mode : None.

Flags : Flags are not affected.

4. HLT : Halts the processor.

Description : This instruction halts the processor. It can be restarted by a valid interrupt or by applying a RESET signal.

No. of Bytes : 1 byte.

Opcode of HLT.

Addressing Mode : None.

Flags : Flags are not affected.

5. SIM : Set Interrupt Mask.

Description : This instruction masks the interrupts ' as desired. It also sends out serial data through the SOD pin. For this instruction command byte must be loaded in the accumulator.

The pattern for command byte is

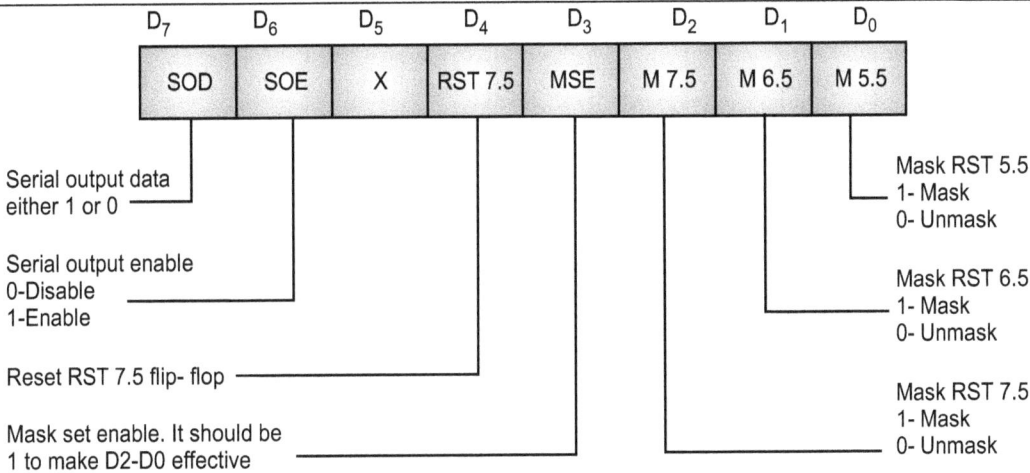

Fig. 3.29

Example :

A = 0EH

D₇	D₆	D₅	D₄	D₃	D₂	D₁	D₀		Register
SOD	SOE	X	RST 7.5	MSE	M 7.5	M 6.5	M 5.5	=	A
0	0	0	0	1	1	1	0		0EH

SIM : This instruction will mask RST 7.5 and RST 6.5 interrupts where as RST,5.5 interrupt will be unmasked. It will also disable serial output.

A = C0H

D₇	D₆	D₅	D₄	D₃	D₂	D₁	D₀		Register
SOD	SOE	X	RST 7.5	MSE	M 7.5	M 6.5	M 5.5	=	A
1	1	0	0	0	0	0	0		C0H

SIM : This instruction will output one on the SOD pin of 8085. Masking will be ineffective because MSE bit is zero in the command byte.

6. RIM : Read Interrupt Mask.

Description : This instruction copies the status of the interrupts into the accumulator. It also reads the serial data through the SID pin. The pattern of the status byte is

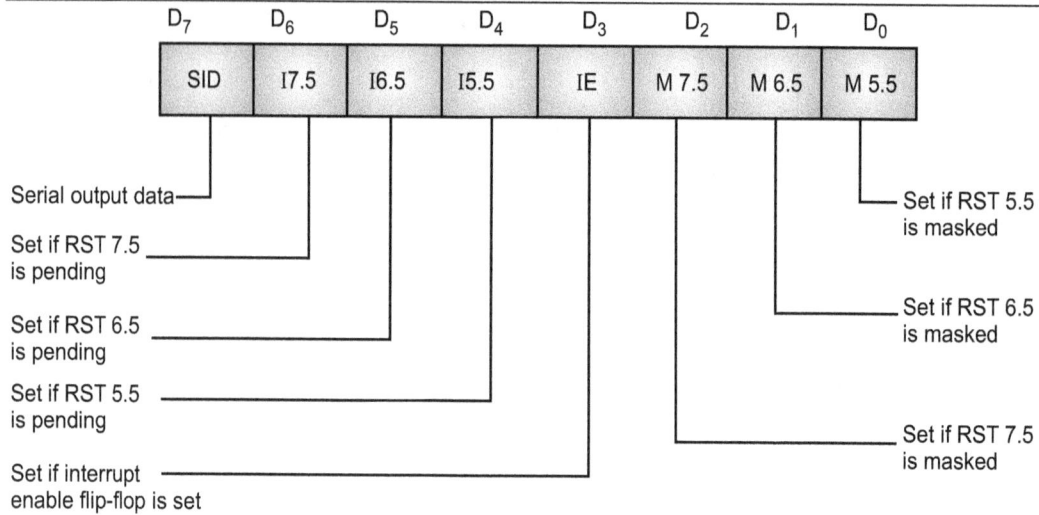

Fig. 3.30

Example

RIM : After execution of RIM instruction if the contents of accumulator
; are 413H then we get following information.

D_7	D_6	D_5	D_4	D_3	D_2	D_1	D_0		Register
SID	I7.5	I6.5	I5.5	IE	M 7.5	M 6.5	M 5.5		A
0	1	0	0	1	0	1	1	=	4BH

i.e. (a) RST 7.5 is pending
 (b) RST 5.5 and RST 6.5 are masked
 (c) Interrupt Enable flip-flop is set
 (d) Serial i/p data is zero.

Data Transfer Group Instructions

Instruction	Description	Operation
MOV r1, r2	(Move Data; Move the content of the one register to another)	[r1] <-- [r2]
MOV r, m	(Move the content of memory register).	r <-- [M]
MOV M, r	(Move the content of register to memory)	M <-- [r]
MVI r, data	(Move immediate data to register).	[r] <-- data
MVI M, data	(Move immediate data to memory)	M <-- data
LXI rp, data 16	(Load register pair immediate)	[rp] <-- data 16 bits, [rh] <-- 8 LSBs of data

LDA addr	(Load Accumulator direct)	[A] <-- [addr].
STA addr.	(Store accumulator direct)	[addr] <-- [A]
LHLD addr.	(Load H-L pair direct)	[L] <-- [addr], [H] <-- [addr+1]
SHLD addr.	(Store H-L pair direct)	[addr] <-- [L], [addr+1] <-- [H]
LDAX rp.	(LOAD accumulator indirect)	[A] <-- [[rp]]
STAX rp.	(Store accumulator indirect)	[[rp]] <-- [A]
XCHG	(Exchange the contents of H-L with D-E pair)	[H-L] <--> [D-E]

1. **MVI r, data (8)** : Move 8 bit immediate data to register r.
   Operation : r ← 8-bit data (byte)
   Description : This instruction directly loads a specified register with an 8-bit data given within the instruction. The register r is an 8-bit general purpose register such as A, B, C, D, E, H and L.
   Number of Bytes : 2 bytes.
   First byte : Opcode of MVI r.
   Second byte : 8-bit data.
   Addressing Mode : Immediate addressing.
   Flags : Flags are not affected.
   Example :
   MVI B, 60H : This instruction will load 60H directly into the B register.

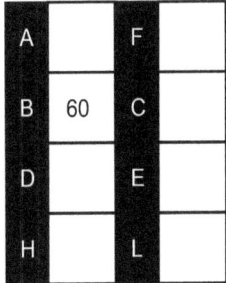

Fig. 3.31

2. **MVI M, data (8)** : Move 8 bit immediate data to memory whose address is in HL register pair.
   Operation : M ← byte or (HL) ← byte
   Description : This instruction directly loads an 8-bit data given within the

instruction into a memory location. The memory location is specified by the contents of HL register pair.

No. Bytes : 2 bytes.

First byte : Opcode of MVI M.

Second byte : 8-bit data.

Addressing Mode : Immediate and indirect addressing.

Flags : Flags are not affected.

Example : H = 20H and L = 50H

MVI M. 40H ; This instruction will load 40H into
; memory whose address is 2050H.

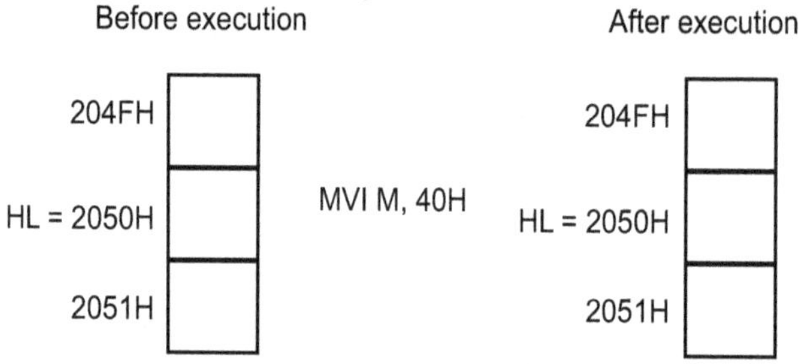

Before execution   After execution

204FH   MVI M, 40H   204FH

HL = 2050H   HL = 2050H

2051H   2051H

Fig. 3.32

3. **MOV rd, rs** : %love data from source register (rs) to destination register (rd).

   Operation : rd ← rs

   Description : This instruction copies data from the source register into destination register. The rs and rd are general purpose registers such as A, B, C, D, E, H and L. The contents of the source register remain unchanged after execution of the instruction.

   No. of Bytes : 1 byte.

   Opcode of MOV rd, rs.

   Addressing Mode : Register addressing.

   Flags : Flags are not affected.

   Example : A = 20

   MOV B, A ; This instruction will copy the contents
   ; of register A (20H) into register B.

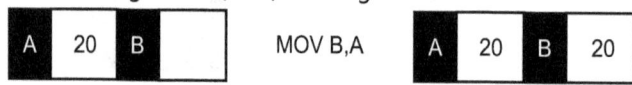

Fig. 3.33

4. **MOV M, rs** : Move data froth source register (rs) to memory whose address is in HL register pair.

   Operation : (HL) ← rs,

   Description : This instruction copies data form the source register into memory location pointed by the HL register pair. The rs is an 8-bit general purpose register such as A, B, C. D, E, H and L.

No. of Bytes : 1 byte.
Opcode of MOV M, rs.
Addressing Mode : Indirect addressing.
Flags : Flags are not affected.
Example : If 14L = 200H, B 3()H.
MOV M, B ; This instruction will, copy the contents
; of o B register (31011) into the memory location
; whose address is specified by HL

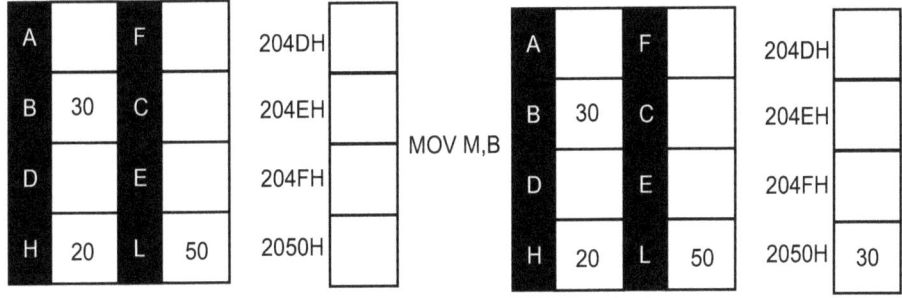

Fig. 3.34

5. **MOV rd, M** : Move data from memory location specified by HL register pair to the, destination register (rd).

Operation : rd (HL)
Description : This instruction copies data from memory location whose-address is specified by HL register into destination register. The contents of the "The rd is an 8-bit general he memory location remain unchanged The rd is an 8-bit general purpose register such as A, B, C, D, E, H and L.

No. of Bytes : 1 byte.
Opcode of MOV rd, M
Addressing Mode : Indirect addressing.
Flags : Flags are not affected.
Example : HL = 2050H, contents at 2050H memory location = 40H
MOV C, M ; This instruction will copy the contents
; of memory location pointed by HL
; register pair (40H) into the C register

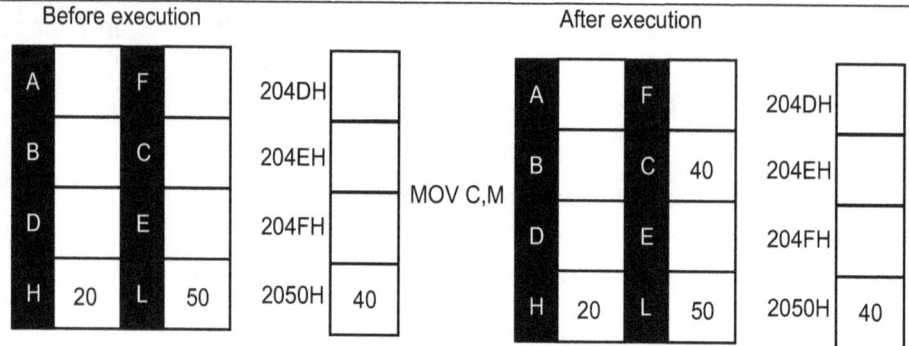

Fig. 3.35

6. **LXI rp, data (16)** : Load 16-bit immediate data to specified register pair.

   Operation : rp ← data (16)

   Description : This instruction loads immediate 16 bit data specified within the instruction i46 register pair or stack pointer. The rp is 16-bit register pair such- as BC, DE, HL or 16-bit stack pointer.

   No. of Bytes : 3 bytes.

   First byte : Opcode of LXI rp.

   Second byte : Low-order byte of 16-bit data.

   Third byte : High order byte of 16-bit data.

   Addressing Mode : Immediate addressing.

   Flags : Flags are not affected.

   Example :

   i) LXI B, 1020H ; This instruction will load 10H into B
   ; register and 20H into C register.

   ii) LXI SP, 27FFH ; This instruction will load 27FFH into stack pointer.

   Before execution 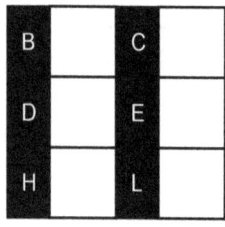 After execution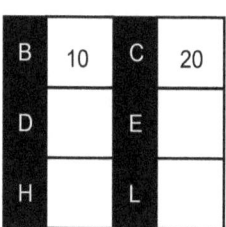

   LXI B,1020H

   Fig. 3.36

7. **STA addr** : Store the contents of A register at address given within the instruction.

   Operation : (addr) ←- A

   Description : This instruction stores the contents of- A , register into the memo location whose address is directly specified within the instruction, The

	contents of A register remain unchanged
No. of Bytes	: 3 bytes.
	First byte : Opcode of STA.
	Second byte: Low order byte of the address.
	Third byte : High order byte of the address.
Addressing Mode	: Direct addressing.
Flags	: Flags are not affected.
Example	: A 50H
	STA 2000H ; This instruction will store the
	; contents of A register (50H) to
	; memory location 2000H.

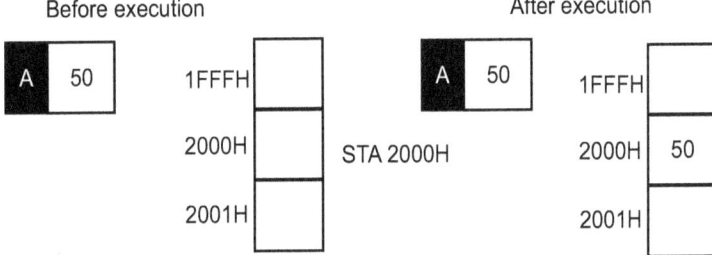

Fig. 3.37

8. **LDA addr** : Load data into A register directly from the address given within the instruction.

Operation	: A ← (addr)
Description	: This instruction copies the contents of the memory location address is given within the instruction into the accumulator. The contents of the memory location remain- unchanged
No. of Bytes	: 3 bytes.
	First byte Opcode of LDA
	Second byte : Low order byte of the address.
	Third byte: High order byte of the address
Addressing Mode	: Direct addressing.
Flags	: Flags are not affected.
Example	: (2000H) = 30H
	LDA 2000H ; This instruction will copy the
	; contents of memory location
	; 2000H i.e. data 30H into the
	; A register

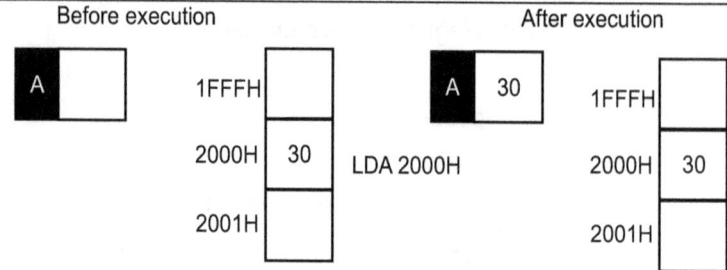

Fig. 3.38

9. **SKLD addr** : Store HL register pair in memory.
   Operation : (addr) ← L and (addr + 1) ← H
   Description : This instruction stores the contents of L register in the memory location given within the instruction and contents -of H register at address next to it. This instruction is used to store the contents of H and L registers directly into the memory. The contents of the H and L registers remain unchanged.
   No. of Bytes : 3 bytes.
   First byte : Opcode of SHLD
   Second byte : Low order byte of the address
   Third byte : High order byte of the address
   Addressing Mode : Direct addressing.
   Flags : Flags are not affected.
   Example : H 30H, L = 60H
   SHLD 2500H ; This instruction will copy
   ; the contents of L register at
   ; address 2500H and the contents
   ; of H register at address 2501H.

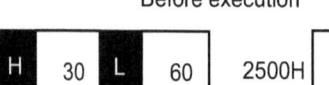
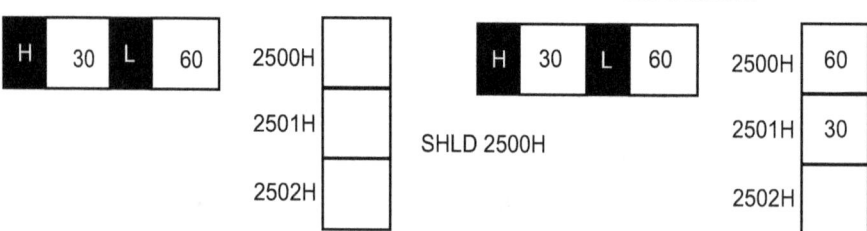

Fig. 3.39

10. **LRLD addr** : Load HL register pair from memory.
    Operation : L ← (addr), H ← (addr + 1)
    Description : This instruction copies the contents of the memory location given within the instruction into the L register and the contents of the next

	memory location into the H register.
No. of Bytes	: 3 bytes.

First byte : Opcode of LHLD
Second byte : Low order byte of the address
Third byte : High-order byte of the address

Addressing Mode : Direct addressing.
Flags : Flags art not affected.
Example :

(2500H) 30H, (2501H) 60H
LHLD 2500 H ; This instruction will copy the
                        ; contents of memory location 2500H
                        ; i.e. data 30H into the L register and
                        ; the contents at memory location
                        ; 2501H i.e. data 60H into the H register.

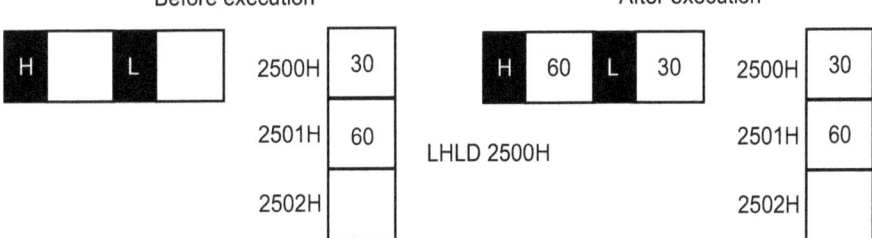

Fig. 3.40

11. STAX rp : Store the contents of A register in memory location whose address is specified by BC or DE register pair.

Operation : (rp) ← A

Description : This instruction copies the contents of accumulator into the memory location whose address is specified by the specified register pair. The rp is BC or DE register pair. This register pair is used as a memory pointer. The contents of the accumulator remain unchanged.

No. of Bytes : 1 byte.

Opcodc-of STAR, rp

Addressing Mode : Register indirect addressing.
Flags : Flags are not affected.
Example : BC = 1020H, A 50H

STAX B ; This instruction will copy the
                       ; contents of A register (50H) to the

; memory location specified
; by RC register pair (1020H).

Before execution

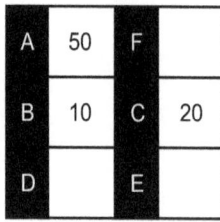 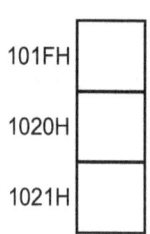

STAX B

After execution

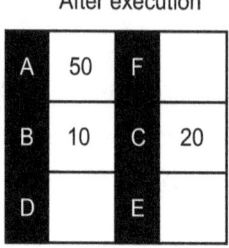 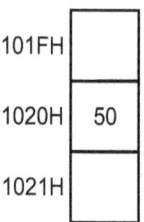

Fig. 3.41

12. LDAX rp : Load A register with the contents of memory location whose address is specified by AC or DE register pair.

Operation : A ← (rp)

Description : Ibis instruction copies the contents of memory location' whose address is specified by the register pair into the accumulator. The rp is BC or DE register pair. The register pair is used as a memory pointer.

No. of Bytes : 1 byte.

Opcode of LDAX rp

Addressing Mode : Register indirect addressing.

Flags : Flags are not affected.

Example : DE 2030H, (2030H) 80H

LDAX D ; This instruction will copy the
; contents of memory location
; specified by DE register pair
; (2030H) into the accumulator.

Before execution

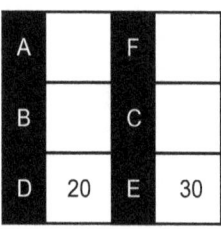 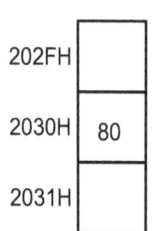

LDAX D

After execution

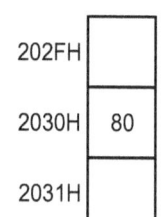

Fig. 3.42

13. XCHG : exchange the contents of H with D and L with E

Operation : H ↔ D and L ↔ E

Description : This instruction -exchanges the contents of the -register H with that of D and of L with that of E.

No. of Bytes : 1 byte.

Opcode of XCHG

Addressing Mode : Register addressing.

Flags : Flags are not affected.

Example : DE = 2040H, HL = 7080H

XCHG : This instruction wilt load the data into registers as follows H = 20H, L 40H, D 70H and E = 80.

Note : 1. There is no single- instruction to transfer data from one memory location to another memory location in 8085.

2. Data transfer instructions do not affect the flags.

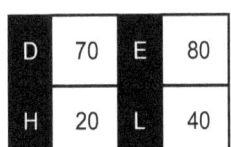

Fig. 3.43

QUESTIONS

1. Explain the Data Addressing modes.
2. Explain the details MOV r_1 Data.
3. Explain PUSH | POP instruction and it's details.
4. What are stack memory Addressing modes ?
5. Brief detail of Register Addressing modes.
6. Explain the different Addressing modes.

7. Explain the stack operation. input / output and machine control group.
8. Explain in details following instructions
   (i) PUSH rp (ii) POP rp (iii) POP psw
9. What is CALL address and RET ?

   Explain the implements of substations
10. Explain in details STAX rp.

✠ ✠ ✠

Unit - IV

ARITHMATIC, LOGIC AND PROGRAM CONTROL INSTRUCTIONS

4.1 INTRODUCTION

An instruction is a binary pattern designed inside a microprocessor to perform a specific function.

- The entire group of instructions that a microprocessor supports is called Instruction Set.
- 8085 has 246 instructions.
- Each instruction is represented by an 8-bit binary value.
- These 8-bits of binary value is called Op-Code or Instruction Byte.

1. Arithmetic Group

The instructions of this group perform arithmetic operations such as addition, subtraction; increment or decrement of the content of a register or memory. Examples are: ADD, SUB, INR, DAD etc.

Any 8-bit number, or the contents of register, or the contents of memory location can be added to the contents of accumulator.

- The result (sum) is stored in the accumulator.
- No two other 8-bit registers can be added directly.
- Example: The contents of register B cannot be added directly to the contents of register C.

2. Logical Group

The Instructions under this group perform logical operation such as AND, OR, compare, rotate etc. Examples are: ANA, XRA, ORA, CMP, and RAL etc.

3. Branch Control Group

This group includes the instructions for conditional and unconditional jump, subroutine call and return, and restart. Examples are: JMP, JC, JZ, CALL, CZ, RST etc.

4.2 ARITHMETIC GROUP INSTRUCTIONS

Instruction	Description	Operation
ADD r	(Add register to accumulator)	[A] <-- [A] + [r]
MOV r, m	(Move the content of memory register).	r <-- [M]
ADD M	(Add memory to accumulator)	[A] <-- [A] + [[H-L]]
ADC r	(Add register with carry to accumulator)	[A] <-- [A] + [r] + [CS]
ADC M	(Add memory with carry to accumulator)	[A] <-- [A] + [[H-L]] [CS]
ADI data	(Add immediate data to accumulator)	[A] <-- [A] + data
ACI data	(Add with carry immediate data to accumulator)	[A] <-- [A] + data + [CS]
DAD rp	(Add register paid to H-L pair)	[H-L] <-- [H-L] + [rp]
SUB r	(Subtract register from accumulator)	[A] <-- [A] – [r]
SUB M	(Subtract memory from accumulator)	[A] <-- [A] – [[H-L]]
SBB r	(Subtract register from accumulator with borrow)	[A] <-- [A] – [r] – [CS]
SBB M	(Subtract memory from accumulator with borrow)	[A] <-- [A] – [[H-L]] – [CS]
SUI data	(Subtract immediate data from accumulator)	[A] <-- [A] – data
SBI data	(Subtract immediate data from accumulator with borrow)	[A] <-- [A] – data – [CS]
INR r	(Increment register content)	[r] <-- [r] +1
INR M	(Increment memory content)	[[H-L]] <-- [[H-L]] + 1
DCR r	(Decrement register content)	[r] <-- [r] – 1
DCR M	(Decrement memory content)	[[H-L]] <-- [[H-L]] – 1
INX rp	(Increment register pair)	[rp] <-- [rp] – 1
DCX rp	(Decrement register pair)	[rp] <-- [rp] -1
DAA	(Decimal adjust accumulator)	-

The instruction DAA is used in the program after ADD, ADI, ACI, ADC, etc instructions. After the execution of ADD, ADC, etc instructions the result is in hexadecimal and it is placed in the accumulator. The DAA instruction operates on this result and gives the final result in the decimal system. It uses carry and auxiliary carry for decimal adjustment. 6 is added to 4 LSBs of the content of the accumulator if their value lies in between A and F or the AC flag is set to 1. Similarly, 6 is also added to 4 MSBs of the content of the accumulator if their value lies in between A and F or the CS flag is set to 1. All status flags are affected. When DAA is used data should be in decimal numbers.

4.2.2 Arithmetic Group

Arithmetic Group Arithmetic group instructions add, subtract, increment or decrement data in registers or in memory. In addition, there is one instruction which adjusts 8-bit data to form BCD numbers.

4.2.2.1 Add

This group consists of following set of instructions
- (1) ADD r
- (2) ADD M
- (3) ADI data (8)
- (4) ADC r
- (5) ADC M
- (6) ACI data (8)
- (7) DAD rp

1. **ADP r** : Add register r to Accumulator.
   Operation : $A \leftarrow A + r$
   Description : This instruction adds the contents. of the specified register to the contents of accumulator and stores result in. the, accumulator. The r is 8-bit general purpose register such as A, BI C, D, E, H and L.
   No. of Bytes : 1 byte.
   Opcode of ADD r.
   Addressing Mode : Register addressing.
   Flags : All flags are Affected.
   Example : A = 20H, C = 30H.
   ADD C ; This instruction will add the contents of C register, i.e. data 30H
   ; to the contents of accumulator, i.e. data 20H and-it will store
   ; the-result 50H in the accumulator.

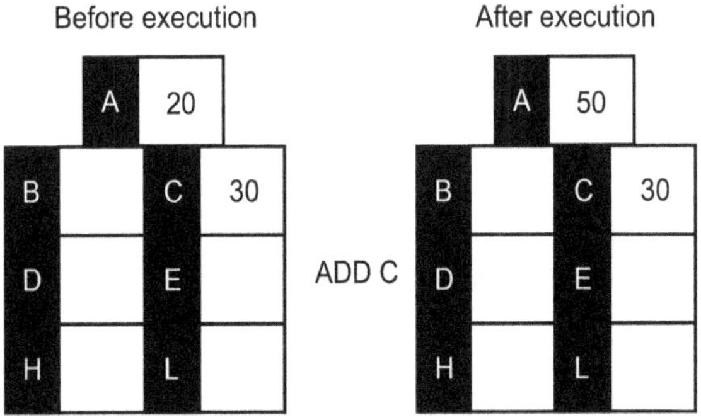

Before execution   After execution

A	20		A	50
---	----		---	----
B		C	30		B		C	30
D		E		ADD C	D		E	
H		L			H		L	

Fig. 4.1

2. **ADD M** : Add data in memory to Accumulator.
   Operation : A ← A + M
   Description : This instruction adds the contents of the memory location pointed by HL register pair to the contents of accumulator and stores result in the accumulator. The HL register pair is used as a memory pointer. This instruction affects all flags.
   No. of Bytes : 1 byte.
   Opcode of ADD M.
   Addressing more : Register indirect addressing.
   Flags : All flags are affected.
   Example : A = 20H, HL = 2050H,
   : (205014) = 1014
   ADD M : This instruction will add the contents of memory location pointed
   ; by HL register pair, 2050H i.e. dam 10H to the contents of
   ; accumulator i.e. data 20H and it will store the result, 30H
   ; in the accumulator.

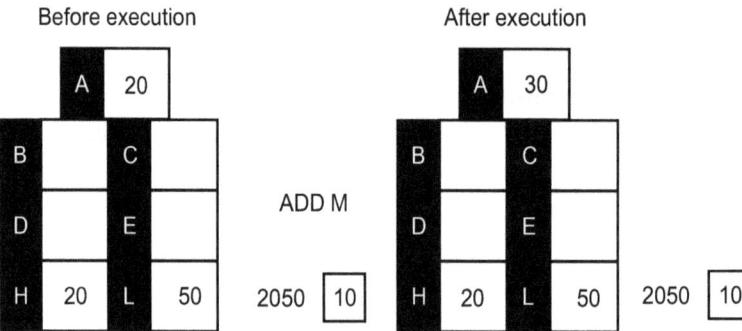

Fig. 4.2

3. **ADI data (8)** : Add immediate 8 bit data to Accumulator.
   Operation : A +- A + data (8)
   Description : This instruction adds the 8 bit data given within the instruction to the contents of accumulator and stores the result in the accumulator.
   No. of Bytes : 2 bytes.
   First byte : Opcode of ADI
   Second byte : 8-bit data
   Addressing Mode : Immediate addressing.
   Flags : All flags are affected.
   Example : A = 50H
   ADI 70H : This instruction will add 70H. to the contents of the accumulator
   ; (50H) and it will store the result in the accumulator (COH).

Fig. 4.3

4. **ADC r** : Add register t with, carry to register A.
   Operation : A +- A + r + CY
   Description : This instruction adds the contents of specified register to, the contents of accumulator with-carry. This means, if the carry flag is set by some previous operation, "it adds 1 and the contents of the specified register to the contents of accumulator, else it adds the contents of the specified register only. The r is 8-bit general purpose register such as A, B, C, D, E, H and L.
   No. of Bytes : 1 byte.
   Opcode of ADC r.
   Addressing Mode : Register addressing.
   Flags : All flags are, affected.
   Example : Carry flag 1, A 50H, C 20H
   ADC C : This instruction will add the contents of C (20H) register to the
   : contents of accumulator (50H) with carry (1) and it will store
   : result, 71H (50H + 20H + 1 = 71H) in the accumulator.

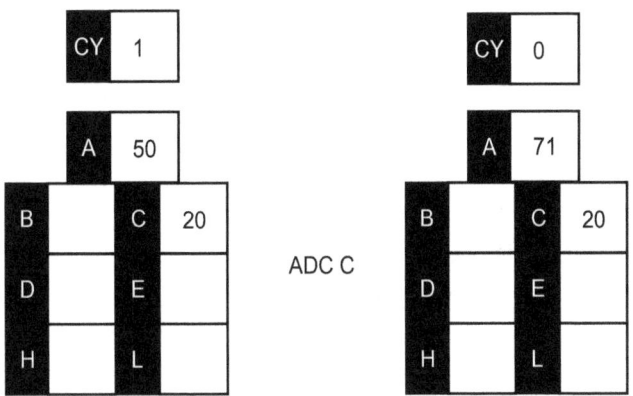

Fig. 4.4

5. **ADC M** : Add data in memory to accumulator with carry.
   Operation : A ← A + M + CY
   Description : This instruction adds the contents of memory location pointed by HL register pair to the contents of accumulator with carry and stores the result, in the, accumulator. HL register pair is used, as a memory pointer.

No. of Bytes	: 1 byte.
	Opcode of ADC M.
Addressing Mode	: Register indirect addressing.
Flags	: All flags are affected.
Example	: Carry flag =, 1, HL = 2050H, A 20H, (20 OH) 30H.
ADC M	: This instruction will add the contents of memory location pointed ; by HL register pair, 2050H, i.e. data 30H to the contents of ; accumulator, i.e. data 20H with carry flag (1). It will store the ; result (30 + 20 + 1 = 51H) in the accumulator.

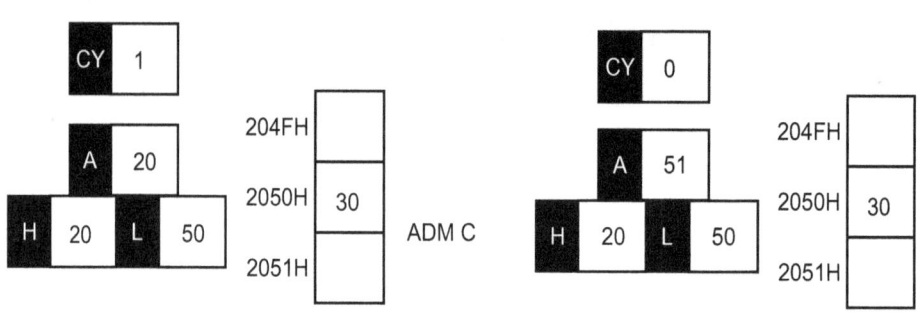

Fig. 4.5

6. **ACI data (8)** : Add 8 bit immediate data to Accumulator with carry.
   Operation : A ← A + data (8) + CY
   Description : This- instruction adds- 8 bit data given within the instruction to the contents of accumulator with carry and stores result in the accumulator.
   No. of Bytes : 2 bytes.
   First byte : Opcode of ACI.
   Second byte : 8-bit data.
   Addressing Mode : Immediate addressing.
   Flags : All flags are affected.
   Example : A = 30H, Carry flag = 1
   ACI 20H ; This instruction will add 20H to the contents of accumulator
   ; i.e. data 30H with carry (1) and stores the result,
   ; 51H (30 + 20 + 1 = 51H) in the accumulator.

Fig. 4.6

7. **DAD rp** : Add register pair rp to 'HL register pair
   Operation : HL ← HL + rp
   Description : This instruction adds the contents of the specified register pair to the contents of the HL register pair and stores the result in the HL register pair. The rp is 16-bit register pair such as BC, DE, HL or, stack pointer. Only higher order register is to be specified for. register; pair within the instruction.
   No. of Bytes : 1 byte.
   Opcode of DAD rp.
   Addressing Mode : Register addressing
   Flags : Only carry flag is not affected.
   Example : DE = 1020H, HL = 2050H
   DAD D : This instruction will add the contents of DE register pair, 1020H to
   ; the contents of HL register pair, 2050H. It will store the result,
   ; 3070H in the HL register-pair.

   Before execution    After execution

      DAD D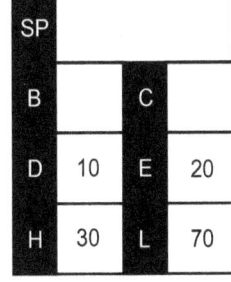

Fig. 4.7

4.2.2.2 Substract

This group consists of the following set of instructions
  (1) SUB r
  (2) SUB M
  (3) SUI data
  (4) SBB r
  (5) SBB M
  (6) SBI data

1. **SUB r** : Subtract specified register from Accumulator
   Operation : A ← A - r
   Description : This instruction subtracts the contents of the specified register from the contents of the accumulator and stores the result in the accumulator. The register r is 8-bit general register such as A, B, C, D, E, H and L.
   No. of Bytes : 1 byte.
   Opcode of SUB r.
   Addressing Mode : Register addressing.
   Flags : All flags are affected. If carry flag = 1, result is negative and is in 2's form ' m and if carry flag 0 remit is positive. 2s complement
   Example : A = 50H, B = 30H.
   SUB B ; This instruction will subtract the contents of B register (30H) from
   ; the contents of accumulator (50H) and stores the result (20H) in
   ; the accumulator.

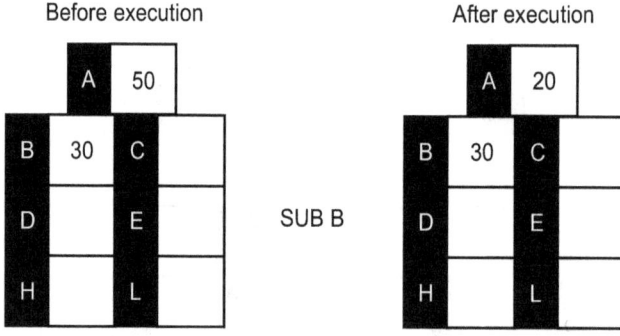

Fig. 4.8

2. **SUB M** : Subtract data in memory from Accumulator.
   Operation : A ← A - M.
   Description : This instruction subtracts the contents of the memory location pointed by HL register pair from the contents accumulator stores the result in the accumulator. The. HL register pair is used as memory pointer.
   No. of Bytes : 1 byte.
   Opcode of SUB M.
   Addressing Mode : Register indirect addressing.
   Flags : All flags are affected.
   Example : HL 1020H, A 50H, (1020H) =.10H
   SUB M ; This instruction will subtract the contents of memory location
   ; pointed by HL register pair, 1020H, i.e. data 10H from the
   ; contents 'accumulator, i.e. data 50H and stores the result (40H) in

; accumulator.

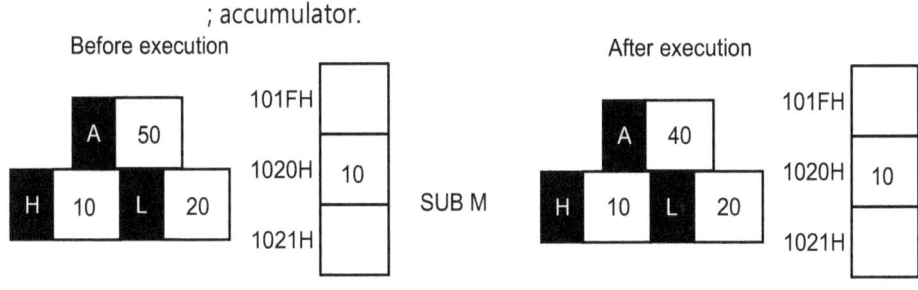

Fig. 4.9

3. **SUI data (8)** : Subtract 8 bit immediate data from the Accumulator.

   Operation : A ← A - data (8)

   Description : This instruction subtracts an 8 bit data given within the instruction from the contents of the accumulator and stores the result in the accumulator.

   No. of Bytes : 2 bytes.

   First byte Opcode of SUI.

   Second byte : 8-bit data.

   Addressing Mode : Immediate addressing.

   Flags : All flags are affected.

   Example : A = 40H,

   SUI 20H ; This instruction will subtract 20H from the contents of accumulator ; (40H). It will store the result (20H) in the accumulator.

4. **SBB r** : Subtract specified register and borrow flag (carry flag) from accumulator.

   Operation : A ← A - r - CY

   Description : This, instruction subtracts the specified register, contents and borrow flag from the accumulator contents. This means, if the carry flag (borrow for subtraction) is set. by some previous operation, it subtracts 1 and the contents of the specified register from the contents of accumulator, else it subtracts the contents of the specified register only. The register r is 8-bit register such as A, B, C, D, E, H and L.

   No. of Bytes : 1 byte.

   Opcode of SBB r.

Addressing Mode : Register addressing.
Flags : All flags are affected.
Example : Carry flag = 1, C = 20H, A 40H
SBB C : This instruction will subtract the contents of C register (20H) and
; carry flag (1) from the contents of accumulator (40H).
; It will store the result (40H - 20H = 1 1FH) in the accumulator.

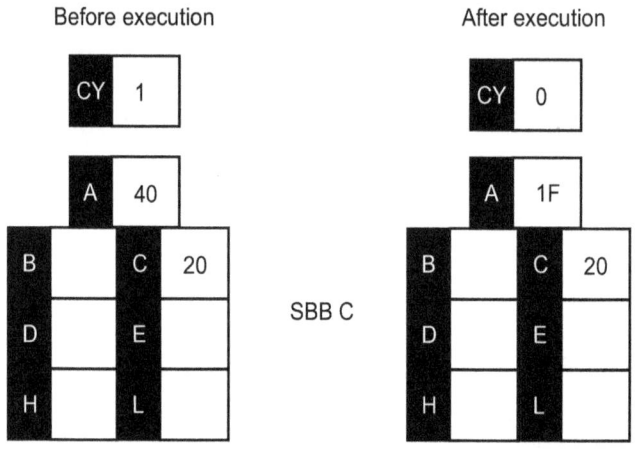

Fig. 4.10

5. **SBB M** : Subtract memory data and borrow flag from Accumulator
   Operation : A ← A – M – CY
   Description : This instruction subtracts the contents of memory location pointed by HL register pair from the contents of accumulator and borrow flag and stores the result in the accumulator.
   No. of Bytes : 1 byte.
   Opcode of SBB M.
   Addressing Mode : Register indirect addressing.
   Flags : All flags are affected.
   Example : Carry flag = 1, HL = 2050H, A 50H, (2050H) 10H.
   SBB M ; This instruction will subtract the contents of memory location
   ; pointed by HL register pair, 2050H, i.e. data 10H and borrow
   ; (Carry flag = 1) from the contents of accumulator (50H) and stores
   ; the result 3FH in the accumulator (50 - 10 – 1 3F).

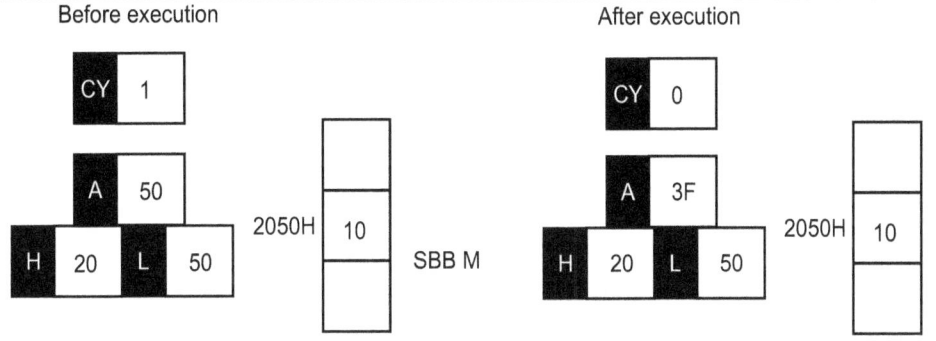

Fig. 4.11

6. **SM data (8)** : Subtract 8 bit immediate data and borrow flag from Accumulator.

   Operation : A ← A - data (8) - CY

   Description : This instruction subtracts 8 bit data given within the instruction and borrow flag from the contents of accumulator and stores the result in the accumulator.

   No. of Bytes : 2 bytes.

   First byte : Opcode of SBI.

   Second byte : 8-bit data

   Addressing Mode : Immediate addressing.

   Flags : All flags are affected.

   Example : Carry flag = 1, A = 50H

   SBI 2014 ; This instruction will subtract 20H and the' carry flag (1) from the
   ; contents of the accumulator (50H). It will store the result
   ; (50H – 20H – 1 2FH) in the accumulator.

Fig. 4.12

4.2.2.3 Decimal Adjust Accumulator

DAA

This instruction adjusts accumulator to sacked BCD (Binary Coded Decimal after adding two BCD numbers.

Instruction Works as Follows :

- If the value of the low, order four bits (D3-Do) in the accumulator is greater than 9 or if auxiliary carry flag is set, the instruction adds 6 (06) to the low-order four bits.

- If the value of the high-order four bits (D7-D4) in the accumulator is greater than 9 or if carry flag is set, the instruction adds 6(60) to the high-order four bits.

Example :

If, A = 0011 1001, 39 BCD

and C = 0001-0010 12 BCD then

ADD C	: Gives A 0100 1011 4BH
DAA	: adds 0110 because, 1011 > 9, A 0101"0001 51
	; BCD

If A 1001 0110 BCD

and D 0000 0111 07 BCD then

ADD D	; Gives A = 1001 1101 9DH
DAA	; adds 01100. becau 1101 > 9,
	; A= 10 11 = A3H
	; 1010 > 9 so adds 0110 0000
	; A ='0000 0011 = 03 BCD, CF 1.
No. of. Bytes	: 1 byte.
	(Opcode of DAA
Flags	: All flags are affected.

4.2.2.4 Increment and Decrement

This group consists of the following set of instructions
 (1) INR r
 (2) INR M
 (3) INX rp
 (4) DCR r
 (5) DCR M
 (6) DCX rp

1. | **INR r** | : Increment specified register. |
   |---|---|
   | **Operation** | : r ← r+ 1 |
   | **Description** | : This instruction increments the contents of specified register by L The result is stored in the same register. The register r is 8-bit general purpose register such as A, B, C, D, E, H and L. |
   | **No of Bytes** | : 1 byte. |
   | | Opcode of INR r. |
   | **Addressing Mode** | : Register addressing. |
   | **Flags** | : All flags except carry flag are affected. |
   | **Example** | : B = 10H |

INR B : This instruction will increment the contents of B register (10H)
; by one and stores the result (10 + 1 = 11 H) in the same i.e. B
; register,

Fig. 4.13

2. **INR M** : Increment data in. memory.
   Operation : M – M + 1
   Description : This instruction increments the contents of memory location pointed by HL register pair by 1. The result is stored at the same memory location. The HL register pair is used as a memory pointer.
   No. of Bytes : 1 byte,
   Opcode of INR M.
   Addressing Mode : Register indirect addressing.
   Flags : All flags except carry: flag are affected.
   Example : HL = 2050H, (20510H) = 30H
   INR M : This instruction will increment the contents of
   ; memory location pointed by HL register pair, 2050H, i.e. data 30H
   ; by one. It will store the result (30 + 1= 31H) at the same place.

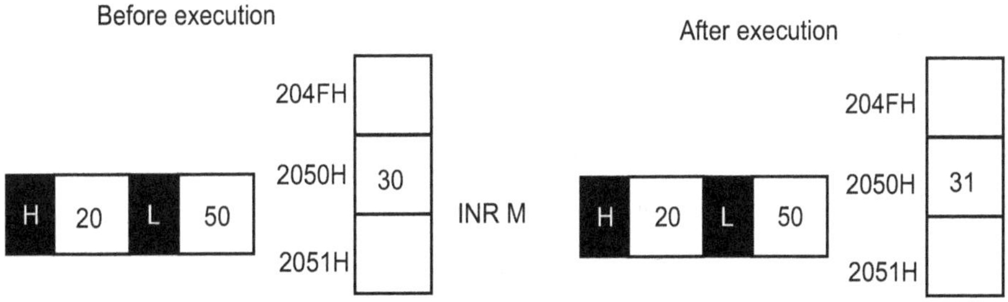

Fig. 4.14

3. **INX rp** : Increments ified register pair
   Operation : rp ← rp + 1

Description	: This instruction increments the contents of register pair by one. The result is stored in the same register pair. The rp is register pair such as BC, DE, HL or stack pointer (SP).
No. of Bytes	: 1 byte.
	Opcode of INX rp.
Addressing Mode	: Register addressing.,
Flags	: No flags are affected.
Example	: HL = IOFFH
INX H	; This instruction will increment the contents of HL register pair ; (IOFFH) by one. It will store the result (10 FF + 1 1100 H) in ; the same Le. HL register pair.

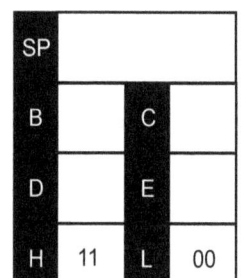

Fig. 4.15

4. **DCR r** : Decrement specified register.

   Operation : $r \leftarrow r - 1$

   Description : This instruction decrements the contents of the specified register by, one. It stores the result in the same register. The register is 8-bit general purpose register such as A, B,C, D, E, H and L.

   No. of Bytes : 1 byte.
   Opcode of DCR r.

   Addressing Mode : Register addressing.

   Flags : All flags except carry flag are affected.

   Example : DE = 20H

   DCX D : This instruction will decrement the contents of DE register pair ; (20H) by one. It will store the result (20 – 1 = 10 FH) in the ; same, DE register pair.

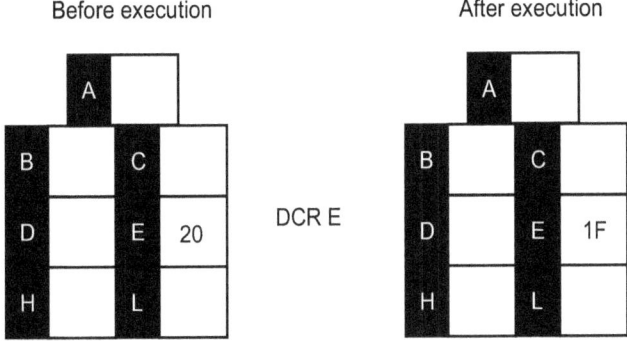

Fig. 4.16

5. **DCR M** : Decrement data in memory.

   Operation : M ← M - 1

   Description : This instruction decrements the contents of memory location pointed by HL register pair by 1. The HL register pair -is used as a memory pointer. The result, is stored in the same memory location.

   No. of Bytes : 1 byte.

   Opcode of DCR M.

   Addressing node : Register indirect addressing.

   Flags : All flags except carry flag are affected.

   Example : HL 2050H, (2050H) = 21H

   DCR M : This instruction will decrement the contents of memory location
   ; pointed by HL register pair, 2050H, i.e. data 21H by one. It will
   ; store the result (21 1 20H) in the same memory location.

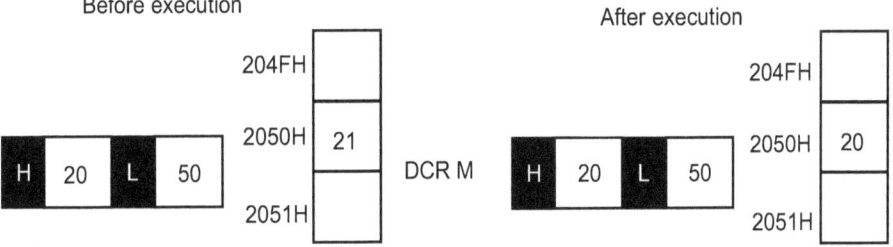

Fig. 4.17

6. **DCX rp** : Decrement specified register pair.

   Operation : rp ← rp − 1

   Description : This instruction decrements the contents of register pair by one. The result is stored, in the same register pair. The rp is register pair such as BC, DE, HL or stack pointer (SP). Only higher order register is. to be specified within the instruction.

   No. of Bytes : 1 byte.

   Opcode of DCX rp.

UNIT IV | 4.15

Addressing Mode : Register addressing.
Flags : No flags are affected.
Example : DE = 1020H
DCX D : This instruction will decrement the contents .of DE register pair
; (1020H) by one and store the result (1020 1. 101FH) in the
; same, DE register pair.

Before execution 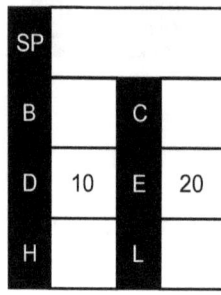 After execution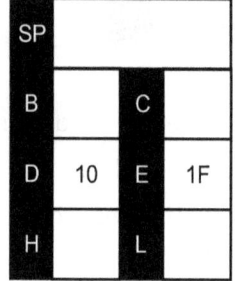

DCX D

Fig. 4.18

4.3 LOGICAL GROUP INSTRUCTIONS

Instruction	Description	Operation
ANA r	(AND register with accumulator)	[A] <-- [A] ^ [r]
ANA M	(AND memory with accumulator)	[A] <-- [A] ^ [[H-L]]
ANI data	AND (immediate data with accumulator)	[A] <-- [A] ^ data
ORA r	(OR register with accumulator)	[A] <-- [A] v [r]
ORA M	(OR memory with accumulator)	[A] <-- [A] v [[H-L]]
ORI data	OR immediate data with accumulator	() [A] <-- [A] v data
XRA r	(EXCLUSIVE – OR register with accumulator)	[A] <-- [A] v [r]
XRA M	(EXCLUSIVE-OR memory with accumulator)	[A] <-- [A] v [[H-L]]
XRI data	(EXCLUSIVE-OR immediate data with accumulator)	[A] <-- [A]
CMA	(Complement the accumulator)	[A] <-- [A]
CMC	(Complement the carry status)	[CS] <-- [CS]
STC	(Set carry status)	[CS] <-- 1
CMP r	(Compare register with accumulator)	[A] – [r]
CMP M	(Compare memory with accumulator)	[A] – [[H-L]]
CPI data	(Compare immediate data with accumulator)	[A] – data

The 2nd byte of the instruction is data, and it is subtracted from the content of the accumulator. The status flags are set according to the result of subtraction. But the result is discarded. The content of the accumulator remains unchanged.

- RLC (Rotate accumulator left) [An+1] <-- [An], [A0] <-- [A7],[CS] <-- [A7].

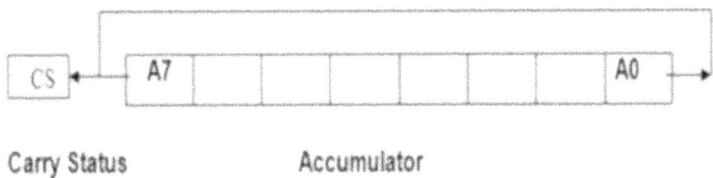

Carry Status   Accumulator

Fig. 4.19

- The content of the accumulator is rotated left by one bit. The seventh bit of the accumulator is moved to carry bit as well as to the zero bit of the accumulator. Only CS flag is affected.
- RRC. (Rotate accumulator right) [A7] <-- [A0], [CS] <-- [A0], [An] <-- [An+1].

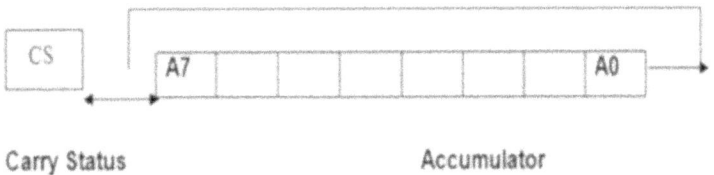

Carry Status   Accumulator

Fig. 4.20

- The content of the accumulator is rotated right by one bit. The zero bit of the accumulator is moved to the seventh bit as well as to carry bit. Only CS flag is affected.
- RAL. (Rotate accumulator left through carry) [An+1] <-- [An], [CS] <-- [A7], [A0] <-- [CS].
- RAR. (Rotate accumulator right through carry) [An] <-- [An+1], [CS] <-- [A0], [A7] <-- [CS]

3.6.4 Logic Group

Logic group instructions perform logic operations such as AND, OR, and XOP, compare data between registers, or between register and memory, rotate and complement data in register.

Logical Operation : This group consists of the following set of instructions.

    (1) ANS r
    (2) ANA M
    (3) ANI data
    (4) XRA r
    (5) XRA M
    (6) XRI data
    (7) ORA r
    (8) ORA M
    (9) ORI data

(10) CMP r
(11) CMP M
(12) CPI data
(13) STC
(14) CMC
(15) CMA

1. **ANA r**   : AND specified register with Accumulator
   Operation   : A ← A ∧ r

   Description   : This instruction logically ANDS the contents of the specified register with the contents of accumulator and stores the result in the accumulator. Each bit in the accumulator is ANDed wtth D0 bit in register r, DI in A with DI in r and so on upto D7 bit. The register r is 8-bit general purpose register such as A, B, C, D, E, H and L.

   No. of Bytes   : 1 byte.
   Opcode of ANA r.

   Addressing Mode : Register addressing.
   Flags   : All flags are affected with carry flag 0 and auxiliary carry
   A C flag = 1

   Example   :

                       ; A 10101010 (AAH) B = 00001111 (0171-1)
   ANA B   ; This instruction will logically AND the contents of B register
   1010 1010   ; with the contents of accumulator. It will store the result (OAH)
   0000 1111   ; in the accumulator.
   0000 1010 0AH

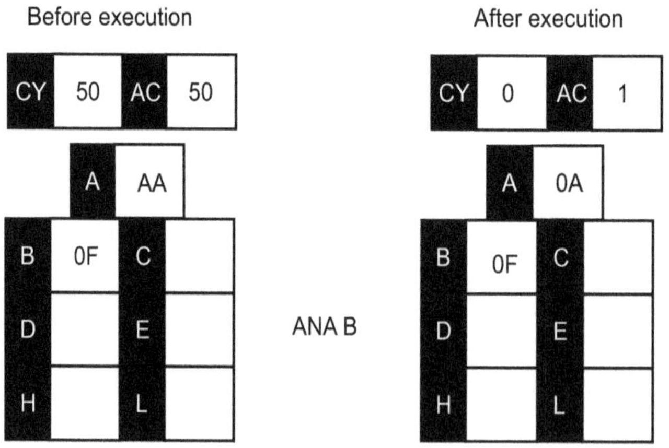

Before execution

| CY | 50 | AC | 50 |

A	AA
B	0F	C	
D		E	
H		L	

ANA B

After execution

| CY | 0 | AC | 1 |

A	0A
B	0F	C	
D		E	
H		L	

Fig. 4.21

2. **ANA M** : AND data in memory with Accumulator

   Operation : A ← A ∧ M

   Description : This instruction logically ANDs the contents of memory location pointed by HL register pair with the contents of accumulator. The result is stored in the accumulator. The HL register pair is used as a memory pointer.

   No. of Bytes : 1 byte.
   Opcode of ANA M.

   Addressing Mode : Register indirect addressing..

   Flags : All flags are affected with carry flag = 0 and auxiliary carry flag = 1.

   Example :

   ; A = 01010101 = (55H), HL 2050H
   ; (2050H) → 10110011 = (B3H)

   ANA M   : This instruction will logically ANDs the contents 4-memory
   0101 0101   ; location pointed by HL register pair (B3H) with the contents
   1011 0011   ; of accumulator (55H). It will store the result (11H) in the accumulator
   0001 0001 = 11 H ;

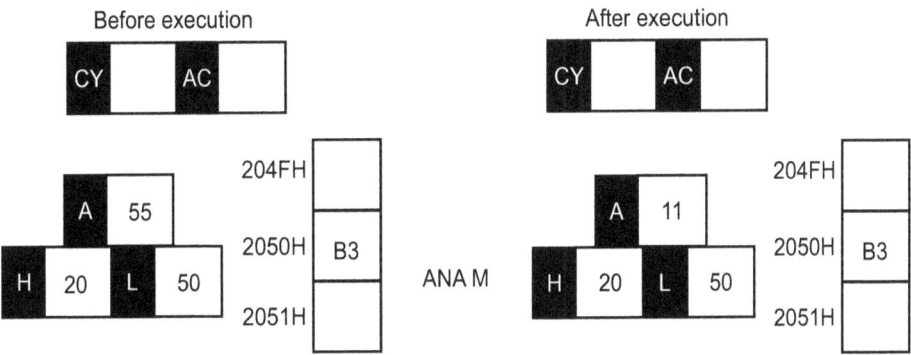

Fig. 4.22

3. **ANI data** : AND 8 bit immediate data with Accumulator

   Operation : A +- A ^ data (8)

   Description : is instruction logically ANDS the 8 bit data given in the instruction with the contents of the accumulator and stores the result in the accumulator.

   No. of Bytes : 2 bytes.
   First byte : Opcode of ANI.

Second byte 8-bit data.

Addressing Mode : Immediate addressing.

Flags : All flags are affected with carry flag 0 and auxiliary carry

Example : A 1011 0011 (B3H)

ANI 3FH ; This instruction will logically AND the contents, of accumulator

1011 0011 ; (B3H) with 3FH. It will store the result (33H) in the accumulator.

0011 1111

0011 0011 33H

Fig. 4.23

4. **XRA r** ; XOR specified register with Accumulator.

Operation : A ← A ⊕ r

Description : Instruction logically XORs the contents of the specified register with the contents of accumulator and stores the result in the accumulator. The register r is 8-bit general purpose register such as A, B, C, D, E, H and L.

No. of Bytes : 1 byte.

Opcode of XRA r.

Addressing Mode : Register addressing.

Flags : All flags are affected with carry flag 0 and auxiliary carry flag = 0

Example : A = 1010 1010 (AAH)

: C - 0010 1101 (2DH)

XRA C : This instruction will logically XOR the contents of C register

1010 1010 : with the contents of accumulator. It will store the result (87H)

0010 1101 : in the accumulator.

1000 0111 = (87H)

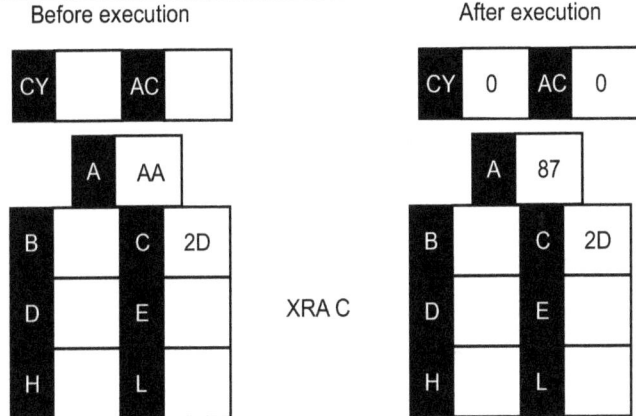

Fig. 4.24

5. **XRA M** : XOR data in memory with Accumulator
   Operation : A +- AS M
   Description : This instruction logically XOR$ the contents of memory location pointed by HL register pair with the contents of accumulator. The HE register pair is used as a memory pointer.
   No. of Bytes : 1 byte.
   Opcode of XRA M.
   Addressing Mode : Register indirect addressing.
   Flags : All flags are affected with carry flag 0 and auxiliary carry
   Example :
   ; A = 0101 0101 = (55H), HL = 2050H,
   ; (2050H) → 1011 0011 = (B3H)

XRA M   ; This instruction will logically XOR the contents of memory
0101 0101   ; location pointed by HL register pair (2050H) i.e. data 133H with
1011 0011   ; the contents of accumulator (55H). It will store the result
               ; (136H) in the accumulator.
1110 0110 E6H

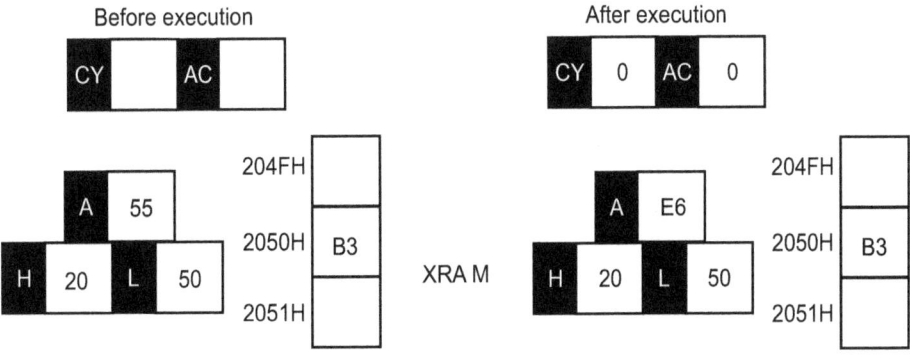

Fig. 4.25

6. **XRI data** : XOR 8 bit immediate data with Accumulator
   Operation : A <– A ⊕ data
   Description : This instruction logically XORs the 8 bit data given in the instruction with the contents of the accumulator and stores the result in the accumulator.
   No. of Bytes : 2 bytes.
   First byte Opcode of XRI..
   Second byte : 8-bit data
   Addressing Mode : immediate addressing.
   Flags : All flags are affected with carry flag 0 and auxiliary carry flag = 0.
   Example :
   ; A = 10110011 = (B3H)

   XRI 39H : This instruction will, logically XOR the contents of accumulator
   1011 0011 : (B3H) with 39H. It will store the result (8AH)'in the accumulator.
   0011 1001
   1000 1010 = 8AH

Fig. 4.26

7. **ORA r** : OR specified register with Accun
   Operation : A <-- A v r
   Description : This instruction logically ORs register with the contents of accumulator and Se accumulator. Each bit in the accumulator is bit in riling register r. i.e. D_0 bit in accumulator is ORed with D0 bit in register r, D_1 in A with D_1 in r and so on upto D_7 bit. The register r is 8bit general purpose register such as A, B, C, D, E, H and L.
   No. of Bytes : 1 byte.
   Opcode of ORA r.
   Addressing Mode : Register addressing.
   Flags : All flags are affected with carry flag 0 and flag 0.
   Example :
   ; A = 1010 1010 (AAH), B = 0001 0010-(12H)
   ORA B ; This instruction will logically OR the contents of B register with

```
1010 1010      ; the contents of accumulator. It will store the rem* (BAH) in
0001 0010      ; the accumulator.
---------
1011 1010 = BAH
```

Contents of registers before execution and after execution are shown.

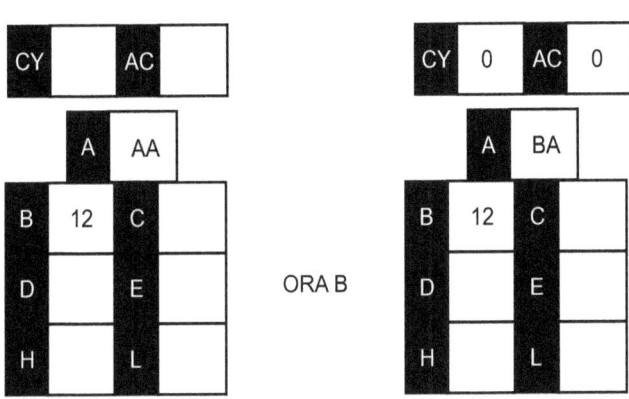

Fig. 4.27

8. **ORA M** : OR data in memory with Accumulator

   Operation : A ← A v M

   Description : This - instruction logically ORs the contents of memory location pointed by HL register pair with the contents of accumulator. The result is stored in the accumulator. The HL register pair is used as a memory pointer.

   No. of Bytes : 1 byte,

   Opcode of ORA M.

   Addressing Mode : Register indirect addressing.

   Flags : All flags are affected with carry flag 0 and auxiliary carry flag = 0.

   Example :

   ```
                ; A. = 0101 0101  (55H), HL  2050H
                ; (2050H) —> 1011 0011 = (B3H)
   ORA M        ; This instruction will logically OR the contents of memory
   0101 0101    ; location pointed by-HL register pair (B3H) with the contents
   1011 0011    ; of accumulator (55 H). It will store the result (F7H) in the
                ; accumulator.
   ```

1111 0111 = F7H

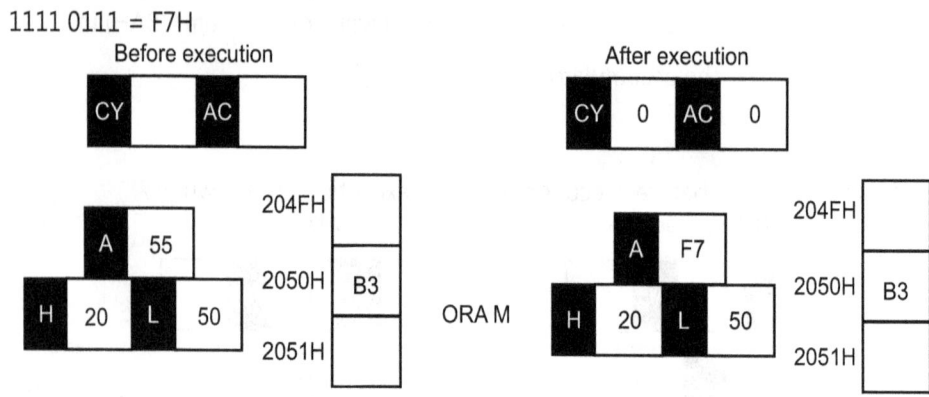

Fig. 4.28

9. **ORI data** : OR 8 bit immediate data with Accumulator.
   Operation : A ← A v data (8)
   Description : This instruction logically ORs the 8 bit data given in the instruction with the contents of the accumulator and stores the result in the accumulator.
   No. of Bytes : 2 bytes.
   First byte : Opcode of ORL
   Second byte : 8-bit data.
   Addressing Mode : Immediate addressing.
   Flags : All flags are affected with carry flag 0 and auxiliary carry flag = 0.
   Example : A= 1011 0011 = (B3H)
   ORI 08H : This instruction will logically OR the contents of accumulator
   1011 0011 : (B3H) with 08H. It will store the result (BBH) in the accumulator.
   0000 1000 ;
   ─────────
   1011 1011 (BBH)

Fig. 4.29

10. **CMP r** : Compare specified register with Accumulator
    Operation : A − r
    Description : This instruction subtracts the contents of the specified register from contents of the accumulator and sets the Condition flags as a result of

the subtraction. It sets zero flag if A = r and sets carry flag if A < r. The register r is 8-bit general purpose register such as A, B, C, D, E, H and L.

Note : The result of the subtraction is not stored in the accumulator, so accumulator contents remain unchanged.

No. of Bytes : 1 byte.
Opcode of CMP r.

Addressing Mode : Register addressing.

Flags : All flags are affected. Result of comparison can be obtained with the help of flags as follows

A > r : CY = 0, Z = 0
A = r : CY = 0, Z = 1
A < r : CY = 1, Z = 0

Example :

; A = 1011 1000 (B8H)-and D 1011 1001 (B9H)

CMP D ; This instruction will compare the contents of D register with the
; Contents of accumulator. Here A < D so carry flag will set after
; the execution of the instruction.

Before execution

After execution

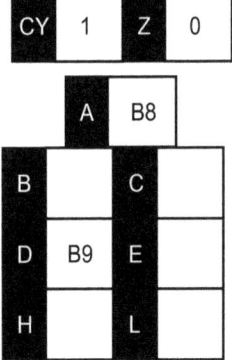

CMP D

Fig. 4.30

11. CMP M : Compare data in memory with Accumulator.

Operation : A – M

Description : This instruction subtracts the contents of the memory location specified by HL register pair from the contents of the accumulator and sets the condition flags as a result of subtraction. It sets zero flag if A = M and sets carry flag if A < M. The HL register pair is used as a memory pointer.

Note : The result of the subtraction is not stored in the accumulator, so

	accumulator contents remain unchanged.
No. of Bytes	: 1 byte.
	Opcode of CMP M.
Addressing Mode	: Register indirect addressing.
Flags	: All flags are affected. Result of comparison can be obtained with the help of flags as follows
	A > M : CY = 0, Z = 0
	A = M : CY = 0, Z = 1
	A < M : CY = 1, Z = 0
Example	;
	; A 1011 1000 (B8H), HL = 2050H
	; and (2050H) = 1011 1000 (B8H)
CMP M	: This instruction will compare the contents of memory location
	; (B8H) and the contents of accumulator. Here A = M so zero
	; flag will set after the execution of the instruction.

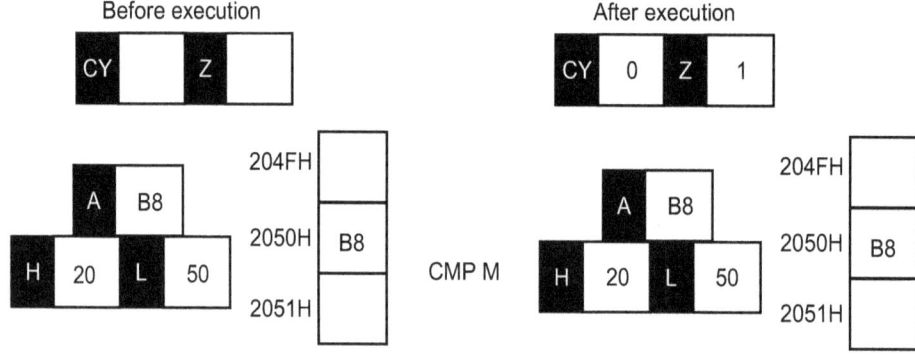

Fig. 4.31

12. **CPI data**	: Compare immediate 8'bit data with Accumulator.
Operation	: A – data
Description	: This instruction subtracts the 8 bit data given in the instruction from the contents of the accumulator and sets the condition flags as a result of subtraction. It sets zero flag if A data and sets carry flag if A < data.
Note	: The, result of the subtraction is not stored in the accumulator, so accumulator contents remain unchanged.
No. of Bytes	: 2 bytes.
	First byte : Opcode of CPI.
	Second byte : 8-bit data.
Addressing Mode	: Immediate addressing.

Flags	: All flags are affected. Result of comparison can be obtained with the help of flags as follows
	A > data : CY = 0, Z = 0
	A = data : CY = 0, Z = 1
	A < data : CY = 1, Z = 0
Example	:
	; A=1011 1010 = (BAH)
CPI 30H	: This instruction will compare 30H with the contents of
	; accumulator (BAH). Here A > data so zero and carry both
	; flags will reset after the execution of the instruction.

Before execution   After execution

CY		Z	

CY	0	AC	0

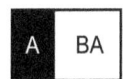
                CPI 30H   

Fig. 4.32

13. STC   : Set carry
   Operation   : CY ← 1
   Description   : This instruction sets carry flag 1
   No. of Bytes   : 1 byte.
                  Opcode of STC.
   Flags   : Carry flag is set all other flags are unaffected.
   Example   : Carry flag = 0
   STC   : This instruction will set the carry flag 1

                  Before execution   After execution

   STC   

Fig. 4.33

14. CMC   : Complement carry
   Operation   : CY ← $\overline{CY}$
   Description   : This instruction complements the carry flag.
   No. of Bytes   : 1 byte.
                  Opcode of CMC.
   Flags   : Carry flag is complemented, the carry flag.
   Example   : Carry flag = 1

CMC : This instruction will complement the carry flag i.e. carry flag = 0

Before execution  CMC After execution

Fig. 4.34

15. CMA : Complement A

Operation : $A \leftarrow \overline{A}$

Description : This instruction complements each bit of the accumulator.

No. of Bytes : 1 byte.
Opcode of CMA.

Addressing Mode : Implied addressing.

Flags : Flags are not affected.

Example : A = 1000 1000 = 88'H

CMA : This instruction will complement each bit of accumulator A = 0111 0111 = 77H

4.3.1.1 Rotate

This group consists of the following set of instructions

    RLC
    RRC
    RAL
    RAR

1. RLC : Rotate Accumulator Left

Operation :

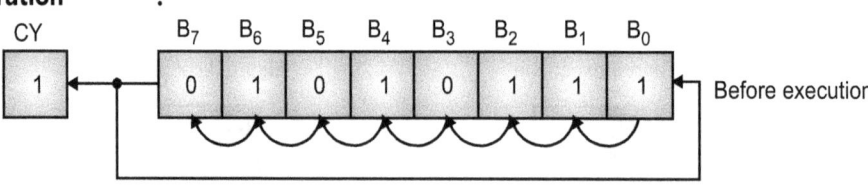

Fig. 4.35

Description : This instruction rotates the contents of the accumulator left by one position. Bit B7 is placed in B0 as well as in CY.

No. of Bytes : 1 byte.
Opcode of RLC.

Addressing Mode : Implied addressing.

Flags	: Carry flag is affected. All other flags are unaffected.
Example	:
RLC	; A = 01010111 (57H) and CY = 1 ; After execution of the instruction the accumulator contents will be ; (1010 1110) AEH and carry flag will reset.

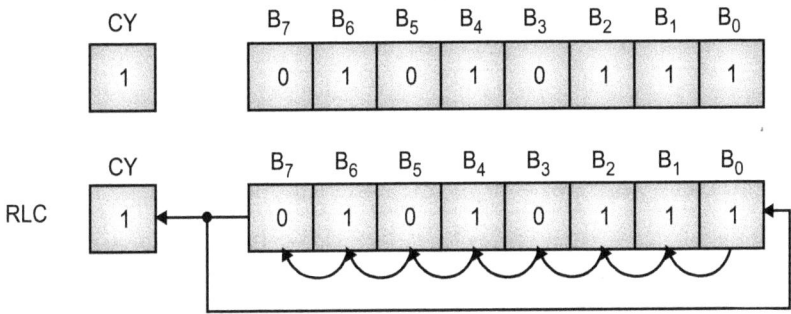

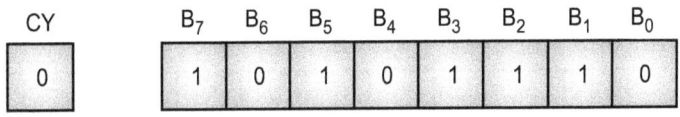

Fig. 4.36

2. **RRC** : Rotate Accumulator right.
   Operation :

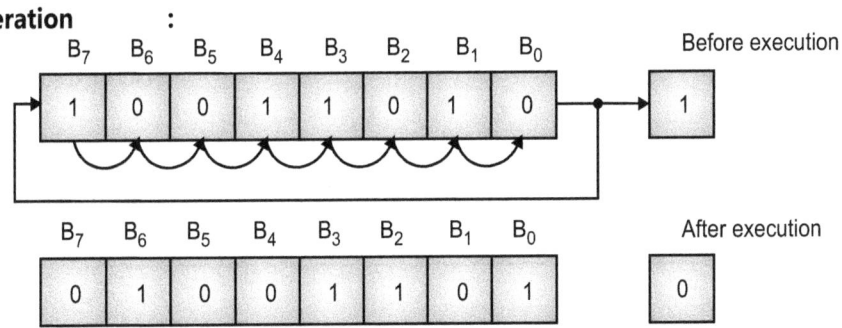

Fig. 4.37

Description	: This instruction- rotates the contents of the accumulator right by one position. Bit B0 is placed in B7 as well as in CY.
No. of Bytes	: 1 byte. Opcode of RRC.
Addressing Mode	: Implied addressing.

Flags : Carry flag is affected. All other flags are unaffected.
Example :

; A = 1001 1010 (9AH) and CY = 1
; After execution of the instruction the accumulator contents will be
; (0100 1101) 4DH and carry flag will reset.
Before execution register A:

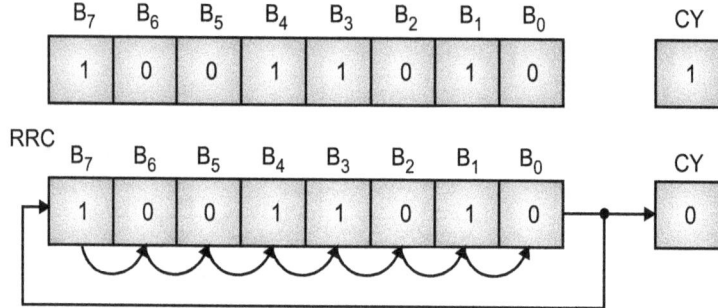

After execution register A:

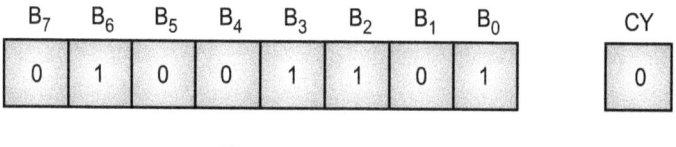

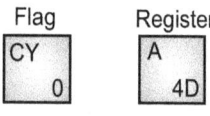

Fig. 4.38

3. **RAL** : Rotate Accumulator left through carry.
   Operation :

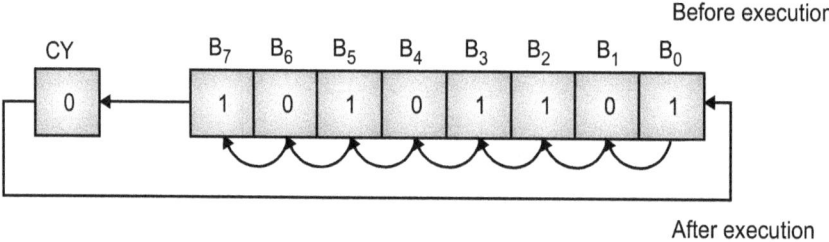

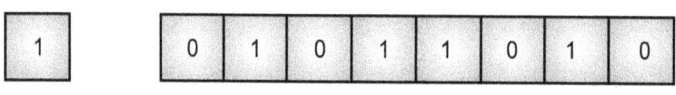

Fig. 4.39

Description : This instruction rotates the contents of the Accumulator left by one position. Pj07 is placed in CY and CY is placed in B_0.

No. of Bytes : 1 byte.
Opcode of RAL.

Addressing Mode : Implied addressing
Flags : Carry flag is affected. All other flags are unaffected.
Example :

; A = 10101101 (ADH) and CY = 0

RAL : After execution of the instruction accumulator contents will be (0101 1010) 5AH and carry flag will set.

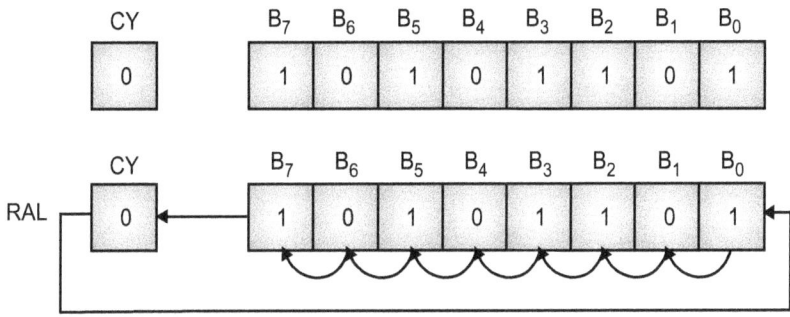

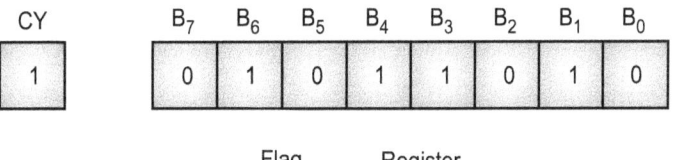

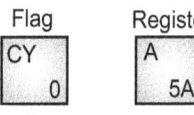

Fig. 4.40

4. **RAR** : Rotate Accumulator right through carry.
   Operation :

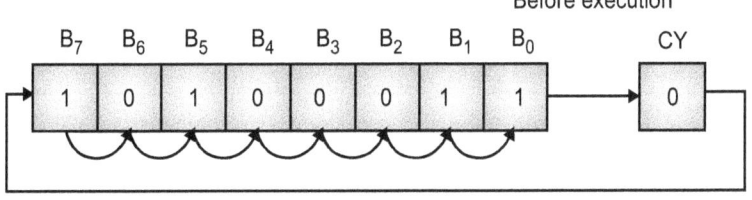

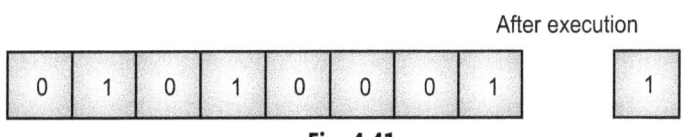

Fig. 4.41

Description : This instruction rotates the contents of the accumulator right by one position. Bit B_0 is placed in CY and CY is placed in B_7.

No. of Bytes : 1 bytes.

Opcode of RAR.

Addressing Mode : Implied addressing.

Flags : Carry flag is affected. All other flags are unaffected.

Example :

RAR : A = 1010 0011'(A3H) and CY = 0

; After execution of the instruction accumulator contents will be

; (0101 0001) 51H and carry flag will set.

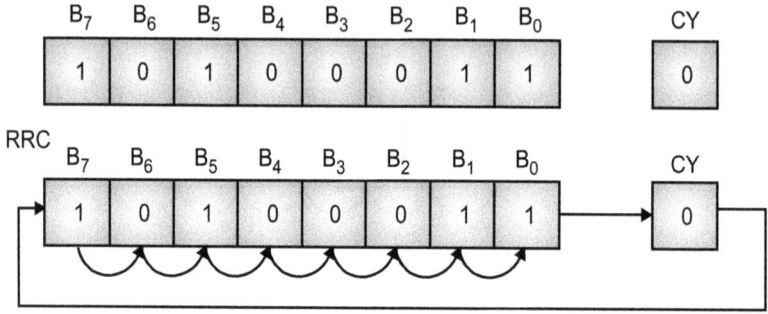

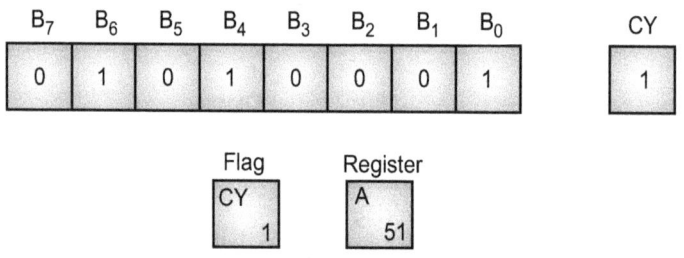

Fig. 4.42

4.4 BRANCH GROUP INSTRUCTIONS

a. JMP addr (label). (Unconditional jump: jump to the instruction specified by the address). [PC] <-- Label.

b. Conditional Jump addr (label): After the execution of the conditional jump instruction the program jumps to the instruction specified by the address (label) if the specified condition is fulfilled. The program proceeds further in the normal sequence if the specified condition is not fulfilled. If the condition is true and program jumps to the specified label, the execution of a conditional jump takes 3 machine cycles: 10 states. If condition is not true, only 2 machine cycles; 7 states are required for the execution of the instruction.

Instruction	Description
JZ addr (label).	(Jump if the result is zero)
JNZ addr (label).	(Jump if the result is not zero)
JC addr (label).	(Jump if there is a carry)
JNC addr (label).	(Jump if there is no carry)
JP addr (label).	(Jump if the result is plus)
JM addr (label).	(Jump if the result is minus)
JPE addr (label).	(Jump if even parity)
JPO addr (label).	(Jump if odd parity)

c. CALL addr (label) (Unconditional CALL: call the subroutine identified by the operand)

CALL instruction is used to call a subroutine. Before the control is transferred to the subroutine, the address of the next instruction of the main program is saved in the stack. The content of the stack pointer is decremented by two to indicate the new stack top. Then the program jumps to subroutine starting at address specified by the label.

d. RET (Return from subroutine)

e. RST n (Restart) Restart is a one-word CALL instruction. The content of the program counter is saved in the stack. The program jumps to the instruction starting at restart location.

4.4.1 Branch Group

The branch group instructions allow the microprocessor to change the sequence of a program, either unconditionally or under certain test conditions. This group include

- Jumps instructions
- Call and Return instructions
- Restart instructions

In this section only jump instructions are explained. The call, return, and restart instructions are associated with the subroutine technique and also require stack operation, hence ate discussed in'the stack group of instructions (section 3.6.5).

JUMP

This group consists of the following set of instructions

(1) JMP addr

(2) J condition qddr

(3) PCHL

1. **JMP addr** : Jump unconditionally to the address.

   Operation : PC ← addr

   Description : This instruction loads the PC with the address given within the instruction and resumes-the program execution from this location.

   No, of Bytes : 3 bytes.

   First byte : Opcode of JMP.

   Second byte : Low order byte of the address.

   Third byte : High order byte of the address.

   Addressing Mode : Immediate addressing.

   Flags : Flags are not affected.

   Example :

   JMP 2000H ; This instruction will load. PC with 2000H and processor will
   ; fetch next instruction from this address.

   Before execution

   | PC | |

   JMP 2000H

   After execution

   | PC | 2000 |

   Fig. 4.43

2. **Condition addr** : Jump conditionally to the, address

   Operation : If condition is true PC ← addr. else PC ← PC + 3

   Description : This instruction causes a jump to an addrew given in the instruction if the desired condition occurs in the program before the execution of the instruction. The table 3.3 shows the possible conditions for jumps.

Table 3.3 : Conditional jumps

Instruction code	Description	Condition for jump
JC	Jump on carry	CY = 1
JNC	Jump on not carry	CY = 0
JP	Jump on positive	S = 0
JM	Jump on minus	S = 1
RE	Jump on parity even	P = 1
JPO	Jump- on parity odd	p = 0
JZ	Jump on zero	Z = 1
JNZ	Jump on pot zero	Z = 0

No. of Bytes : 3 bytes.

First byte : Opcode of J condition.

Second byte : Low order byte of the address.

Third byte : High order byte of the address.

Addressing Mode : Immediate addressing-

Flags : Flags are not affected. Flags are checked

Example : Carry flag = 1

JC 2000H ; This instruction will cause a jump to an address 2000H

; i.e. program counter will load with 2000H since CF 1.

Before execution   After execution

PC   1   PC   1

PC   [   ]   JC 2000H   PC   2000

Fig. 4.44

3. **PCHL** : Load HL contents into program counter.

   Operation : PC ← HL

   Description : This instruction loads the contents of HL register pair into the program counter. Thus the program, control is transferred to the location whose address is in HL register pair.

No. of Bytes : 1 byte.

Opcode of PCHL.

Addressing Mode : Register addressing.

Flags : Flags are not affected.

Example : HL = 6000H

PCHL : This instruction will load 6000H into the program counter

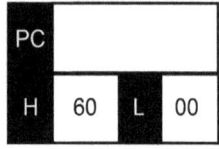

Fig. 4.45

Note : This is effectively one byte unconditional jump instruction, provided that the address of the jump is stored in HL register pair.

QUESTIONS

1. Explain the Arithmetic instruction in details.
2. Explain multiplication and subtraction instruction in detail.
3. Explain the Basic instruction in details
4. Explain following instruction
   1. JUMP   2. CALL   3. Shift and Rotate
5. Explain the different types of instructions group.
6. Explain in details Decimal Adjust Accumulator and How works. Explain step by step.
7. Define the increment and Decrement instructions.
8. Explain different types of logical group instructions.
9. Explain following instruction
   (i) ORA M   (ii) ORI data   (iii) cmp r
10. Explain different types of Branch group instructions.

✠ ✠ ✠

Unit - V

INTERRUPTS AND THE 80386 MICROPROCESSOR

5.1 INTERRUPTS

Interrupt is a mechanism by which an I/O or an instruction can suspend the normal execution of processor and get itself serviced. Generally, a particular task is assigned to that interrupt signal. In the microprocessor based system the interrupts are used for data transfer between the peripheral devices and the microprocessor. The processor will check the interrupts always at the 2nd T-state of last machine cycle.

Interrupt Service Routine (ISR): A small program or a routine that when executed services the corresponding interrupting source is called as an ISR.

Maskable/Non-Maskable Interrupt: An interrupt that can be disabled by writing some instruction is known as Maskable Interrupt otherwise it is called Non-Maskable Interrupt.

There are two types of interrupts used in 8085 Microprocessor:

- **Hardware Interrupts:** Also called vectored interrupts / non maskable
- **Software Interrupts:** Also called non vectored / maskable / restart interrupts (From RST0 to RST7)

There are 6 pins available in 8085 for hardware interrupts which generates signals.

(i) TRAP

(ii) RST 7.5

(iii) RST6.5

(iv) RST5.5

(v) INTR

(vi) INTA

Execution of Interrupts:

When there is an interrupt requests to the Microprocessor then after accepting the interrupts Microprocessor send the INTA (active low) signal to the peripheral. The vectored address of particular interrupt is stored in program counter. The processor executes an interrupt service routine (ISR) addressed in program counter.

Hardware interrupts:

- An external device initiates the hardware interrupts and placing an appropriate signal at the interrupt pin of the processor.
- If the interrupt is accepted then the processor executes an interrupt service routine.

The 8085 has five hardware interrupts
(1) TRAP   (2) RST 7.5   (3) RST 6.5   (4) RST 5.5   (5) INTR

Table 5.1

Interrupt	Vector address
RST 7.5	$003C_H$
RST 6.5	0034_H
RST 5.5	$002C_H$
TRAP	0024_H

TRAP :
- This interrupt is a non-maskable interrupt. It is unaffected by any mask or interrupt enable.
- TRAP bas the highest priority and vectored interrupt.
- TRAP interrupt is edge and level triggered. This means hat the TRAP must go high and remain high until it is acknowledged.
- In sudden power failure, it executes a ISR and send the data from main memory to backup memory.
- The signal, which overrides the TRAP, is HOLD signal. (i.e., If the processor receives HOLD and TRAP at the same time then HOLD is recognized first and then TRAP is recognized).
- There are two ways to clear TRAP interrupt.
  1. By resetting microprocessor (External signal)
  2. By giving a high TRAP ACKNOWLEDGE (Internal signal)

RST 7.5 :
- The RST 7.5 interrupt is a maskable interrupt.
- It has the second highest priority.
- It is edge sensitive. ie. Input goes to high and no need to maintain high state until it recognized.
- Maskable interrupt. It is disabled by,
  1. DI instruction
  2. System or processor reset.
  3. After reorganization of interrupt.
- Enabled by EI instruction.

RST 6.5 and 5.5 :
- The RST 6.5 and RST 5.5 both are level triggered. i.e. Input goes to high and stay high until it recognized.

- Maskable interrupt. It is disabled by,
  1. DI, SIM instruction
  2. System or processor reset.
  3. After reorganization of interrupt.
- Enabled by EI instruction.
- The RST 6.5 has the third priority whereas RST 5.5 has the fourth priority.

INTR:
- INTR is a maskable interrupt. It is disabled by,
  1. DI, SIM instruction
  2. System or processor reset.
  3. After reorganization of interrupt.
- Enabled by EI instruction.
- Non- vectored interrupt. After receiving INTA (active low) signal, it has to supply the address of ISR.
- It has lowest priority.
- It is a level sensitive interrupts i.e. Input goes to high and it is necessary to maintain high state until it recognized.
- The following sequence of events occurs when INTR signal goes high.
1. The 8085 checks the status of INTR signal during execution of each instruction.
2. If INTR signal is high, then 8085 complete its current instruction and sends active low interrupt acknowledge signal, if the interrupt is enabled.
3. In response to the INTA acknowledge signal, external logic places an instruction OPCODE on the data bus. In the case of multi-byte instruction, additional interrupt acknowledge machine cycles are generated by the 8085 to transfer the additional bytes into the microprocessor.
4. On receiving the instruction, the 8085 save the address of next instruction on stack and execute received instruction.

Software Interrupts: A software interrupts is a particular instructions that can be inserted into the desired location in the program. There are eight Software interrupts in 8085 Microprocessor. From RST0 to RST7.

(i) RST0
(ii) RST1
(iii) RST2
(iv) RST3
(v) RST4
(vi) RST5
(vii) RST6
(viii) RST7

They allow the microprocessor to transfer program control from the main program to the subroutine program. After completing the subroutine program, the program control returns back to the main program.

We can calculate the vector address of these interrupts using the formula given below:

Vector Address = Interrupt Number * 8. So we can find simply vector address. For Example:

  RST2: vector address = 2*8 = 16
  RST1: vector address = 1*8 = 08
  RST3: vector address = 3*8 = 24

SIM and RIM for Interrupts:

- The 8085 provide additional masking facility for RST 7.5, RST 6.5 and RST 5.5 using SIM instruction.
- The status of these interrupts can be read by executing RIM instruction.
- The masking or unmasking of RST 7.5, RST 6.5 and RST 5.5 interrupts can be performed by moving an 8-bit data to accumulator and then executing SIM instruction.
- The format of the 8-bit data is shown below.

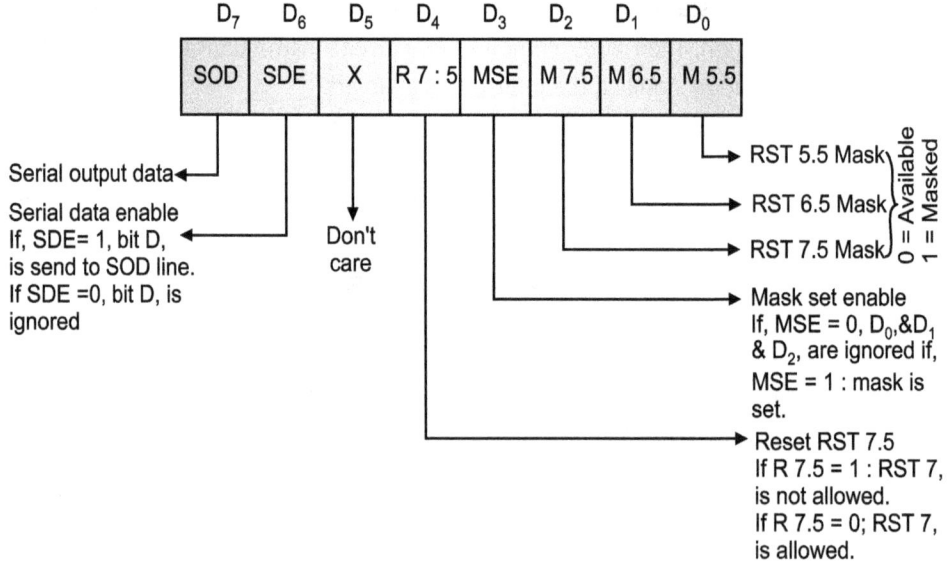

Fig. 5.1

- The status of pending interrupts can be read from accumulator after executing RIM instruction.
- When RIM instruction is executed an 8-bit data is loaded in accumulator, which can be interpreted as shown in fig.

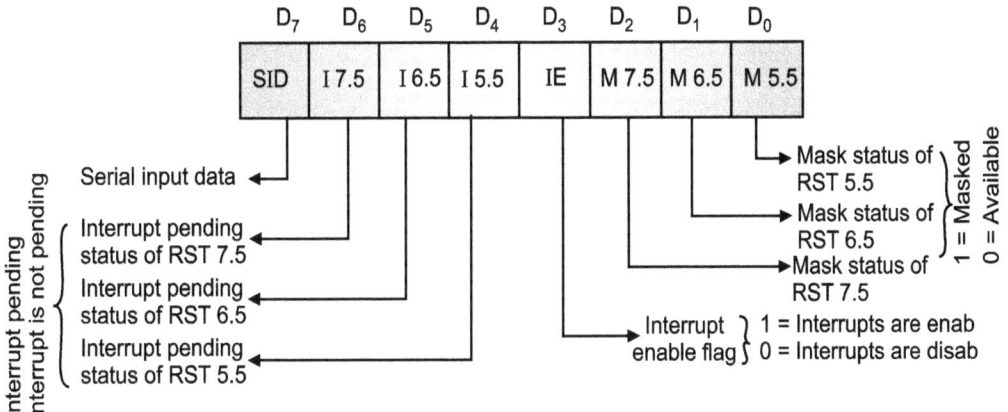

Fig. 5.2

Table 5.2

Interrupt Type	Trigger	Priority	Maskable	Vector address
TRAP	Edge and Level	1st	No	0024H
RST 7.5	Edge	2nd	Yes	003CH
RST 6.5	Level	3rd	Yes	0034H
RST 5.5	Level	4th	Yes	003CH
INTR	Level	5th	Yes	-

5.2 CONTROL INSTRUCTIONS

NOP: (No operation) No operation to be performed.

HLT: (Halt and enter wait state) The CPU finishes executing the current instruction And halts any further execution.

DI: (Disable Interrupt System) The interrupt enable flip-flop is reset and all the Interrupts except the TRAP are disabled. No flags are affected.

EI: (Enable Interrupt System) The interrupt enable flip-flop is set and all interrupts are enabled. No flags are affected.

5.3 80386 MICROPROCESSOR

The 80386DX is a 32-bit processor that supports, 8-bit/16-bit/32-bit data operands. The 80386 instruction set is upward compatible with all its predecessors. The 80386 can run 8086 applications under protected mode in its virtual 8086 mode of operation. With its 32-bit address bus, the 80386 can address upto 4Gbytes of physical memory. The physical memory is organised in terms of segments of 4Gbytes size at maximum. The 80386 CPU supports 16K (16384) number of segments and thus the total virtual memory space is 4 Gbytes x 16K = 64 terrabytes. The memory management section of 80386 supports the virtual memory, paging and four levels of protection, maintaining full compatibility with 80286. The concept of paging is introduced in 80386 that enables it to organise the available physical memory in terms of pages of size 4Kbytes each, under the segmented memory. The 80386 can be supported by 80387 for mathematical data processing. The 80386 offers a set of total eight debug registers DR_0-DR_7 for hardware debugging and control. The 80386 has an on-chip address translation cache. The 80386 is available in another version-80386SX, which has identical architecture as 80386DX with the difference that it has only a 16-bit data bus and 24-bit address bus. This low cost, low power version of 80386 may be used in a number of applications. 80386DX is available in a 132-pin grid array package and has 20 MHz and 33 MHz versions.

The internal architecture of 80386 is divided into three sections viz., central processing unit, memory management unit and bus interface unit. The central processing unit is further divided in to execution unit and instruction unit. The execution unit has eight general purpose and eight special purpose registers which are either used for handling data or calculating offset addresses. The instruction unit decodes the opcode bytes received from the 16-byte instruction code queue and arranges them in a 3-instruction decoded-instruction queue, after decoding them so as to pass it to the control section for deriving the necessary control signals. The barrel shifter increases the speed of all shift and rotate operations. The multiply/divide logic implements the bit-shift-rotate algorithms to complete the operations in minimum time. Even 32-bit multiplications can be executed within one microsecond by the multiply/divide logic.

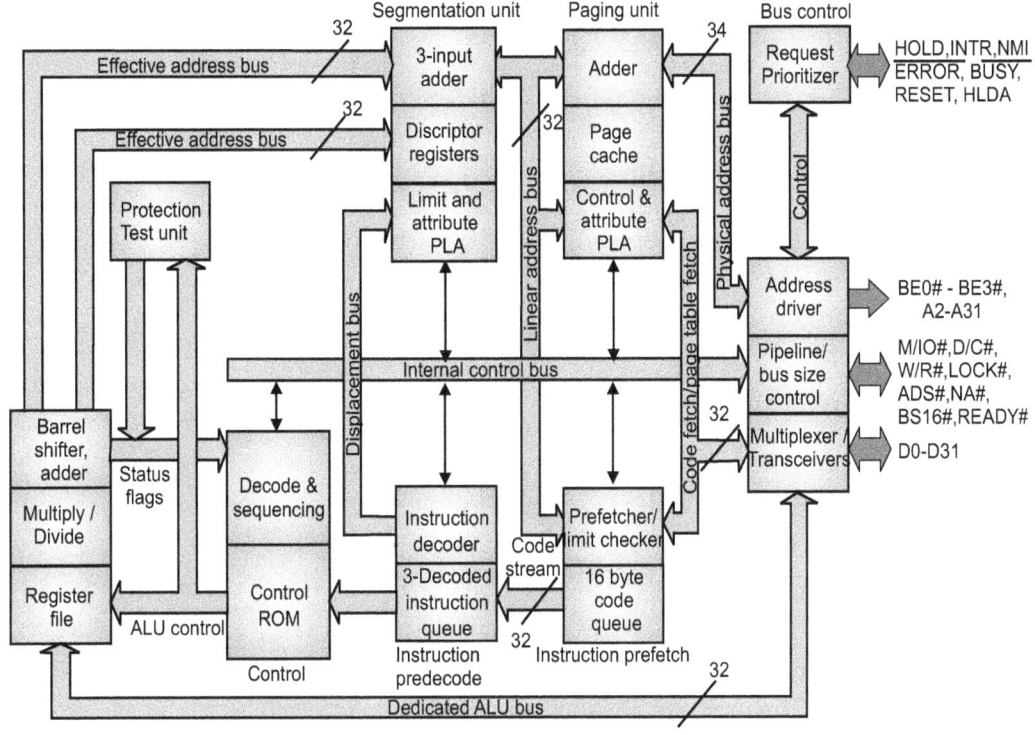

Fig. 5.3 : 80386 architecture

The memory management unit (MMU) consists of a segmentation unit and a paging unit. The segmentation unit allows the use of two address components, viz. segment and offset for relocability and sharing of code and data. The segmentation unit allows segments of size 4Gbytes at maximum. The paging unit organizes the physical memory in terms of pages of 4Kbytes size each. The paging unit works under the control of the segmentation unit, i.e. each segment is further divided into pages. The virtual memory is also organized in terms of segments and pages by the memory management unit.

The segmentation unit provides a four level protection mechanism for protecting and isolating the system's code and data from those of the application program. The paging unit converts linear addresses into physical addresses. The control and attribute PLA checks the privileges at the page level. Each of the pages maintains the paging information of the task. The limit and attribute PIA checks segment limits and attributes at segment level to avoid invalid accesses to code and data in the memory segments.

The bus control unit has a prioritizer to resolve the priority of the various bus requests. This controls the access of the bus. The address driver drives the bus enable and address signals A_0-A_{31}. The pipeline and dynamic bus sizing units handle the related control signals. The data buffers interface the internal data bus with the system bus.

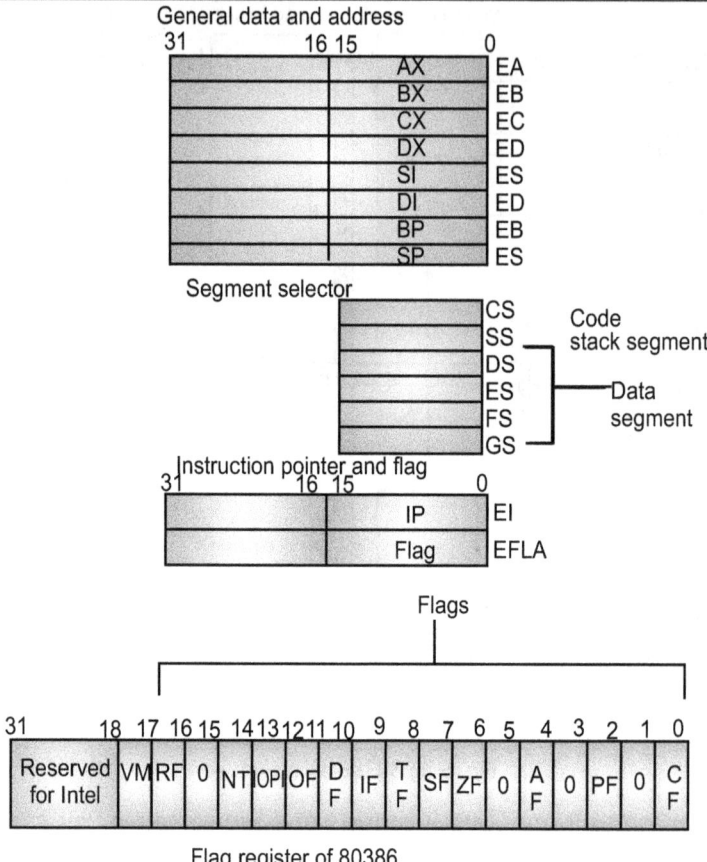

Fig. 5.4 : Registers and flags in 80386

The 80386 has eight 32 - bit general purpose registers which may be used as either 8 bit or 16 bit registers.

- A 32 - bit register known as an extended register, is represented by the register name with prefix E.
- **Example :** A 32 bit register corresponding to AX is EAX, similarly BX is EBX etc.
- The 16 bit registers BP, SP, SI and DI in 8086 are now available with their extended size of 32 bit and are names as EBP,ESP,ESI and EDI.
- AX represents the lower 16 bit of the 32 bit register EAX.
- BP, SP, SI, DI represents the lower 16 bit of their 32 bit counterparts, and can be used as independent 16 bit registers.
- The six segment registers available in 80386 are CS, SS, DS, ES, FS and GS.
- The CS and SS are the code and the stack segment registers respectively, while DS, ES, FS, GS are 4 data segment registers.
- A 16 bit instruction pointer IP is available along with 32 bit counterpart EIP.

- Flag Register of 80386: The Flag register of 80386 is a 32 bit register. Out of the 32 bits, Intel has reserved bits D18 to D31, D5 and D3, while D1 is always set at 1. Two extra new flags are added to the 80286 flag to derive the flag register of 80386. They are VM and RF flags.
- **VM - Virtual Mode Flag:** If this flag is set, the 80386 enters the virtual 8086 mode within the protection mode. This is to be set only when the 80386 is in protected mode. In this mode, if any privileged instruction is executed an exception 13 is generated. This bit can be set using IRET instruction or any task switch operation only in the protected mode.
- **RF- Resume Flag:** This flag is used with the debug register breakpoints. It is checked at the starting of every instruction cycle and if it is set, any debug fault is ignored during the instruction cycle. The RF is automatically reset after successful execution of every instruction, except for IRET and POPF instructions.
- Also, it is not automatically cleared after the successful execution of JMP, CALL and INT instruction causing a task switch. These instruction are used to set the RF to the value specified by the memory data available at the stack.
- **Segment Descriptor Registers:** This registers are not available for programmers, rather they are internally used to store the descriptor information, like attributes, limit and base addresses of segments.
- The six segment registers have corresponding six 73 bit descriptor registers. Each of them contains 32 bit base address, 32 bit base limit and 9 bit attributes. These are automatically loaded when the corresponding segments are loaded with selectors.
- **Control Registers:** The 80386 has three 32 bit control registers CR0, CR2 and CR3 to hold global machine status independent of the executed task. Load and store instructions are available to access these registers.
- System Address Registers: Four special registers are defined to refer to the descriptor tables supported by 80386.
- The 80386 supports four types of descriptor table, viz. global descriptor table (GDT), interrupt descriptor table (IDT), local descriptor table (LDT) and task state segment descriptor (TSS).
- **Debug and Test Registers:** Intel has provide a set of 8 debug registers for hardware debugging. Out of these eight registers DR0 to DR7, two registers DR4 and DR5 are Intel reserved.
- The initial four registers DR0 to DR3 store four program controllable breakpoint addresses, while DR6 and DR7 respectively hold breakpoint status and breakpoint control information.
- Two more test register are provided by 80386 for page cacheing namely test control and test status register.

- **ADDRESSING MODES**: The 80386 supports overall eleven addressing modes to facilitate efficient execution of higher level language programs.
- In case of all those modes, the 80386 can now have 32-bit immediate or 32-bit register operands or displacements.
- The 80386 has a family of scaled modes. In case of scaled modes, any of the index register values can be multiplied by a valid scale factor to obtain the displacement.
- The valid scale factor are 1, 2, 4 and 8.
- The different scaled modes are as follows.
- Scaled Indexed Mode: Contents of the an index register are multiplied by a scale factor that may be added further to get the operand offset.
- Based Scaled Indexed Mode: Contents of the an index register are multiplied by a scale factor and then added to base register to obtain the offset.
- Based Scaled Indexed Mode with Displacement: The Contents of the an index register are multiplied by a scaling factor and the result is added to a base register and a displacement to get the offset of an operand.

Features :
- More highly pipelined than 80286
- Instruction fetching, instruction decoding, instruction execution and memory management are all carried out in parallel.
- 32-bit data bus
- 32-bit non-multiplexed address bus
- 2^{32} = 4 Gigabyte of physical memory
- 2^{46} or 64 Terabyte of virtual memory.

5.3.1 The Memory System

The physical memory system of the 80386 is 4G bytes in size and is addressed as such. If virtual addressing is used, 64T bytes are mapped into the 4G bytes of physical space by the memory management unit and descriptors. (Note that virtual addressing allows a program to be larger than 4G bytes if a method of swapping with a very large hard disk drive exists.

The memory is divided into four 8-bit wide memory banks, each containing up to IG bytes of memory. This 32-bit wide memory organization allows bytes, words, or double words of memory data to access directly. The 80386DX transfers up to a 32-bit wide number in a single memory cycle, whereas the early 8088 requires four cycles to accomplish the same transfer, and the 80286 and 80386SX require two cycles. The data width is important, especially with single-precision floating-point numbers that are 32 bits wide. High-level software normally uses floating-point numbers for data storage, so 32-bit memory locations speed the execution of high level software when it is written to take advantage of this wider memory.

Each memory byte is numbered in hexadecimal as they were in prior versions of the family. The difference is that the 80386DX uses a 32-bit wide memory address, with memory bytes numbered from location 00000000H to FFFFFH.

The two memory banks in the 8086, 80286, and 80386SX system are accessed via $\overline{BLE}$ (A0 on the 8086 and 80286) and $\overline{BHE}$. In the 80386DX, the memory banks are accessed via four bank enable signals. This arrangement allows a single byte to be accessed when one bank enable signal is activated by the microprocessor. It also allows a word to be addressed when two bank enable signals are activated. In most cases, a word is addressed in bank 0 and I or in bank 2 and 3. Memory location 00000000H is in bank 0, location 00000001H is in bank 1, location 00000002H is in bank 2, and location 00000003H is in bank 3. The 80386DX does not contain address connections A0 and A1 because these have been encoded as the bank enable signals. Likewise, the 80386SX does not contain the A0 address pin because it is encoded in $\overline{BLE}$ and $\overline{BHE}$ signals.

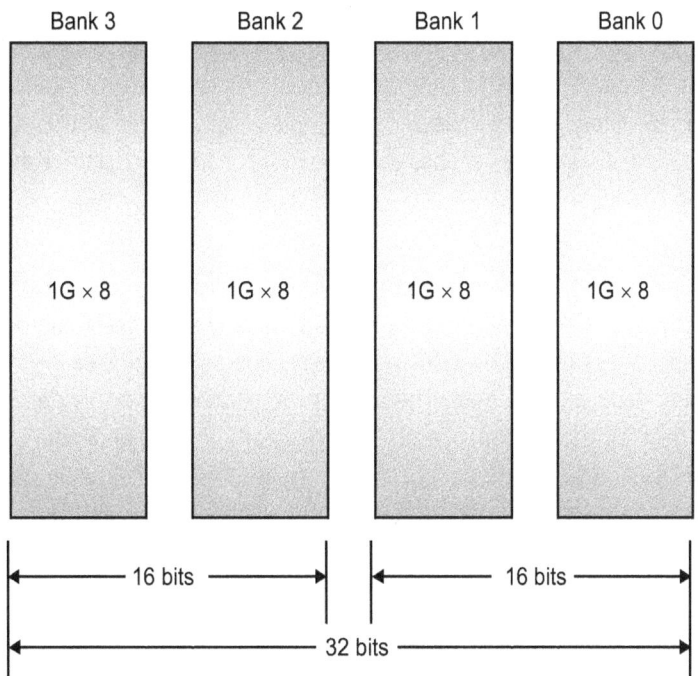

Fig. 5.5 : The memory system for 80386

5.3.1.1 Pipelines and Caches

The cache memory is a buffer that allows the 80386 to function more efficiently with lower DRAM speeds. A pipeline is a special way of handling memory accesses so the memory has additional time to access data. A 16 MHz 80386 allows memory devices with access times of 50 ns or less to operate at full speed. Obviously, there are few DRAMs currently available with these access times. In fact, the fastest DRAMs currently in use have an access time of 60 ns or longer. This means that some technique must be found to interface these memory devices, which are slower than required by the microprocessor. Three techniques are available: interleaved memory, caching, and a pipeline.

The pipeline is the preferred means of interfacing memory because the 80386 microprocessor supports pipelined memory accesses. Pipelining allows memory an extra clocking period to access data. The extra clock extends the access time from 50 ns to 81 ns on an 80386 operating with a 16MHz clock. The pipe, as it is often called, is set up by the microprocessor. When an instruction is fetched from memory, the microprocessor often has extra time before the next instruction is fetched. During this extra time, the address of the next instruction is sent out from the address bus ahead of time. This extra time is used to allow additional access time to slower memory components.

Not all memory references can take advantage of the pipe, which means that some memory cycles are not pipelined. These non-pipelined memory cycles request one wait state if the normal pipeline cycle requires no wait states. Overall, a pipe is a cost-saving feature that reduces the access time required by the memory system in low-speed systems.

Not all systems can take advantage of the pipe. Those systems typically operate at 20, 25, or 33 MHz. In these higher-speed systems, another technique must be used to increase the memory system speed. The cache memory system improves overall performance of the memory systems for data that are accessed more than once. Note that the 80486 contains an internal cache called a level one cache and the 80386 can only contain an external cache called a level two cache.

5.3.1.2 Cache

A cache is a high-speed memory system that is placed between the microprocessor and the DRAM memory system. Cache memory devices are usually static RAM memory components with access times of less than 25 ns. In many cases, we see level 2 cache memory systems with sizes between 32K and 1M byte. The size of the cache memory is determined more by the application than by the microprocessor. If a program is small and refers to little memory data, a small cache is beneficial. If a program is large and references large blocks of memory, the largest cache size possible is recommended. In many cases, a 64K-byte cache improves speed sufficiently, but the maximum benefit is often derived from a 256K-byte cache. It has been found that increasing the cache size much beyond 256K provides little benefit to the operating speed of the system that contains an 80386 microprocessor.

5.3.2 Interleaved Memory Systems

An interleaved memory system is another method of improving the speed of a system. Its only disadvantage is that it costs considerably more memory because of its structure. Interleaved memory systems are present in some systems, so memory access times can be lengthened without the need for wait states. In some systems, an interleaved memory may still require wait states, but may reduce their number. An interleaved memory system requires two or more complete sets of address buses and a controller that provides addresses for each bus. Systems that employ two complete buses are called a two-way interleave; systems that use four complete buses are called a four-way interleave.

An interleaved memory is divided into two or four parts. For example, if an interleaved memory system is developed for the 80386SX microprocessor, one part contains the 16-bit addresses 000000H to 000001H, 000004H to 000005H, etc.; the other part contains addresses 000002 to 000003, 000006H to 000007H, etc. While the microprocessor accesses locations 000000H to 000001H, the interleave control logic generates the address strobe signal for locations 000002H to 000003H. This selects and accesses the word at location 000002H to 000003H, while the microprocessor processes the word at location 000000H to 000001H. This process alternates memory sections, thus increasing the performance of the memory system.

Interleaving lengthens the amount of access time provided to the memory because the address is generated to select the memory before the microprocessor accesses it. This is because the microprocessor pipelines memory addresses, sending the next address out before the data are read from the last address.

The problem with interleaving, although not major, is that the memory addresses must be accessed so that each section is alternately addressed. This does not always happen as a program executes. Under normal program execution, the microprocessor alternately addresses memory approximately 93 percent of the time. For the remaining 7 percent, the microprocessor addresses data in the same memory section, which means that in these 7 percent of the memory accesses, the memory system must cause wait states because of the reduced access time. The access time is reduced because the memory must wait until the previous data are transferred before it can obtain its address. This leaves the memory with less access time; therefore, a wait state is required for accesses in the same memory bank.

The interleave controller is a complex logic circuit. First, if the SEL input is inactive (logic 0), then the $\overline{\text{WAIT}}$ signal is logic 1. Also, both ALE0 and ALE1, used to strobe the address to the memory sections, are both logic 1s, causing the latches connected to them to become transparent.

As soon as the SEL input becomes logic 1, this circuit begins to function. The Al input is used to determine which latch (U2B or U5A) becomes logic 0, selecting a section of the memory. Also the ALE pin that becomes logic 0 is compared with the previous state of the ALE pins. If the same section of memory is accessed a second time, the $\overline{\text{WAIT}}$ signal becomes a logic 0, requesting a wait state.

Fig. 5.6 illustrates an interleaved memory system. The memory in each bank is 16-bits wide. If accesses to memory require 8-bit data, the system causes wait states, in most cases. As a program executes, the 80386SX fetches instruction 16-bits at a time from normally sequential memory locations. Program execution uses interleaving in most cases. If a system is going to access mostly 8-bit data, it is doubtful that memory interleaving will reduce the number of wait states.

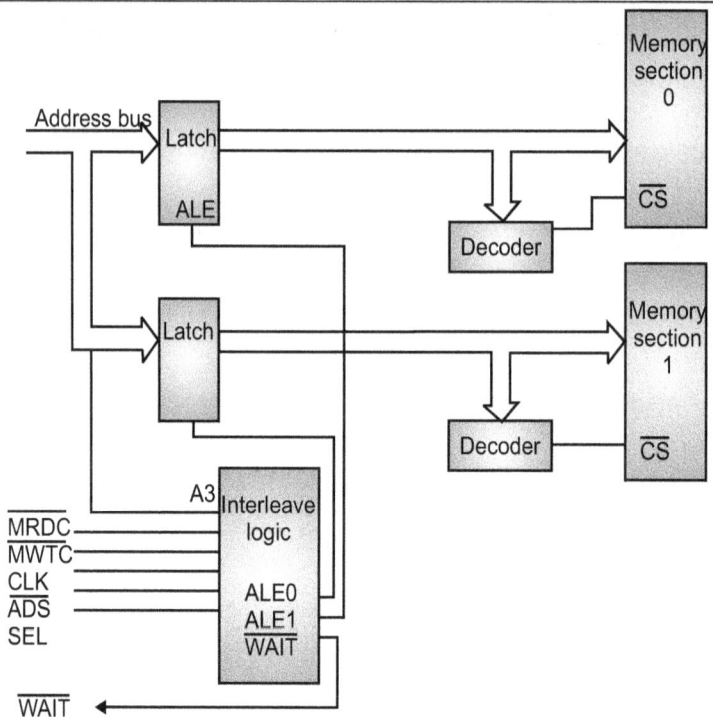

Fig. 5.6 : An interleaved memory system showing the address Latches and the interleaved logic circuit.

The access time allowed by an interleaved system, such as the one shown in Fig. 5.6, is increased to 112 ns from 69 ns by using a 16 MHz system clock. (If a wait state is inserted, access time with a 16 MHz clock is 136 ns, which means that an interleaved system performs at about the same rate as a system with one wait state.) If the clock is increased to 20 MHz, the interleaved memory requires 89.6 ns, where standard, non-interleaved memory interfaces allow 48 ns for memory access. At this higher clock rate, 80 ns DRAMs function properly, without wait states when the memory addresses are interleaved. If an access to the same section occurs, then a wait state is inserted.

5.3.3 The Input / Output System

The 80386 input/output system is the same as that found in any Intel 8086 family microprocessor-based systems. There are 64K different bytes of I/O space available if isolated I/O is implemented. With isolated I/O, the IN and OUT instructions are used to transfer I/O data between the microprocessor and I/O devices. The I/O port address appears on address bus connections AI5- A2, with used to select a byte, word, or double word of I/O data. If memory-mapped I/O is implemented, then the number of I/O locations can be any amount up to 4G bytes. With memory-mapped 110, any instruction that transfers data between the microprocessor and memory system can be used for I/O transfers because the I/O device is treated as a memory device. Almost all 80386 systems use isolated 1/O because of the I/O protection scheme provided by the 80386 in protected mode operation.

Fig. 5.7 shows the I/O map for the 80386 microprocessor. Unlike the I/O map of earlier Intel microprocessors, which were 16-bits wide, the 80386 uses a full 32-bit wide I/O system divided into four banks. This is identical to the memory system, which is also divided into four banks. Most I/O transfers are 8-bits wide because we often use ASCII code (a 7-bit code) for transferring alphanumeric data between the microprocessor and printers and keyboards. This may change if Unicode, a 16-bit alphanumeric code, becomes common and replaces ASCII code. Recently, I/O devices that are 16 bits and even 32-bits wide have appeared for systems such as disk memory and video display interfaces. These wider I/O paths increase the data transfer rate between the microprocessor and the I/O device when compared to 8-bit transfers.

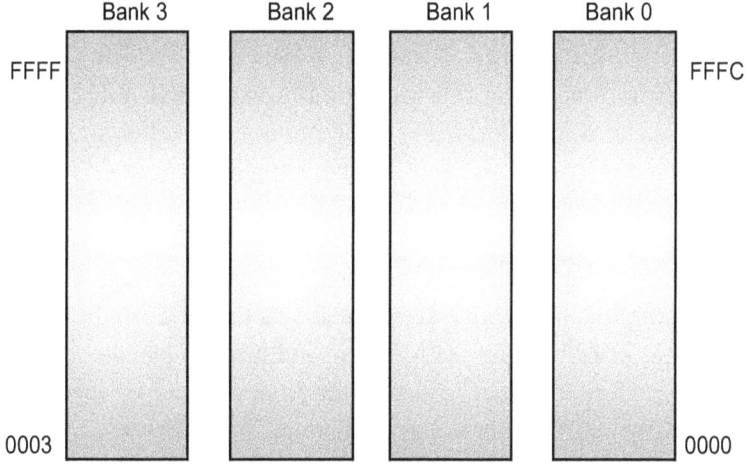

Fig. 5.7 : The isolated I/O map for the 80386 microprocessor

The I/O locations are numbered from 0000H to FFFFH. A portion of the I/O map is designated for the 80387 arithmetic coprocessor. Although the port numbers for the coprocessor are well above the normal I/O map, it is important that they be taken into account when decoding I/O space (overlaps). The coprocessor uses I/O location 800000F8H to 800000FFH for communications between the 80387 and 80386. The 80287 numeric coprocessor designed to use with the 80286 uses the I/O addresses 00F8H to 00FFH for coprocessor communications. Because we often decode only address connections A15 to A2 to select an I/O device, be aware that the coprocessor will activate devices 00F8H to 00FFH unless address line A31 is also decoded. This should present no problem because you really should not be using I/O ports 00F8H to 00FFH for any purpose.

The only new feature that was added to the 80386 with respect to I/O is the I/O privilege information added to the tail end of the TSS when the 80386 is operated in protected mode. As described in the section on memory management, an I/O location can be blocked or inhibited in the protected mode. If the blocked I/O location is addressed, an interrupt (type 13, general fault) is generated. This scheme is added so that I/O access can be prohibited in a multiuser environment. Blocking is an extension of the protected mode operation, as are privilege levels.

5.4 80386 MEMORY MANAGEMENT

The Memory-Management Unit (MMU) within the 80386 is similar to the MMU inside the 80286, except that the 80386 contains a paging unit not found in the 80286. The MMU performs the task of converting linear addresses, as they appear as outputs from a program, into physical addresses that access a physical memory location located anywhere within the memory system. The 80386 uses the paging mechanism to allocate any physical address to any logical address. Therefore, even though the program is accessing memory location A0000H with an instruction, the actual physical address could be memory location 100000H or any other location if paging is enabled. This feature allows virtually any software, written to operate at any memory to function in an 80386 because any linear location can become any physical location. Intel microprocessors did not have this flexibility. Paging is used with DOS to relocate 80386 and 80486 memory at addresses above FFFFFH and into spaces between ROMs at locations D0000 to DFFFFH and other areas as they are available. The area between ROMs is often referred to as upper memory; the area above FFFFFH is referred to as extended memory.

5.4.1 Descriptors and Selectors

The 80386 uses descriptors in much the same fashion as the 80286. In both microprocessors, a descriptor is a series of eight bytes that describe and locate a memory segment. A selector (segment register) is used to index a descriptor from a table of descriptors. The main difference between the 80286 and 80386 is that the latter has two additional selectors (FS and GS) and the most-significant two bytes of the descriptor are defined for the 80386. Another difference is that 80386 descriptors use a 32-bit base address and a 20-bit limit, instead of the 24-bit base address and a 16-bit limit found on the 80286.

The 80286 addresses a 16M-byte memory space with its 24-bit base address and has a segment length limit of 64K bytes, due to the 16-bit limit. The 80386 addresses a 4G-byte memory space with its 32-bit base address and has a segment length limit of 1M bytes or 4G bytes, due to a 20-bit limit that is used in two different ways. The 20-bit limit can access a segment with a length of 1M byte if the granularity bit (G) =0. If G = 1, the 20-bit limit allows a segment length of 4g bytes. The granularity bit is found in the 80386 descriptor. If G =0, the number stored in the limit is interpreted directly as a limit, allowing it to contain any limit between 00000H and FFFFFH for a segment size up to 1M byte. If G = 1, the number stored in the limit is interpreted as 00000XXXH to FFFFFXXXH, where the XXX is any value between 000H and FFFH. This allows the limit of the segment to range between 0 bytes to 40 bytes in steps of 4K bytes. A limit of 00001 H indicates that the limit is 4K bytes when G = 1 and 1 byte when G =0. An example is a segment that begins at physical address 10000000H. If the limit is 0000lH and G = 0, this segment begins at 10000000H and ends at 10000001H. If G = 1 with the same limit (00001H), the segment begins at location 10000000H and ends at location 10001FFFH.

Fig. 5.8 shows how the 80386 addresses a memory segment in the protected mode using a selector and a descriptor. Note that this is identical to the way that a segment is addressed by the 80286. The difference is the size of the segment accessed by the 80386. The selector uses its leftmost 13 bits to select a descriptor from a descriptor table. The TI bit indicates either the local (TI = 1) or global (TI = 0) descriptor table. The rightmost two bits of the selector define the requested privilege level of the access.

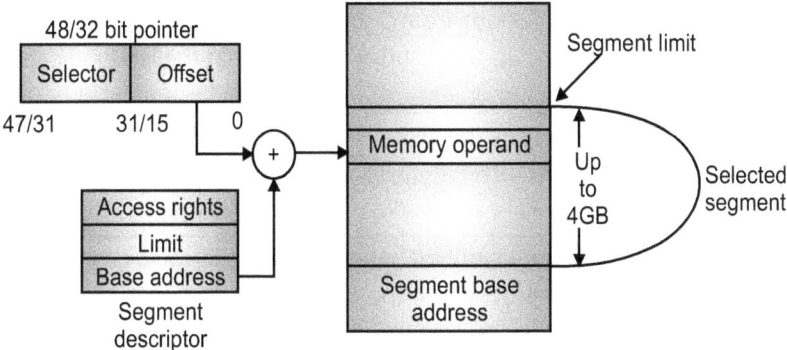

Fig. 5.8 : Protected mode addressing using a segment register as a selector

Because the selector uses a 13-bit code to access a descriptor, there are at most 8192 descriptors in each table local or global. Because each segment (in an 80386) can be 4G bytes in length, we can access 16,384 segments at a time with the two descriptor tables. This allows the 80386 to access a virtual memory size of MT bytes. Of course, only 4G bytes of memory actually exist in the memory system (1T byte = 1024G bytes). If a program requires more than 4G bytes of memory at a time, it can be swapped between the memory system and a disk drive or other form of large volume storage.

The 80386 uses descriptor tables for both global (GDT) and local (LDT) descriptors. A third descriptor table appears for interrupt (IDT) descriptors or gates. The first six bytes of the descriptor are the same as in the 80286, which allows 80286 software to be upward compatible with the 80386. (An 80286 descriptor used 00H for its most significant two bytes.) Fig. 5.9 shows the 80286 and 80386 descriptor. The base address is 32 bits in the 80386, the limit is 20 bits, and a G bit selects the limit multiplier (1 or 4K times). The fields in the descriptor for the 80386 are defined as follows:

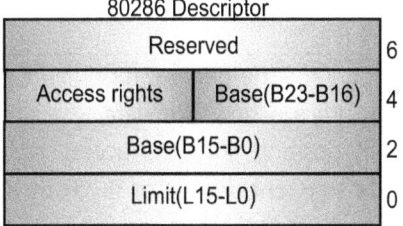 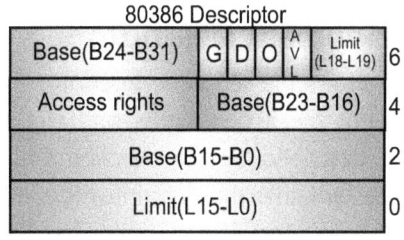

Fig. 5.9 : The descriptors for the 80286 and 80386 microprocessors

Table 5.2 : 80286 /80386 microprocessor

Pin Number	Discretion
Base (B31 to B0)	Defines the starting 32-bit address of the segment within the 4G-byte physical address space of the 80386 microprocessor.
Limit (L19 to L0)	Defines the limit of the segment in units of bytes if the G bit = 0, or in units of 4K bytes if G = 1. This allows a segment to be of any length from 1 byte to 1M bytes if G =0, and from 4K bytes to 4G bytes if G = 1. Recall that the limit indicates the last byte in a segment.
Access Rights	Determines privilege level and other information about the segment. This byte varies with different types of descriptors and is elaborated with each descriptor type.
G	The granularity bit selects a multiplier of 1 or 4K times for the limit field, if G =0, the multiplier is 1; if G = 1, the multiplier is 4K.
D	Selects the default register size. if D =0, the registers are 16-bits wide, as in the 80286; if D = 1, they are 32-bits wide, as in the 80386. This bit determines whether prefixes are required for 32-bit data and index registers. if D =0, then a prefix is required to access 32-bit registers and to use 32-bit pointers. If D = 1, then a prefix is required to access 16-bit registers and I6-bitpointers. The USE16 and USE32 directives appended to the SEGMENT statement in assembly language control the setting of the D bit. In the real mode, it is always assumed that the registers are 16- bits wide, so any instruction that references a 32-bit register or pointer must be prefixed. The current version of DOS assumes D =0.
AVL	This bit is available to the operating system to use in any way that it sees fit. It often indicates that the segment described by the descriptor is available.

Descriptors appear in two forms in the 80386 microprocessor: the segment descriptor and the system descriptor. The segment descriptor defines data, stack, and code segments; the system descriptor defines information about the system's tables, tasks, and gates.

5.4.2 Segment Descriptors

Fig. 5.10 shows the segment descriptor. This descriptor fits the general form, as dictated in Fig. 5.9, but the access rights bits are defined to indicate how the data, stack, or code segment described by the descriptor functions. Bit position 4 of the access rights byte determines whether the descriptor is a data or code segment descriptor (S=1) or a system segment descriptor (S = 0). Note that the labels used for these bits may vary in different versions of Intel literature, but they perform the same tasks.

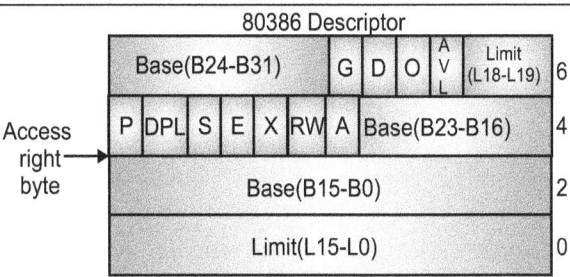

Fig. 5.10 : The format of the 80386 segment descriptor.

Following is a description of the access rights bits and their function in the segment descriptor:

Pin Number	Discretion
P	Present is a logic I to indicate that the segment is present. If P = 0 and the segment is accessed through the descriptor, a type 11 interrupt occurs. This interrupt indicates that a segment was accessed that is not present in the system.
DPL	Descriptor privilege level sets the privilege level of the descriptor, where 00 has the highest privilege and 11 has the lowest. This is used to protect access to segments. If a segment is accessed with a privilege level that is lower (higher in number) than the DPL, a privilege violation interrupt occurs. Privilege levels are used in multiuser systems to prevent access to an area of the system memory.
S	Segment indicates a data or code segment descriptor (S = 1), or a system segment descriptor (S = 0).
E	Executable selects a data (stack) segment (E = 0) or a code segment (E = 1). E also defines the function of the next two bits (X and RW).
X	If E = 0, then X indicates the direction of expansion for the data segment. If X=0, the segment expands upward, as in a data segment; if X = 1, the segment expands downward as in a stack segment. IfE = 1, then X indicates whether the privilege level of the code segment is ignored (X = 0) or observed (X = 1).
RW	If E = 0, then RW indicates that the data segment may be written (RW = 1) or not written (RW = 0): If E = 1, then RW indicates that the code segment may be read (RW= I) or not read (RW=0).
A	Accessed is set each time that the microprocessor accesses the segment. It is sometimes used by the operating system to keep track of which segments have been accessed.

5.4.3 System Descriptor

The system descriptor is illustrated in Fig. 5.11. There are 16 possible system descriptor types (Table below shows the different descriptor types), but not all are used the 80386 microprocessor. Some of these types are defined for the 80286 so that the 80286 software is compatible with the 80386. Some of the types are new and unique to the 80386; some have yet to be defined and are reserved for future Intel products.

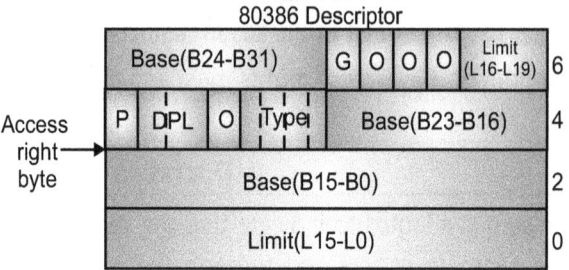

Fig. 5.11 : The general format of an 80386 system descriptor

Table 5.5 : 80386 System descriptor types

Type	Purpose
0000	Invalid
0001	Available 80286 TSS
0010	LDT
0011	Busy 80286 TSS
0100	80286 call gate
0101	Task gate (80286 or 80386)
0110	80286 interrupt gate
0111	80286 trap gate
1000	Invalid
1001	Available 80386 TSS
1010	Reserved for future intel products
1011	Busy 80386 TSS
1100	80386 call gate
1101	Reserved for future intel products
1110	80386 interrupt gate
1111	80836 trap gate

5.4.4 Descriptor Tables

The descriptor tables define all the segments used in the 80386 when it operates in the protected mode. There are three types of descriptor tables: the global descriptor table (GDT), the local descriptor table (LDT), and the interrupt descriptor table (IDT). The registers used by the 80386 to address these three tables are called the global descriptor table register (GDTR), the local descriptor table register (LDTR), and the interrupt descriptor table register (IDTR). These registers are loaded with the LGDT, LLDT, and LIDT instructions, respectively.

The descriptor table is a variable-length array of data, with each entry holding an 8-byte long descriptor. The local and global descriptor tables hold up to 8192 entries each, and the interrupt descriptor table holds up to 256 entries. A descriptor is indexed from either the local or global descriptor table by the selector that appears in a segment register. Fig. 5.12 shows a segment register and the selector that it holds in the protected mode. The leftmost 13 bits index a descriptor, the TI bit selects either the local (TI = 1) or global (TI = 0) descriptor table, and the RPL bits indicate the requested privilege level.

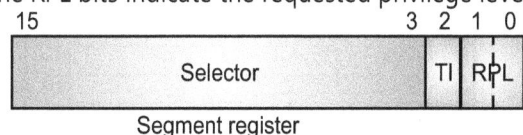

Fig. 5.12 : A segment register

Whenever a new selector is placed into one of the segment registers, the 80386 accesses one of the descriptor tables and automatically loads the descriptor into a program-invisible cache portion of the segment register. As long as the selector remains the same in the segment register, no additional accesses are required to the descriptor table. The operation of fetching a new descriptor from the descriptor table is program-invisible because the microprocessor automatically accomplishes this each time that the segment register contents are changed in the protected mode.

5.4.5 The Task State Segment (TSS)

The task state segment (TSS) descriptor contains information about the location, size, and privilege level of the task state segment, just as any other descriptor. The difference is that the TSS described by the TSS descriptor does not contains data or code. It contains the state of the task and linkage so tasks can be nested (one task can call a second, which can call a third, and so forth). The TSS descriptor is addressed by the task register (TR). The contents of the TR are changed by the LTR instruction. Whenever the protected mode program executes a far JMP or CALL instruction, the contents of TR are also changed. The LTR instruction is used to initially access a task during system initialization. After initialization, the CALL or JUMP instructions normally switch tasks. In most cases, we use the CALL instruction to initiate a new task.

The TSS is illustrated in Fig. As can be seen, the TSS is quite a formidable section of memory, containing many different types of information. The first word of the TSS is labeled back-link. This is the selector that is used, on a return (RET or IRET), to link back to the prior TSS by loading the back-link selector into the TR. The following word must contain a 0.

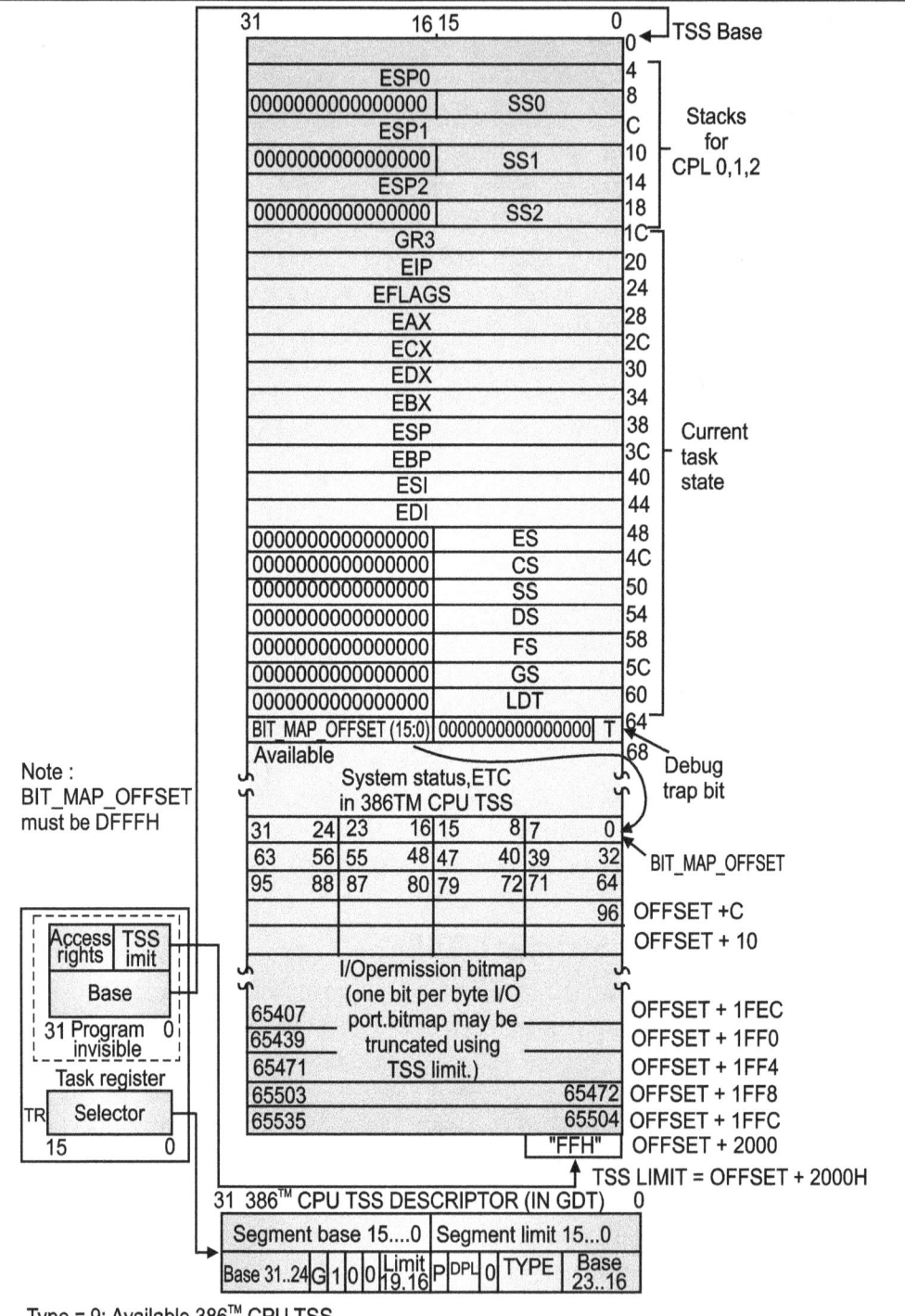

Fig. 5.13 : The task state segment (TSS) descriptor.

The second through the seventh double words contain the ESP and ESS values for privilage levels 0 to 2. These are required in case the current task is interrupted so these privilege level (PL) stacks can be addressed. The eighth word (offset ICH) contains the contents of CR3, which stores the base address of the prior state's page directory register. This must be restored if paging is in effect. The contents of the next 17 doublewords are loaded into the registers indicated. Whenever a task is accessed, the entire state of the machine (all of the registers) is stored in these memory locations and then reloaded from the same locations in the new TSS. The last word (offset 66H) contains the I/O permission bit map base address.

The I/O permission bit map allows the TSS to block 110 operations to inhibited I/O port addresses via an I/O permission denial interrupt. The permission denial interrupt is type number 13, the general protection fault interrupt. The I/O permission bit map base address is the offset address from the start of the TSS. This allows the same permission map to be used by many TSSs.

Each I/O permission bit map is 64K bits long (8K bytes), beginning at the offset address indicated by the I/O permission bit map base address. The first byte of the I/O permission bit map contains I/O permission for I/O ports 0000H to 0007H. The rightmost bit contains the permission for port number 000011. The leftmost bit contains the permission for port number 0007H. This sequence continues for the very last port address (FFFFH) stored in the leftmost bit of the last byte of the I/O permission bit map. A logic 0 placed in an I/O permission bit map bit enables the I/O port address, while a logic I inhibits or blocks the I/O port address. At present, only Windows NT uses the 110 permission scheme to disable I/O ports dependent on the application or the user.

The operation of a task switch, which requires only 17µs to execute, includes the following steps:

Step 1 : The gate contains the address of the procedure or location jumped to by the task switch. It also contains the selector number of the TSS descriptor and the number of words transferred from the caller to the user stack area for parameter passing.

Step 2 : The selector is loaded into TR from the gate. (This step is accomplished by a CALL or JMP that refers to a valid TSS descriptor.)

Step 3 : The TR selects the TSS.

Step 4 : The current state is saved in the current TSS and the new TSS is accessed with the state of the new task (all the registers) loaded into the microprocessor. The current state is saved at the TSS selector currently found in the TR. Once the current state is saved, a new value (by the JMP or CALL) for the TSS selector is loaded into TR and the new state is loaded from the new TSS.

The return from a task is accomplished by the following steps:

Step 1 : The current state of the microprocessor is saved in the current TSS.

Step 2 : The back-link selector is loaded to the TR to access the prior TSS so that the prior state of the machine can be returned to and be restored to the microprocessor. The return for a called TSS is accomplished by the IRET instruction.

5.5 VIRTUAL 8086 MODE

In its protected mode of operation, 80386DX provides a virtual 8086 operating environment to execute the 8086 programs. The real mode also can be used to execute the 8086 programs along with the capabilities of 80386, like protection and a few additional instructions. However, once the 80386 enters the protected mode from the real mode, it cannot return back to the real mode without a reset operation. Thus, the virtual 8086 mode of operation of 80386, offers an advantage of executing 8086 programs while in protected mode.

The address forming mechanism in the virtual 8086 mode is exactly identical with that of 8086 real mode. In virtual mode, 8086 can address 1Mbytes of physical memory that maybe anywhere in the 4Gbytes address space of the protected mode of 80386. Like 80386 real mode, the addresses in virtual 8086 mode lie within 1Mbytes of memory. In virtual mode, the paging mechanism and protection capabilities are available at the service of the programmers (note that the 80386 supports multiprogramming, hence more than one programmer may use the CPU at a time). Paging unit may not be necessarily enabled in virtual mode, but may be needed to run the 8086 programs which require more than 1Mbyte of memory for memory management functions.

In virtual mode, the paging unit allows only 256 pages, each of 4Kbytes size. Each of the pages may be located anywhere within the maximum 4Gbytes of physical memory. The virtual mode allows the multiprogramming of 8086 applications. Fig. 5.14 shows how the memory is managed in multitasking virtual 8086 environment.

The virtual 8086 mode executes all the programs at privilege level 3. Any of the other programmers may deny access to the virtual mode programs or data. However, the real mode programs are executed at the highest privilege level, i.e. level 0. Note that the instructions to prepare the processor for protected mode can only be executed at level 0.

The virtual mode may be entered using an IRET instruction at CPL=0 or a task switch at any CPL, while executing any task whose TSS is having a flag image with VM flag set to 1. The IRET instruction may be used to set the VM flag and consequently enter the virtual mode. The PUSHF and POPF instructions are unable to read or set the VM bit, as they do not access it. Even in the virtual mode, all the interrupts and exceptions are handled by the protected mode interrupt handler. To return to the protected mode from the virtual mode, any interrupt or exception may be used. As a part of interrupt service routine, the VM bit may be reset to zero to pull back the 80386 into protected mode.

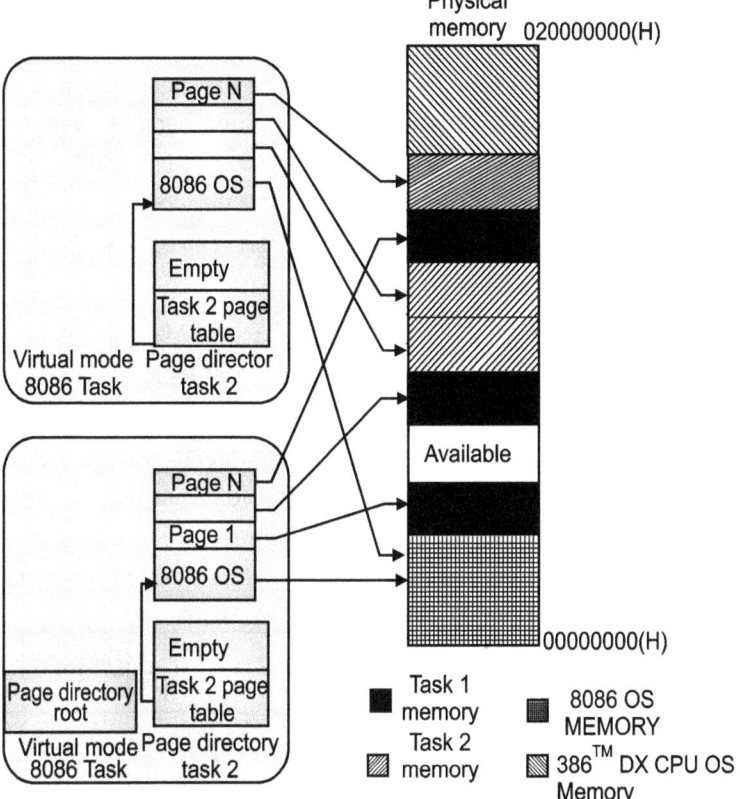

Fig. 5.14 : Memory Management in Virtual 8086 Mode (Multitasking)

5.6 PAGING

5.6.1 Paging Operation

Paging is one of the memory management techniques used for virtual memory multitasking operating systems. The segmentation scheme may divide the physical memory into variable size segments but the paging divides the memory into fixed size pages. The segments are supposed to be the logical segments of the program, but the pages do not have any logical relation with the program. The pages are just the fixed size portions of the program module or data. The advantage of the paging scheme is that the complete segment of a task need not be in the physical memory at any time. Only a few pages of the segments, which are required currently for the execution need to available in the physical memory. Thus the memory requirement of the task is substantially reduced, relinquishing the available memory for other tasks. Whenever the other pages of the task are required for execution, they may be fetched from the secondary storage. The previous pages which are executed need not be available in the memory, and hence the space occupied by them may be relinquished for other tasks. Thus the paging mechanism provides an effective technique to manage the physical memory for multitasking systems.

Paging Unit : The paging unit of 80386 uses a two level table mechanism to convert the linear addresses provided by segmentation unit into physical addresses. The paging unit converts the complete map of a task into pages, each of size 4K. The task is further handled in terms of its pages, rather than segments. The paging unit handles every task in terms of three components namely page directory, page tables and the page itself.

Page Descriptor Base Register : The control register CR2 is used to store the 32-bit linear address at which the previous page fault was detected. The CR3 is used as page direct physical base address register, to store the physical starting address of the page directory. The lower 12 bits of CR3 are always zero (page size 2^{12} =4K) to ensure the page size aligned directory. A move operation to CR3 automatically loads the page table entry caches and a task switch operation, to load CR0 suitably.

Page Directory : This is at the most 4Kbytes in size. Each directory entry is of four bytes, thus a total of 1024 entries are allowed in a directory. The following Fig. 5.15 shows a typical directory entry. The upper 10 bits of the linear address are used as an index to the corresponding page directory entry. The page directory entries point to page tables.

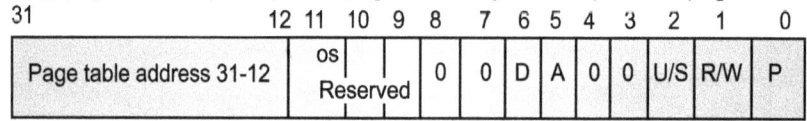

Fig. 5.15 : Page directory entry

Page Tables : Each page table is of 4Kbytes in size and may contain a maximum of 1024 entries. The page table entries contain the starting address of the page and the statistical information about the page as shown if Fig. 5.16. The upper 20-bit page frame address is combined with the lower 12 bits of the linear address. The address bits A_{12}-A_{21} are used to select the 1024 page table entries. The page tables can be shared between the tasks.

Fig. 5.16 : Page table entry

The P-bit of the above entries indicate, if the entry can be used in address translation. If P = 1, the entry can be used in address translation, otherwise, it cannot be used. The P-bit of the currently executed page is always high. The accessed bit A is set by 80386 before any access to the page. If A = 1, the page is accessed, otherwise, it is unaccessed. The D bit (Dirty bit) is set before a write operation to the page is carried out. The D-bit is undefined for page directory entries. The OS reserved bits are defined by the operating system software.

The user/supervisor (U/S) bit and read/write (R/W) bit are used to provide protection. These bits can be decoded as shown in the Table to provide protection under the four level protection model. The level 0 is supposed to have the highest privilege, while the level 3 is supposed to have the least privilege.

Table 5.6

U/S	R/W	Permitted for level 3	Permitted for levels 2,1 or 0
0	0	None	Read/Write
0	1	None	Read/Write
1	0	Read only	Read/Write
1	1	Read-Write	Read/Write

5.6.2 Conversion of a Linear Address to a Physical Address

The paging unit receives a 32-bit linear address from the segmentation unit. The upper 20 linear address bits (A_{12}-A_{31}) are compared with all the 32 entries in the translation look a side buffer to check if it matches with any of the entries. If it matches, the 32-bit physical address is calculated from the matching TLB entry and placed on the address bus.

For converting all the linear addresses to physical addresses, if the conversion process uses the two level paging for every conversion, a considerable time will be wasted in the process. Hence, to optimize this a 32-entry (32 x 4bytes) page table cache is provided which stores the 32 recently accessed page table entries. Whenever a linear address is to be converted to physical address, it is first checked to see, whether it corresponds to any of the page table cache entries. This page table cache is called as translation look-aside buffer (TLB).

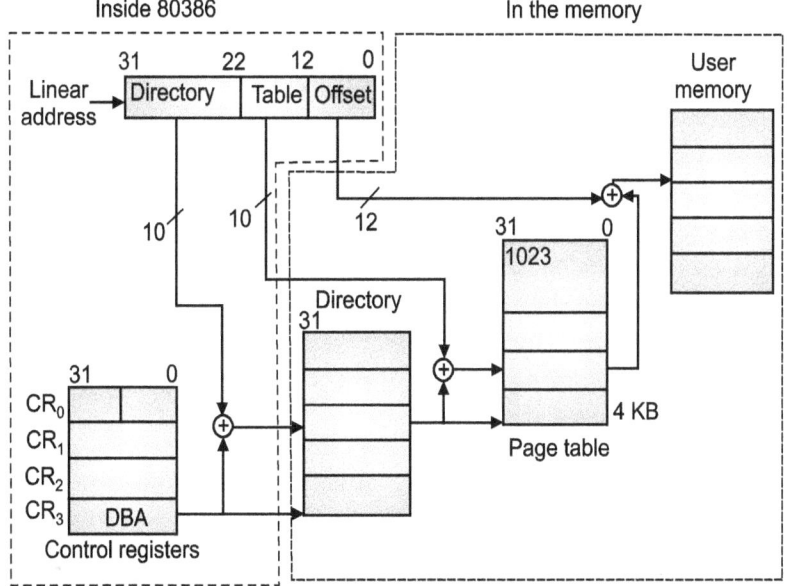

DBA- Physical directory base address

Fig. 5.17 : Paging mechanism of 80386

If the page table entry is not in TLB, the 80386 reads the appropriate page directory entry. It then checks the P-bit of the directory entry. If P = 1, it indicates that the page table is in the memory. Then 80386 refers to the appropriate page table entry and sets the accessed bit A. If

P=1, in the page table entry, the page is available in the memory. Then the processor updates the A and D bits and accesses the page. The upper 20 bits of the linear address, read from the page-table are stored in TLB for future possible access. If P=0, the processor generates a page fault exception number 14. This exception is also generated, if page protection rules are violated. Every time a page fault exception is generated, the CR2 is loaded with the page fault address. Fig. 5.18 shows the overall paging operation with TLB.

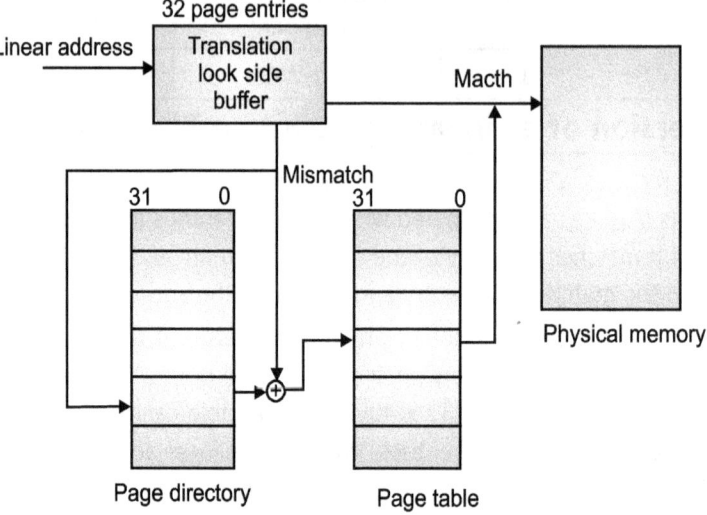

Fig. 5.18 : Paging operation with TLB

QUESTIONS

1. What is interrupt? Why it is required?
2. What are the different types of interrupts?
3. Explain hardware interrupts?
4. Arrange the interrupts on the basis of highest priority to lowest priority.
5. Explain the software interrupts.
6. Draw and explain 80386 microprocessor.
7. What are the different types of registers used in 80386 microprocessor.
8. Explain the memory system in 80386 microprocessor.
9. Explain the memory management in 80386 microprocessor.
10. Describe virtual mode of 8086 mode.
11. Explain memory paging mechanism.

✠ ✠ ✠

Unit - VI

PENTIUM, PENTIUM PRO AND PENTIUM 4 MICROPROCESSOR

6.1 DEVELOPMENT OF MICROPROCESSORS

Pentium, Family of microprocessors developed by Intel Corp. Introduced in 1993 as the successor to Intel's 80486 microprocessor, the Pentium contained two processors on a single chip and about 3.3 million transistors. Using a CISC (complex instruction set computer) architecture, its main features were a 32-bit address bus, a 64-bit data bus, built-in floating-point and memory-management units, and two 8KB caches. It was available with processor speeds ranging from 60 megahertz (MHz) to 200 MHz. The Pentium quickly became the processor of choice for personal computers. It was superseded by ever faster and more powerful processors, the Pentium Pro (1995), the Pentium II (1997), the Pentium III (1999), and the Pentium 4 (2000).

Microprocessors have undergone significant evolution over the past four decades. This development is clearly perceptible to a common user, especially, in terms of phenomenal growth in capabilities of personal computers. Development of some of the microprocessors can be given as follows.

Table 6.1

IC	Numbers	Specification	Year
Intel	4004	4 bit (2300 PMOS transistors)	1971
Intel	8080	8 bit (NMOS)	1974
	8085	8 bit	
Intel	8088	16 bit	1978
	8086	16 bit	
Intel	80186	16 bit	1982
	80286	16 bit	
Intel	80386	32 bit (275000 transistors)	1985
Intel	80486 SX DX	32 bit 32 bit (built in floating point unit)	1989

...Cont.

Intel 80586 I		1993
MMX	64 bit	1997
Celeron II		1999
III		2000
IV		
Z-80 (Zilog)	8 bit	1976
Motorola Power PC 601	32-bit	1993
602		1995
603		

6.2 COMPARISON BETWEEN 8085 AND 8086

Size : 8085 is 8 bit microprocessor whereas 8086 is 16 bit microprocessor.

Address Bus : 8085 has 16 bit address bus and 8086 has 20 bit address bus.

Memory : 8085 can access upto 2^{16} = 64 Kb of memory whereas 8086 can access upto 2^{20} = 1 MB of memory.

Instruction Queue : 8085 doesn't have an instruction queue whereas 8086 has instruction queue.

Pipelining : 8085 does not support pipelined architecture whereas 8086 supports pipelined architecture.

Multiprocessing Support : 8085 does not support multiprocessing support whereas 8086 supports.

I/O :- 8085 can address 2^8 = 256 I/O's and 8086 can access 2^{16} = 65,536 I/O's

Arithmetic Support : 8085 only supports integer and decimal whereas 8086 supports integer, decimal and ASCII arithmetic.

Multiplication and Division : 8085 doesn't support whereas 8086 supports.

Operating Modes : 8085 supports only single operating mode whereas 8086 operates in two modes real mode and protected mode.

External Hardware : 8085 requires less external hardware whereas 8086 requires more external hardware.

Cost : The cost of 8085 is low and 8086 is high.

Memory Segmentation : In 8085, memory space is not segmented but in 8086, memory space is segmented.

6.3 PENTIUM ARCHITECTURE

The Pentium family of processors originated from the 80486 microprocessor. The term "Pentium processor" refers to a family of microprocessors that share a common architecture and instruction set. The first Pentium processors were introduced in 1993. It runs at a clock frequency of either 60 or 66 MHz and has 3.1 million transistors. Some of the features of Pentium architecture are

- Complex Instruction Set Computer (CISC) architecture with Reduced Instruction Set Computer (RISC) performance.
- 64-Bit Bus
- Upward code compatibility.
- Pentium processor uses Superscalar architecture and hence can issue multiple instructions per cycle.
- Multiple Instruction Issue (MII) capability.
- Pentium processor executes instructions in five stages. This staging, or pipelining, allows the processor to overlap multiple instructions so that it takes less time to execute two instructions in a row.
- The Pentium processor fetches the branch target instruction before it executes the branch instruction.
- The Pentium processor has two separate 8-kilobyte (KB) caches on chip, one for instructions and one for data. It allows the Pentium processor to fetch data and instructions from the cache simultaneously.
- When data is modified, only the data in the cache is changed. Memory data is changed only when the Pentium processor replaces the modified data in the cache with a different set of data
- The Pentium processor has been optimized to run critical instructions in fewer clock cycles than the 80486 processor.

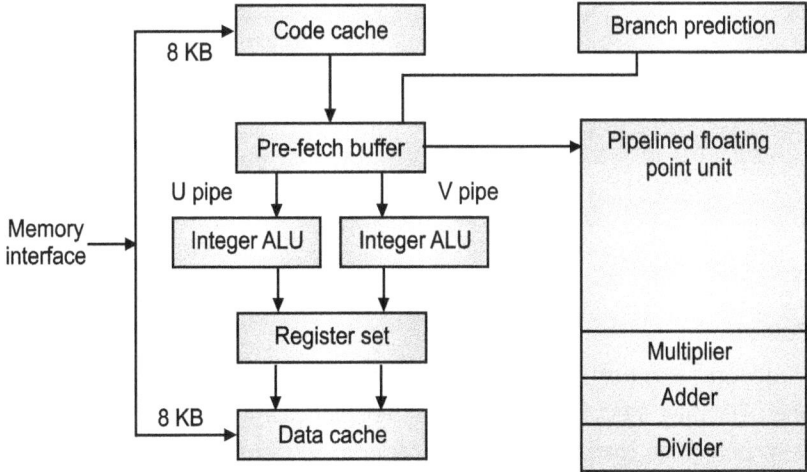

Fig. 6.1 : Superscalar architecture of pentium

The Pentium processor has two primary operating modes
1. **Protected Mode**: In this mode all instructions and architectural features are available, providing the highest performance and capability. This is the recommended mode that all new applications and operating systems should target.
2. **Real-Address Mode**: This mode provides the programming environment of the Intel 8086 processor, with a few extensions. Reset initialization places the processor in real mode where, with a single instruction, it can switch to protected mode

The Pentium's basic integer pipeline is five stages long, with the stages broken down as follows:
1. **Pre-Fetch/Fetch**: Instructions are fetched from the instruction cache and aligned in pre-fetch buffers for decoding.
2. **Decode1**: Instructions are decoded into the Pentium's internal instruction format. Branch prediction also takes place at this stage.
3. **Decode2**: Same as above, and microcode ROM kicks in here, if necessary. Also, address computations take place at this stage.
4. **Execute**: The integer hardware executes the instruction.
5. **Write-Back**: The results of the computation are written back to the register file.

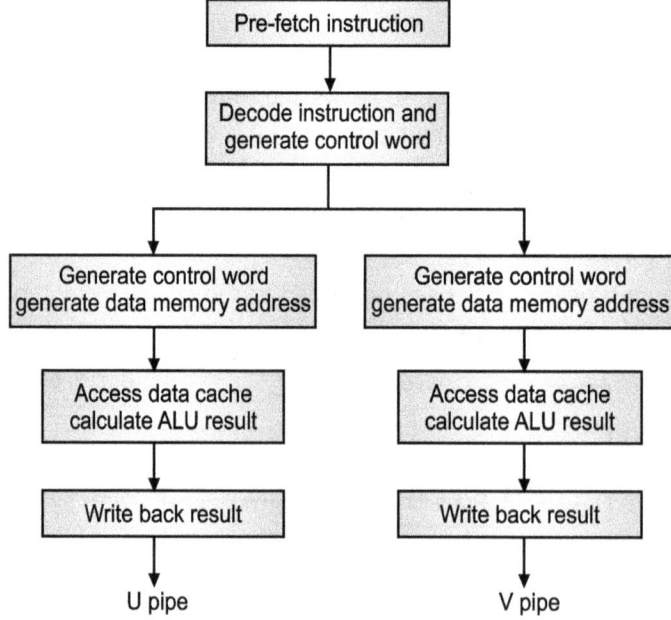

Fig. 6.2 : Pentium pipeline stages

Floating Point Unit :

There are 8 general-purpose 80-bit Floating point registers. Floating point unit has 8 stages of pipelining. First five are similar to integer unit. Since the possibility of error is more in Floating Point unit (FPU) than in integer unit, additional error checking stage is there in FPU. The floating point unit as shown in Fig. 6.3.

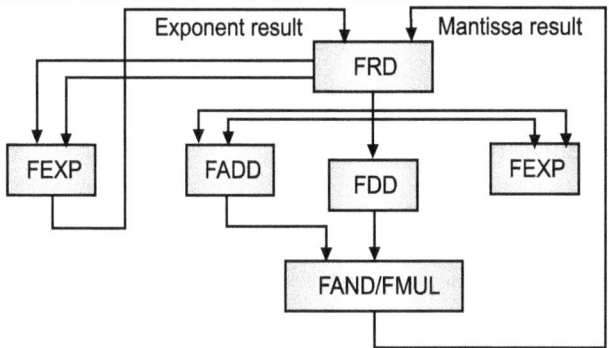

Fig. 6.3 : Floating point unit

FRD : Floating Point Rounding

FDD : Floating Point Division

FADD : Floating Point Addition

FEXP : Floating Point Exponent

FAND : Floating Point And

FMUL : Floating Point Multiply

6.4 INTEL 80386 – A 32-BIT MICROPROCESSOR WITH MEMORY PAGING FACILITY

Intel 80386 is a logical extension of the 80286 microprocessor. The basic architecture of 80386 is given here.

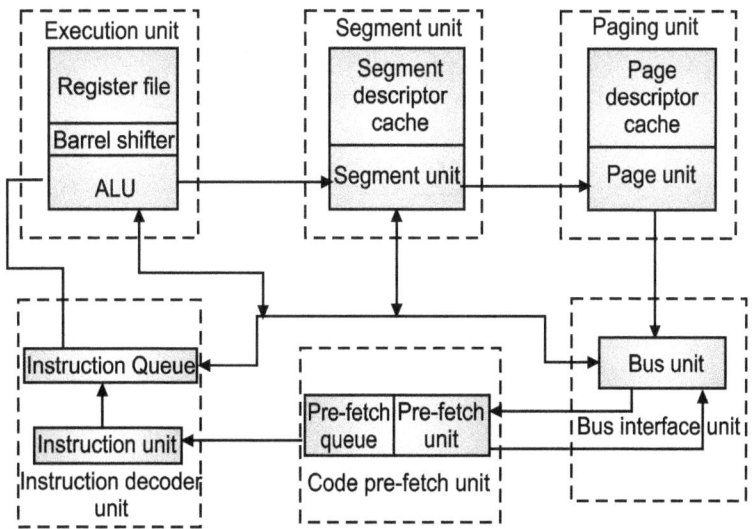

Fig. 6.4 : Basic architecture of 80386 microprocessor

Features of 80386 :
- More highly pipelined than 80286
- Instruction fetching, instruction decoding, instruction execution and memory management are all carried out in parallel.
- 32-bit data bus
- 32-bit non-multiplexed address bus
- 2^{32} = 4 Gigabyte of physical memory
- 2^{46} or 64 Terabyte of virtual memory.

6.5 REGISTERS OF PENTIUM MICROPROCESSOR

The Intel architectures as a set just do not have enough registers to satisfy most assembly language programmers. Still, the processors have been around for a LONG time, and they have a sufficient number of registers to do whatever is necessary general purpose use, we get

32-bit	16-bit	8-bit	8-bit	
			(high part of 16)	(low part of 16)
EAX	AX	AH	AL	
EBX	BX	BH	BL	
ECX	CX	CH	CL	
EDX	DX	DH	DL	

EBP	BP
ESI	SI
EDI	DI
ESP	SP

There are a few more, but we won't use or discuss them. They are only used for memory accessibility in the segmented memory model.

Pointer Registers :

As an operand,

    EBP is a frame pointer

    ESP is a stack pointer

Flag Register :

Many bits used for controlling the action of the processor and setting state are in the register called EFLAGS. This register contains the condition codes :

OF	Overflow flag
SF	Sign flag
ZF	Zero flag
PF	Parity flag
CF	Carry flag

The settings of these flags are checked in conditional control instructions. Many instructions set one or more of the flags.

(Note that we only utilized SF and ZF in SASM.)

There are many other bits in the EFLAGS register : TO BE DISCUSSED LATER.

The use of the EFLAGS register is implied in instructions.

6.6　ACCESSING MEMORY

There are 2 memory models supported in the Pentium architecture.

(Actually it is the 486 and more recent models that support 2 models.)

In both models, memory is accessed using an address. It is the way that addresses are formed (within the processor) that differs in the 2 models.

FLAT MEMORY MODEL

The memory model that we use. AND, the memory model that every other manufactures' processors also use.

SEGMENTED MEMORY MODEL

Different parts of a program are assumed to be in their own, set-aside portions of memory. These portions are called segments.

An address is formed from 2 pieces : a segment location and an offset within a segment.

Note that each of these pieces can be shorter (contain fewer bits) than a whole address. This is much of the reason that Intel chose this form of memory model for its earliest single-chip processors.

There are segments for :

    code

    data

    stack

    other

Which segment something is in can be implied by the memory access involved. An instruction fetch will always be looking in the code segment. A push instruction (we'll talk about this with chapter 11) always accesses the stack segment. Etc.

6.7 REAL ADDRESS MODE OF 80386

After reset, the 80386 starts from the memory location FFFFFFF0 H under real address mode. In real address mode, 80386 works as a fast 8086 with 32 bit registers and data types. The addressing techniques, memory size, interrupt handling in this mode of 80386 are similar to the real addressing mode of 80286. In real address mode, the default operand size is 16 bit but 32 bit operands and addressing modes may be used with the help of override prefixer.

Maximum physical memory = 1Mega byte
0000 0000 to 000FFFFF (A_0 - A_{19}).
Maximum virtual memory :
$2^{14} \times 2^{32} = 2^{46}$ bytes or 64 Terabytes.

6.7.1 Protected Virtual Addressing Mode (PVAM)

80386 operates in two memory management modes in PVAM. They are given as follows

1. **Non Paged Mode :**

   MMU operates similar to 80286. Virtual addresses are represented with a selector component and an offset component. The selector component is used to index a descriptor in a descriptor table. The descriptor contains the 32 bit physical base address for the segment. The offset part of the virtual address is added to the base address to produce the actual physical address. The offset part of a virtual address can be 16 or 32 bits so segment can be as large as 4 gigabytes.

   Hence the virtual memory size is
   $$2^{13} * 2 * 2^{32} = 2^{46} \text{ bytes or 64 Terabytes.}$$

   Advantage of Segmentation of Memory : Segments corresponds to code and data structures in the program. Hence segmentation is useful.

   Limitation of Segmentation of Memory : If we need only a part of memory, even then we have to swap the whole segment content. This will increase the time for execution.

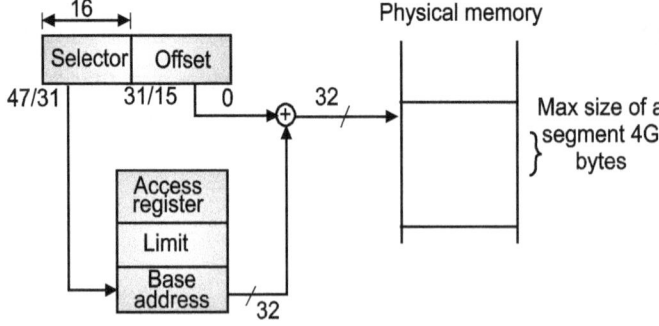

Fig 6.5

Paged Mode :

In this mode, instead of segments, 4 kbytes of fixed page length are used.

Limitation : Pages do not correspond to the logical structure of the program.

Advantage : Pages can be quickly swapped.

Conversion of Linear Address into Physical Address :

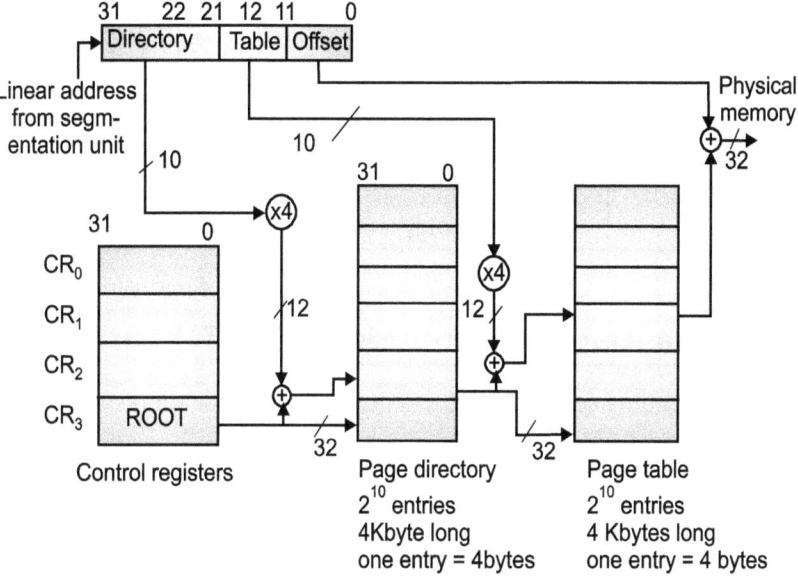

Fig. 6.6 : Address translation mechanism in 80386 paging unit

Page Directory :

Page directory entry

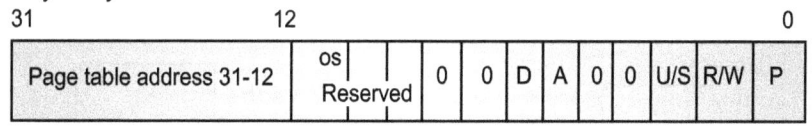

Fig. 6.7

Page Table Entry :

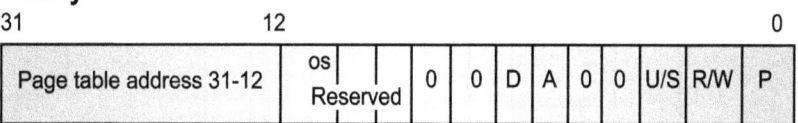

Fig. 6.8

P = entry can be used in address translation

P = 1 Yes

P = 0 No

A = accessed

    A = 1 page is accessed

       = 0 page is unaccessed

D = dirty bit

Dirty bit is set before any write operation to the page.

Dirty bit is undefined for page directory entries.

U/S and R/W bits are used to provide protection.

Table 6.2

U/S	R/W	Permitted for level3	Permitted for levels 2,1,0
0	0	None	Read/Write
0	1	None	Read/Write
1	0	Read only	Read/Write
1	1	Read-write	Read/Write

6.7.2 Use of Translation Look-aside Buffer (TLB) in 80386

It is cumbersome and time consuming to calculate the physical address from linear address for every memory location. A Translation Look-aside Buffer (TLB) simplifies the process. TLB is a page table cache, which stores the 32 recently accessed page table entries.

The paging unit receives a 32-bit linear address from the segmentation unit. The upper 20 bits of the linear address is compared with all 32-entries in the translation look-aside buffer (TLB) to check if it matches with any of the entries. If it matches, the 32-bit physical address is calculated from matching TLB entry and placed on the address bus.

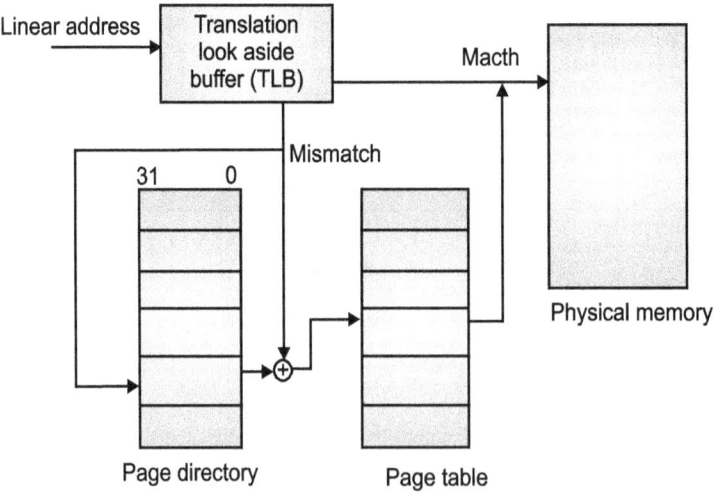

Fig. 6.9 : TLB organization in 80386

Structure of TLB :

TLB has 4 sets of eight entries each. Each entry consists of a TAG and a DATA. Tags are 24 bit wide. They contain 20 upper bits of linear address, a valid bit and three attribute bits. The Data portion of each entry contains higher 20 bits of the Physical address.

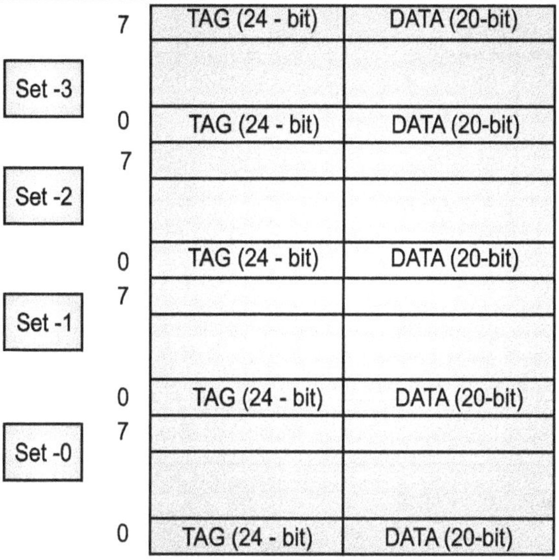

Fig. 6.10 : Structure of TLB

6.8 PENTIUM PRO MICRO-ARCHITECTURE

The Pentium Pro micro-architecture is a three-way superscalar, pipelined architecture. The three-way superscalar architecture is capable of decoding, dispatching, and retrieving three instructions per clock cycle. The Pentium Pro process family utilizes a decoupled 14-stage super pipeline that supports out-of-order instruction execution to facilitate the high level of instruction throughput. The Pentium Pro micro-architecture is illustrated in Fig. 6.11. The Pentium Pro micro-architecture pipeline is divided into four sections the 1st level and 2nd level caches, the front end, the out-of-order execution core, and the retire section. The sections of the pipeline are supplied instructions and data through the bus interface unit.

- The Pentium Pro processor micro-architecture utilizes two cache levels to provide a steady stream of instructions and data to the instruction execution pipeline.
- The L1 cache provides an 8-Kbyte instruction cache and an 8-Kbyte data cache, both closely coupled to the pipeline.
- The L2 cache is a 256-Kbyte, 512-Kbyte, 1-Mbyte, or 2-Mbyte static RAM that is coupled to the core processor through a full clock-speed 64-bit cache bus. The pipelined L2 cache connects to the processor via a 64-bit, full-frequency bus.
- The four-way set associative L2 cache employs 32-byte cache lines and contains 8 bits of error correcting code for each 64 bits of data.
- The nonblocking L1 and L2 caches permit multiple cache misses to proceed in parallel; cache hits proceed in parallel; cache hits proceed during outstanding cache misses to other addresses.

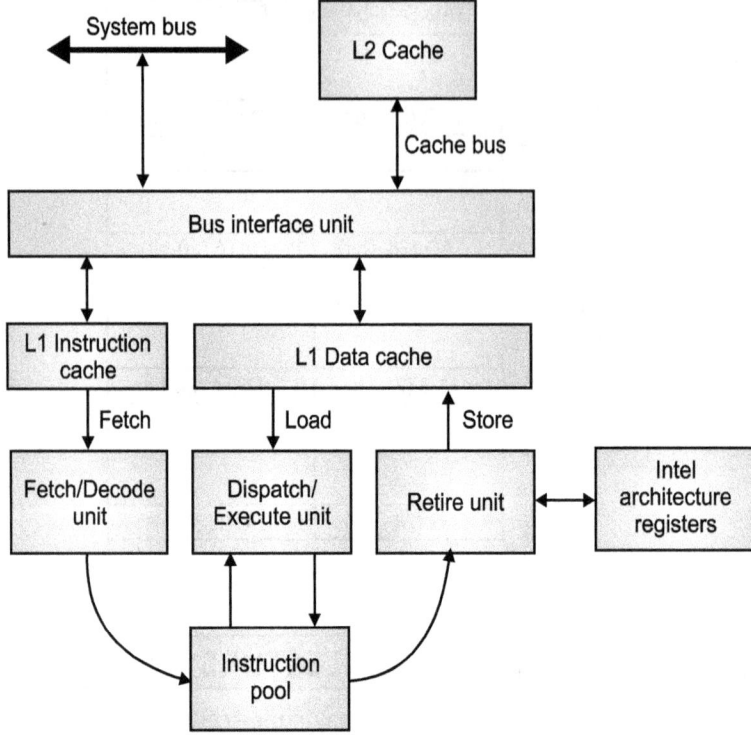

Fig. 6.11 : Pentium pro processing units and their Interface with the memory subsystem

- The Pentium Pro processor micro-architecture utilizes "dynamic execution", an out-of-order execution scheme. Dynamic execution incorporates deep branch prediction, dynamic data flow analysis, and speculative execution.
- Branch prediction is a technique utilized to deliver high performance in pipelined micro-architectures. Branch prediction allows the processor to decode instructions beyond branches to keep the instruction pipeline full.
- The Pentium Pro processor implements an optimized branch prediction algorithm to predict the direction of the instruction stream through multiple levels of branches, procedure calls, and returns. The microprocessor tries to predict whether the branch instruction will jump or not, based on a record of what this branch has done previously. If it has jumped the last four times then chances are high that it will also jump this time.
- The microprocessor decides which instruction to load next into the pipeline based on this prediction, before it knows for sure. This is called speculative execution. If the prediction turns out to be wrong, then it has to flush the pipeline and discard all calculations that were based on this prediction. But if the prediction was correct, then it has saved a lot of time.

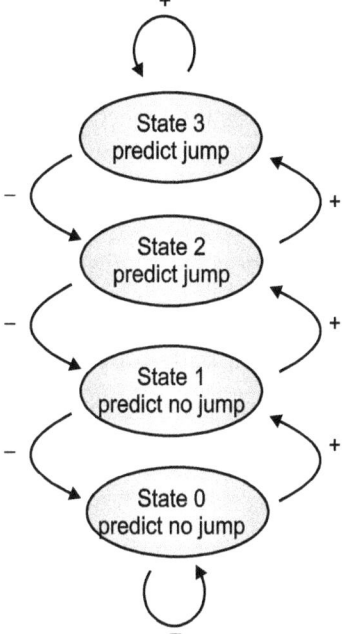

Fig. 6.12 : Branch prediction state diagram

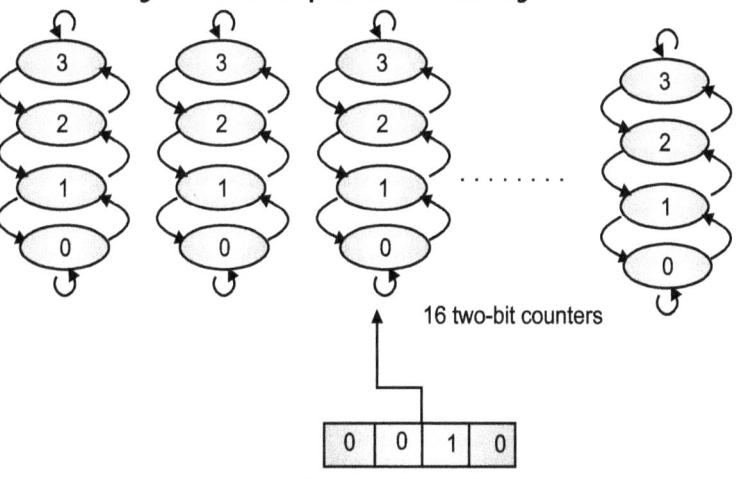

Fig. 6.13 : Pentium Pro 2 level branch prediction.

The Pentium Pro branch prediction is based on the state diagram in Fig. 6.13. The branch state follows the +arrows when the branch instruction jumps, and the -arrows when not jumping. The branch instruction is predicted to jump next time if in state 2 or 3, and to not jump when in state 0 or 1. When a branch does not have an entry in the BTB (branch target buffer) it is predicted to not jump. The first time it jumps it gets an entry in the BTB. The Pentium Pro branch prediction state diagram is a two-bit counter with saturation. The counter is incremented when jumping and decremented when not jumping. The branch instruction is predicted to jump the next time if the counter is in state 2 or 3, and to not jump if in state 0 or 1. This mechanism ensures the branch has to deviate twice from what it does most of the time before the prediction changes.

The improvement in the Pentium Pro processors is achieved by two-level branch prediction. The first level is a shift register that stores the history of the last four events for any branch instruction. This gives sixteen possible bit patterns. You get a pattern of 0000 if the branch did not jump the last four times, and a pattern of 1111 after four times of jumping. The second level in the branch prediction mechanism is constituted of sixteen 2-bit counters of the type in fig. 3a. Level one is a four bit shift register storing the history of the last four events. This four bit pattern is used to select which of the 16 two-bit counters to use for the next prediction. The advantage of the Pentium Pro branch prediction mechanism is that it can learn to recognize repetitive patterns. [3]

Dynamic data flow analysis is the real-time analysis of the flow of data through the processor to determine data and register dependencies. Analysis of data and register dependencies provide opportunities for out-of-order instruction execution. The out-of-order execution core simultaneously monitors multiple instructions and executes instructions in the order that optimizes the processor's multiple execution units. The out-of-order execution core ensures data integrity. The out-of-order execution maintains the executions units work level when cache misses and data dependencies among instructions occur.

6.9 THE PENTIUM 4 ARCHITECTURE

- The Pentium-4 has emerged in a historical context. Its history started with the 8088/8086 microprocessor technology which was correctly conceived in the CISC mould, appropriate for that epoch. Only later when the RISC concept became prevalent, Intel had to decide either to dump the 8086-CISC architecture or to be clever. To dump would mean to render all software based on the 8086 obsolete which would lose Intel its customer base. But the 8086 technology was unsustainable in the face of RISC architectures such as employed by Sun in their SPARC-station. Intel was faced with a dilemma Software required the 8086-CISC instruction set, hardware required a RISC concept. Their solution to this dilemma was *pure magic*, to invent a CPU that would *read* the 8086-CISC code from the software and translate that code into RISC "microcode" operations which would run on a RISC architecture. From the outside, the Pentium reads CISC code, on the inside, it runs RISC code.

There are two ways to approach an analysis of microprocessor architecture. The first is takes a "systems" point of view, and looks at how the various components of the microprocessor work together. The second takes a "dynamic" point of view, looking at how the microprocessor deals with instructions as time flows in other words as instructions pass through a processing pipeline. Here we shall present both approaches.

There are two major groups of components in the P4, (i) the "Front End" which reads IA-32 CISC code and translates this into a stream of micro-operations "mu-ops" and then issues these to the (ii) "Execution Engine" which carries out RISC operations. The Front End has branch prediction logic which uses past history of the program execution tp speculate which IA-32 CISC instructions should be executed next. It then fetches these from the L2 instruction cache, and decodes them and stores them into the L1 Instruction Cache as mu-ops. It also knows what IA-32 CISC instructions have been decoded and stored, so does not need to decode a the same CISC instruction which appears further down the program code.

The Execution engine uses out-of-order (OOO) logic so that mu-ops are re-ordered in sequence so as to keep the machine's execution components, such as the ALUs and the cache as busy as possible. This allows several mu-ops to be processed simultaneously, assuming there are no dependencies. Following processing by the ALUs the instructions are re-ordered by the Retirement Unit to recover the original program code order. This logic also reports branch history back to the Front End allowing branch prediction to occur. Up to 126 mu-ops can be in flight at the same time and also 48 load and 24 store mu-ops. The Allocator searches for the resources required by each mu-op (such as values in registers), and when these become available they are assigned by the Allocator to the mu-op which is then released into the pipeline. The Register Renamer takes the set of 8 IA-32 CISC registers (eax, ebx, ecx, etc) and assigns them to the 128 RISC registers in the machine. This is because in the original program, a register such as eax could be referred to by many lines of code which may been translated to mu-ops in the L1 cache. Each instance of eax could be unique, holding a different value. The Register Renaming logic stores a table of names so that an instruction coming down the pipeline can know which RISC register corresponds to its own instance of eax. The Schedulers decide when each mu-op is ready to execute by monitoring the availability of their input operands. And whether there is an ALU resource waiting for a job. There are multiple schedulers which feed the various ALUs.

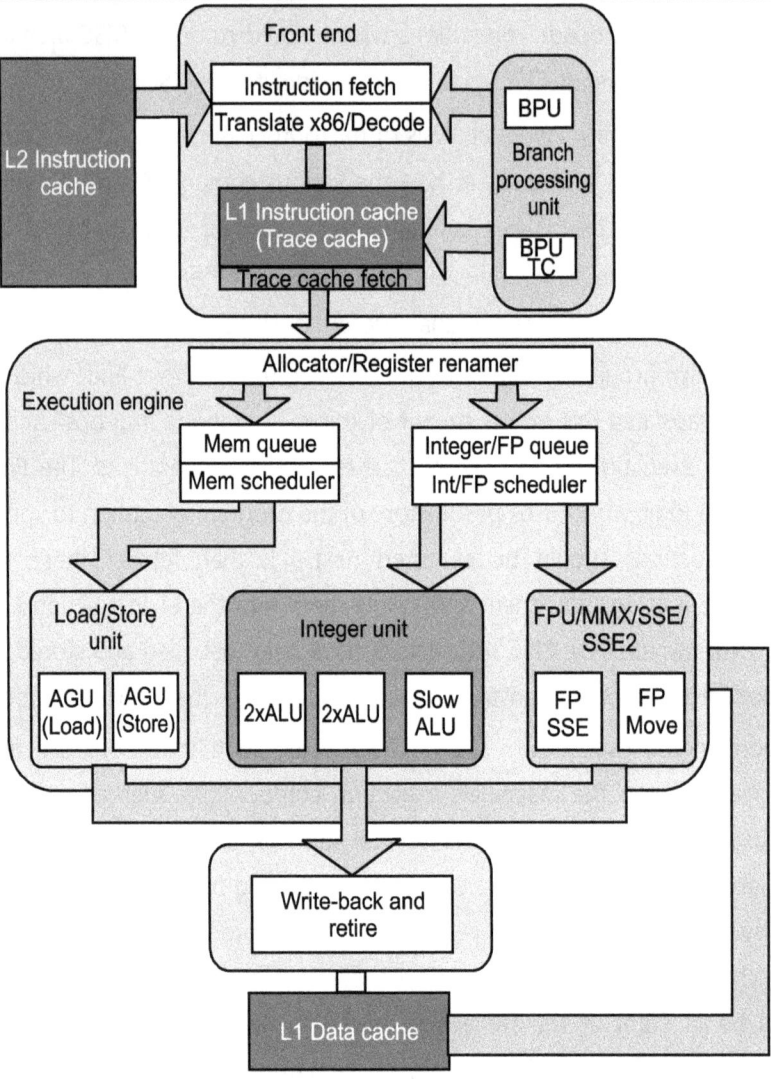

Fig. 6.14

6.9.1 Specifications of the Pentium 4 3GHz Processor

Hyperthreading and a neat clean 800MHz System Bus
- Clock Speed 3GHz
- 800MHz "Quad Pumped" Front Side Bus
- Hyperthreading Technology for increased performance in Multi-tasking and Multi-threaded applications
- .13 micron manufacturing process
- 512K on chip, Full Speed L2 Cache
- Rapid Execution Engine - ALU clocked at 2X frequency of core
- 128bit Floating Point/Multimedia unit

- "Hyper Pipelined" Technology for extremely high clock speeds
- Intel "NetBurst" micro-architecture
- Supported by the Intel® i875P and i865G chipsets, with Hyperthreading support
- Internet Streaming SIMD Extensions 2
- Intel® MMX? media enhancement technology
- Memory cacheability up to 4 GB of addressable memory space and system memory scalability up to 64 GB of physical memory
- Support for uni-processor designs
- 1.525V operating voltage range

6.10 OPTIMAL MEMORY TO MATCH INTEL PENTIUM 4 PROCESSOR

Choosing proper memory for your Pentium 4 based system is a pretty complicated task. We did our best to answer the most frequently asked questions regarding this matter. How do memory timings affect the overall system performance? Would it be better to use high-speed overclocker memory for CPU overclocking? What is more important for Pentium 4 systems high memory working frequency or low latency? Find all answers in our article!

Intel's transition of the Pentium 4 processor family to the 800MHz system bus was an important event not for the CPU market only, but for the memory market as well. Pentium 4 CPUs with 800MHz FSB required new chipsets.

We have them now the i875 and i865 chipset families, which also allow using dual-channel DDR400 SDRAM for the memory subsystem. Moreover, the use of DDR400 SDRAM with these processors is not only possible, but even necessary to reach the highest performance. It's not only because DDR400 SDRAM and the 800MHz bus can work synchronously, thus eliminating the latencies that occur otherwise.

The main advantage of this combination is that the bandwidths of the memory and system buses match each other. The 64-bit Quad Pumped Bus of the modern Pentium 4 CPU working at 800MHz provides a bandwidth of 6.4 GB/s. This is the exact match of the bandwidth of two DDR400 SDRAM channels. This is the main reason for us to say that the dual channel DDR400 if the optimal memory subsystem for the top-end Pentium 4 processor today.

It should also be mentioned that Intel spends much effort to promote the 800MHz bus into the masses. Intel's plans for the next year don't contain Pentium 4 models with a slower bus. The Quad Pumped Bus with 400 and 533 MHz frequency will only remain within the value Celeron processor family.

Thus, the DDR400 dual-channel chipsets have been given the green light. Until the arrival of DDR II memory, scheduled for the middle of 2004, these chipsets will remain the top-end solution for the high-performance Pentium 4 platform.

6.10.1 Hyper-Threading Technology

Hyper-threading is a technology developed by Intel Corporation. It is used in certain Pentium 4 processors and all Intel Xeon processors. Hyper-threading technology, commonly referred to as "HT Technology," enables the processor to execute two threads, or sets of instructions, at the same time. Since hyper-threading allows two streams to be executed in parallel, it is almost like having two separate processors working together.

While hyper-threading can improve processing performance, software must support multiple processors to take advantage of the technology. Fortunately, recent versions of both Windows andLinux support multiple processors and therefore benefit from hyper-threading. For example, a videoplaying in Windows Media Player should not be slowed down by a Web page loading in Internet Explorer. Hyper-threading allows the two programs to be processed as separate threads at the same time. However, individual programs can only take advantage of Intel's HT Technology if they have been programmed to support multiple processors.

The Pentium 4 3.06 GHz processor is the first Intel desktop processor in history that can process two independent threads at the same time. With a SMT enabled OS like Win2000/XP, Linux, etc. the operation system will identify the P4 3.06 GHz CPU as two *logical* processors that share thesingle physical CPU's resources. A physical processor can be thought of as the chip itself, whereas a logica processor is what the computer sees with Hyper-Threading enabled the computer can have one physical processor installed in the motherboard, but the computer will see two logical processors, and treat the system as if there were actually two processors. Even when we put a regular processor under 100% load, we're never fully utilizing 100% of the execution units. With a HyperThreading enabled processor those spare execution units can used towards computing other things now.

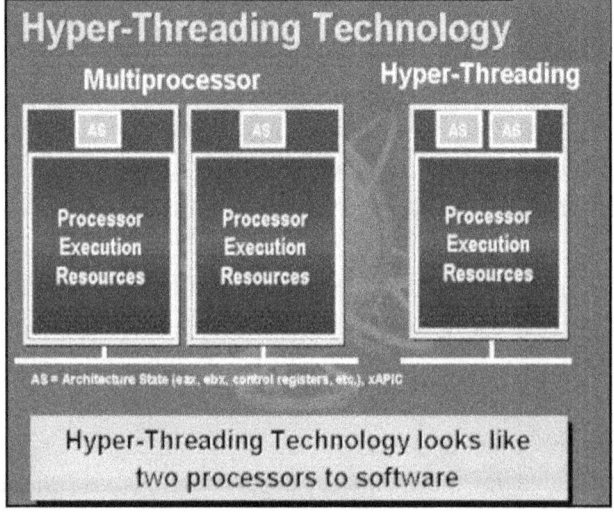

Fig. 6.15 : Hyper threading

CPU Utilization :

As you can see from the slides above (from the Intel Developer Forum) the single Superscalar processor is busy computing information however about half the processor remains unused. In the Multiprocessing portion of the demonstration we see a dual CPU system working on two separate threads, however again about 50% of both CPU's remain unutilized.

In the last Hyper Threading enabled processor, both threads are simultaneously being computed, and the CPU's efficiency has increased from around 50% to over 90%!

The last example is of dual Hyper Threading enabled processors which can work on four independent threads at the same time. Again CPU efficiency is around 90% (and in this case there would be four logical processors, and two physical processors).

While this all sounds very good in the above example, it's also about the most ideal situation ever - so let's get back to the real world.

As the above sample shows, there is a bit of overlapping when computing threads. In the execution units which are "overlapped", the processor now it has twice as much work to do and would not be any faster then a regular Superscalar processor working on the same information separately.

If you were to run two pieces of software that are completely different, and use different execution units, your system performance should get a noticeable boost however!

The operating system will also play a key role in how well Hyper Threading works. The OS assigns operations to the independent logical processors, and so if it's determined that one of the logical CPU's is to remain idle, the OS will issue a HALT command to the free logical processor thus devoting all of the other system resources to the working logical processor.

Hyper Threading has the potential to significantly boost system performance under certain circumstances. As more and more software is written specifically for Hyper Threading, the performance differences will grow larger. It didn't take long for software developers to adopt SSE2, hopefully they'll jump on the Hyper Threading bandwagon quickly and the consumer will see the benefit of this ingenuous technology quickly.

6.11 DIFFERENCE BETWEEN PENTIUM 3 & PENTIUM 4

The most notable difference between a Pentium 3 and a Pentium 4 processor is the speed. The Pentium 3 maxes out at 1.33 GHz while the Pentium 4 blazes up to a maximum of 3.46 GHz. But these processors have other characteristics that affect the performance and reliability of your computer.

1. **Caches :**

   The Pentium 4 processor has a cache size of 512 KB and up, while the Pentium 3 processor has about 256 KB and maxes out at 512 KB.

2. **Size :**

   The Pentium 3 processors were bulky and took up a lot of space on the motherboard. As with each new generation of the Pentium, the Pentium 4 processors are significantly smaller.

3. **Technology :**

   The Pentium 4 has "hyper threading" which allows the computer to multitask more efficiently and effectively.

4. **Architecture :**

   The Pentium 3 lacks the "NetBurst" architecture of the newer version. The Pentium 4 thus allows for advanced graphics, video and multimedia processing.

5. **Bandwidth :**

   The Pentium 3 had a maximum of 133 MHz and 64 bits wide bus with a peak bandwidth of 1.064 GB. The Pentium 4 has a maximum of 400 MHz

6.12 COMPARISON BETWEEN PENTIUM 1,2,3 AND 4

Table 6.3

General Details	Name	Pentium	Pentium Pro	Pentium II	Pentium III	Pentium 4
	Family/Generation	80586, 5th Generation	80686, 6th Generation	80686, 6th Generation, MMX	80686, 6th Generation, MMX, SSE	Intel NetBurst MicroArchitecture 42M transistors
Clock Frequencies	CPU Core Speed	75, 90, 100, 120, 133, 150, 166, 200 MHz	133, 150, 166, 180, 200 MHz	333 Mhz	600E, 650E, ..., 850E MHz	1.4GHz
	External Bus Speed	50, 60, or 66 MHz	60 or 66 MHz, GTL+	66 MHz, GTL+	100 MHz GTL+ (Slot 1), AGTL+ (Slot 2)	400MHz

...Cont.

Processor Core	Generic Details	CISC, In-order and Pipelined Execution	RISC, Out-of-order and Speculative Execution	RISC, Out-of-order and Speculative Execution	RISC, Out-of-order and Speculative Execution	RISC, Out-Of-Order and Speculative Execution
	Specific Details	Dual Pipeline Design	20 Entry RS, 40 Entry ROB	20 Entry RS, 40 Entry ROB	20 Entry RS, 40 Entry ROB	
	Registers	32 Bit Integer, 80 Bit FP	32 Bit Integer, 80 Bit FP, 40 Entry RAT	32 Bit Integer, 80 Bit FP, 64 Bit MM, 40 Entry RAT	32 Bit Integer, 80 Bit FP, 64 Bit MM, 128 Bit SSE, 40 Entry RAT	GP : 32 FPU : 80 MMX : 64 XMM : 128
	Pipeline Depth	2 (Shared) plus 2x 3 (Dual Pipeline) Stages	12 (In-order) plus 2 (Out-of-order) Stages	12 (In-order) plus 2 (Out-of-order) Stages	12 (In-order) plus 2 (Out-of-order) Stages	20 stages
	Execution Units	2x Integer, Pipelined FPU	2x ALU, Load, Store Adress, Store Data, Pipelined FPU	2x ALU/MMX, Load, Store Adress, Store Data, Pipelined FPU	2x ALU/MMX/SSE, Load, Store Adress, Store Data, Pipelined FPU	2*DDR ALU/MMX/SSE2, Load, Store Address, Store Data, Pipelined FPU
Processor Buses	Address Bus Width	32 Bit	36 Bit	36 Bit	36 Bit	36Bit

...Cont.

	Data Bus Width	64 Bit	64 Bit, separate 64 Bit Backside L2 Cache Bus	64 Bit, separate 64 Bit Backside L2 Cache Bus	64 Bit separate 64+8 Bit Backside L2 Cache Bus with ECC (0.25 µm) separate 256+32 Bit Backside L2 Cache Bus with ECC (0.18 µm)	64Bit
	Physical Memory	2^32 Bit = 4 GB	2^36 Bit = 64 GB	2^36 Bit = 64 GB	2^36 Bit = 64 GB	2^36Bit=64 GB
	Virtual Memory	(8,190 + 8,192) × 4 GB = 65,528 GB (~64 TB)	(8,190 + 8,192) × 4 GB = 65,528 GB (~64 TB)	(8,190 + 8,192) × 4 GB = 65,528 GB (~64 TB)	(8,190 + 8,192) × 4 GB = 65,528 GB (~64 TB)	(8,190+8,192)*4GB =65,528GB(~64TB)
	Multiprocessing	SMP, 2 Processors, using integrated local APICs	SMP, 4 Processors, using integrated local APICs	SMP, 2 Processors, using integrated local APICs	SMP, 2 Processors, using integrated local APICs	SMP, 2 Processors APICs
Processor Caches	**Level 0**	N/A	N/A	N/A	N/A	N/A

...Cont.

Level	Type					
Level 1	Code	8 KB, 2-Way, 32 Byte/Line, SI, 2x Fetch Port (supports Split-line Acess), Snoop Port (for SMC), LRU	8 KB, 4-Way, 32 Byte/Line, SI, Fetch Port, Internal and External Snoop Port (for SMC/XMC), LRU	16 KB, 4-Way, 32 Byte/Line, SI, Fetch Port, Internal and External Snoop Port (for SMC/XMC), LRU	16 KB, 4-Way, 32 Byte/Line, SI, Fetch Port, Internal and External Snoop Port (for SMC/XMC), LRU	8KB, 4-Way, 64B/line
	Data	8 KB, 2-Way, 32 Byte/Line, MESI, Non-blocking, Dual-ported, Snoop Port, 8 Banks, LRU	8 KB, 2-Way, 32 Byte/Line, MESI, Non-blocking, Dual-ported, Snoop Port, Write Allocate, 8 Banks, LRU	16 KB, 4-Way, 32 Byte/Line, MESI, Non-blocking, Dual-ported, Snoop Port, Write Allocate, 8 Banks, LRU	16 KB, 4-Way, 32 Byte/Line, MESI, Non-blocking, Dual-ported, Snoop Port, Write Allocate, 8 Banks, LRU	Trace Cache: 12000uOPS
Level 2		External, depends on Motherboard	256 KB..1 MB, 4-Way, 32 Byte/Line, Non-blocking, 64 GB cacheable, using 1 or 2 Dies inside Package	256 KB, 4-Way, 32 Byte/Line, Non-blocking, 64 GB cacheable,	Unified, 256 KB, 8-Way, 32 Byte/Line, MESI Non-blocking, 64 GB cacheable, LRU	256KB, 8-Way, 128B/line

...Cont.

Processor Buffers	Read Buffer		32 Byte for Code Cache 32 Byte for Data Cache	4x 32 Byte	4x 32 Byte	4x 32 Byte (Shared)	
	Write Buffer		2x 8 Byte (supports Dual Pipeline Design) 3x 32 Byte (Line Replacement Write Buffer, Internal and External Snoop Write Buffer)	32 Byte	32 Byte		
	Prefetch Queue		2x 32 Byte (supports Dual Pipeline Design) SMC can be observed up to 94 Byte ahead	32 Byte	32 Byte	32 Byte	
	Branch Prediction	Static	Yes	Yes	Yes	Yes	Yes
		Dynamic	256 Entries, 4-Way, 4-State	512 Entries, 4-Way, providing 16x 4-State Pattern Recognition	512 Entries, 4-Way, providing 16x 4-State Pattern Recognition	512 Entries, 4-Way, providing 16x 4-State Pattern Recognition	
		RSB	N/A	4 Entries	4 Entries	4 Entries	
	TLB		4KB CODE 32 Entries, 4-Way, LRU	4KB CODE 32 Entries, 4-Way, LRU	4KB CODE 32 Entries, 4-Way, LRU	4KB CODE 32 Entries, 4-Way, LRU	4KB CODE

...Cont.

		Col1	Col2	Col3	Col4	Col5
		4MB CODE N/A (uses 4 KB Code Entries)	LARGE CODE 2 Entries, Full, LRU	LARGE CODE 2 Entries, Full, LRU	LARGE CODE 2 Entries, Full, LRU	LARGE CODE
		4KB DATA 64 Entries, 4-Way, LRU	4KB DATA 64 Entries, 4-Way, LRU	4KB DATA 64 Entries, 4-Way, LRU	4KB DATA 64 Entries, 4-Way, LRU	4KB DATA
		4MB DATA 8 Entries, 4-Way, LRU	LARGE DATA 8 Entries, 4-Way, LRU	LARGE DATA 8 Entries, 4-Way, LRU	LARGE DATA 8 Entries, 4-Way, LRU	LARGE DATA
Instruction Set	Regular	IA-32	IA-32	IA-32	IA-32	IA-32
	Floating Point	Integrated	Integrated	Integrated	Integrated	Integrated
	Multi Media	N/A	N/A	MMX, FXSAVE/FXR STOR	MMX, SSE	MMX, SSE2
	Processor Modes	Real, Protected, Virtual, Paging, SMM, Probe Mode	Real, Protected, Virtual, Paging, SMM, Probe Mode	Real, Protected, Virtual, Paging, SMM, Probe Mode	Real, Protected, Virtual, Paging, SMM, Probe Mode	Real, Protected, Virtual, Paging, SMM, Probe Mode

6.13 CPUID

- CPUID dumps detail information about the CPU(s) gathered from the CPUID instruction, and also determines the exact model of CPU(s) from that information.
- It dumps all information available from the CPUID instruction. The exact collection of information available varies between manufacturers and processors. The following information is available consistently on all modern CPUs

  vendor_id

  version information (1/eax)

miscellaneous (1/ebx)

feature information (1/ecx)

- It also produces synthetic fields based on information from multiple CPUID functions. Currently, the synthetic fields are the exact model of each CPU (but see LIMITATIONS below) as (synth); the multiprocessing characteristics including the number of cores per chip (c) and the number of hyperthreads per core (t) as (multi-processing synth); and a decoding of the APIC physical ID as (APIC synth).

- The determination of the model is based on the following information

    version information (1/eax), processor type

    version information (1/eax), family

    version information (1/eax), model

    version information (1/eax), stepping id

    version information (1/eax), extended family

    version information (1/eax), extended model

- feature information (1/ecx), virtual machine extensions

    brand id (1/ebx)

    brand (0x80000004)

    cache and TLB information (2)

    deterministic cache parameters (4/eax), extra processor cores

    AMD extended brand id (0x80000001/ebx)

    AMD extended processor signature (0x80000001/eax)

    Transmeta processor revision ID (0x80860001/ebx & ecx)

- The determination of the multiprocessing characteristics and decoding of APIC physical ID is based on the following information :

    feature information (1/edx), hyper-threading / multi-core supported

    miscellaneous (1/ebx), cpu count

    deterministic cache parameters (4/eax), extra processor cores on this die

    x2APIC features / processor topology (0xb)

    AMD feature flags (0x80000001/ecx)

    AMD Logical CPU cores (0x80000008/ecx), number of logical CPU cores - 1

- In addition, a simpler and coarser determination of the CPU is performed using only the information listed above under version information (1/eax). It is provided as (simple synth) under version information (1/eax). However, it tends to be unable to distinguish between various modern CPUs.

Options

cpuid accepts the following command line arguments :

-1=cpu : Display information only for the first CPU. This cuts down on the output on a multiprocessor system, and is useful when certain that all CPUs are identical.

-f =FILE

> Read raw hex information from FILE instead of from executions of the cpuid instruction.

-h=help, Display help information.

-i=inst : Use the CPUID instruction. The information it provides is reliable. It is not necessary to be root to use this option. (This option is the default.)

-k=kernel

> Use the CPUID kernel module. The information does not seem to be reliable on all combinations of CPU type and kernel version. Typically, it is necessary to be root to use this option.

-r=raw : Display only raw hex information with no decoding.

-v=version : Display cpuid version.

6.13.1 Limitations of CPUID

There are numerous cases where there is no way to distinguish between various CPUs in the (synth) information. In some cases, the sizes of caches, number of cores, brand strings, etc., can be used to distinguish multiple CPUs with the same family and model. But there are cases where that information is insufficient. Whenever cpuid is unable to distinguish between multiple CPUs, it will list all known possibilities.

If you believe that a certain processor should be distinguishable from another and it isn't, please inform the author of this tool.

The (multi-processing synth) information is unreliable on many processors. It faithfully reports the information provided by the CPUID instruction and decodes it as recommended by the processor manufacturers, but often that information is incorrect. The information seems to indicate the architecture's capabilities, rather than what the particular chip actually does. In particular, it seems commonplace to claim the presence of multiple hyper threads when there is only one.

QUESTIONS

1. Draw and explain the architecture of Pentium Processor.
2. Explain the memory system used in Pentium Processor.
3. What are the different types of registers are used in Pentium Processor.
4. Describe memory management in Pentium Processor.
5. Draw architecture of Pentium pro microprocessor and explain.
6. Draw architecture of Pentium 4 microprocessor and explain.
7. Explain hyper threading technology.
8. What is CPUID? Explain.
9. Compare Pentium, Pentium pro and Pentium 4 microprocessor.

✠ ✠ ✠

www.ingramcontent.com/pod-product-compliance
Lightning Source LLC
Chambersburg PA
CBHW081919170426
43200CB00014B/2763